MW00773815

Uncomputable

Uncomputable

Play and Politics In the Long Digital Age

Alexander R. Galloway

VERSO

London • New York

First published by Verso 2021
© Alexander R. Galloway 2021

All rights reserved

The moral rights of the author have been asserted

1 3 5 7 9 10 8 6 4 2

Verso
UK: 6 Meard Street, London W1F 0EG
US: 20 Jay Street, Suite 1010, Brooklyn, NY 11201
versobooks.com

Verso is the imprint of New Left Books

ISBN-13: 978-1-83976-398-4
ISBN-13: 978-1-83976-399-1 (UK EBK)
ISBN-13: 978-1-83976-400-4 (US EBK)

British Library Cataloguing in Publication Data
A catalogue record for this book is available from the British Library

Library of Congress Cataloging-in-Publication Data
Library of Congress Control Number: 2021941169

Typeset in Minion by Hewer Text UK Ltd, Edinburgh
Printed and bound by CPI Group (UK) Ltd, Croydon CR0 4YY

For JJ

Contents

List of Illustrations   ix

A Letter from Paris   xiii

Introduction   1

I. Photography

1. Petrified Photography   15
2. Dimensions Without Depth   25
3. The Parallel Image   35
4. Photographic Modeling   44
5. Our Best Machines Are Made of Sunshine   51

II. Weaving

6. Spider Work   61
7. The Crumb Machine   69
8. Regular Irregularity   82
9. Algebraic Weaving   90
10. Webs Rewoven   98

III. The Digital

11. From One to Two   107
12. The Cybernetic Hypothesis   116
13. Latticework   125
14. A Regular Discrete Framework   131

IV. Computable Creatures

15. Experiments in Bionumeric Evolution   141
16. Conjectural Biology   149
17. Intensity and Survival   160
18. Parallel Causality   165

V. Crystalline War

19. Times of Crisis   177
20. The Game of War   188
21. A Nostalgic Algorithm?   197
22. Some Problems with the Data   203
23. Crystal Aesthetics   208

VI. Black Box

24. Black Box Cypher   215
25. Black Box Function   222
26. The Tyranny of Structurelessness   229
27. The Tragedy of Interactivity   234
28. Toward a Practical Nonexistence   240

Afterword: A Note on Method   247
Acknowledgments   259
Index   261

List of Illustrations

1. François Willème's reverse panopticon, a photographic studio with twenty-four cameras at the perimeter directed inward toward a central subject.   17

2. François Willème, unfinished photosculpture: portrait head of a woman, c. 1861.   22

3. Étienne-Jules Marey, vibrations of a flexible rod, 1887.   28

4. Albert Londe's 1891 chronophotographic camera with twelve apertures.   32

5. James Ensor, "Self-Portrait with Masks," 1899.   33

6. Braune and Fischer, test subject wearing the chronophotographic suit used for the documentation and analysis of human locomotion.   45

7. Braune and Fischer, model of human locomotion.   48

8. Woodcut depicting Charles Babbage's Difference Engine No. 1.   71

9. Didier-Petit & Co., "À la mémoire de J. M. Jacquard" (detail), 1839.   78

10. The polynomial $(a + b + c + d + e + f)^2$ rendered
    using Ada K. Dietz's technique.   86

11. Ada K. Dietz, *Algebraic Expressions in Handwoven
    Textiles* (Louisville, KY: Little Loomhouse, 1949),
    cover block print by Ruth Foster.   92

12. Ada K. Dietz, "AKD-6-2-SW," c. 1947 (reproduction
    2020).   96

13. High-speed mechanical wire drive used at the
    Institute for Advanced Study.   108

14. Oscillogram of word reproduced from magnetic wire,
    before and after limiting.   111

15. Oscillographic production of letters.   114

16. "An arrangement of meteorological stations designed
    to fit with the chief mechanical properties of the
    atmosphere . . . Pressure to be observed at the centre
    of each shaded chequer, velocity at the centre of
    each white chequer."   127

17. Detail from Nils Aall Barricelli's 1953 demonstration
    of bionumeric evolution showing both chaotic and
    stable gene clusters. The relatively chaotic center region
    depicts processes of mutation and disorganization.
    Texture fields on the right and left represent different
    bionumeric organisms.   143

18. Composite image from Nils Aall Barricelli's 1953
    demonstration of bionumeric evolution.   156

19. A 2010 restaging of Nils Aall Barricelli's original 1953
    experiments, with the vertical axis scaled down by a
    factor of 8 to reveal a longer span of evolutionary time.
    Texture fields represent different organisms. Borders
    between textures indicate that an organism has perished,
    mutated, or otherwise evolved. Striped or interwoven
    textures contain multiple organisms in symbiosis.   157

20. Étienne-Jules Marey, smoke trails encounter an
    obstacle creating turbulence, 1901.   166

21. Guy Brossollet, "Non-Battle."   178

22. Konrad Wachsmann, "Grapevine Structure," 1953.   184

23. Playing Guy Debord's Game of War.   189

24. Visualization of combat relationships for the South
    player in Guy Debord's The Game of War, "Turn 22′."   206

25. Visualization of combat relationships for the South
    player in Guy Debord's The Game of War, "Turn 44′."   207

A Letter from Paris

About ten years ago in the springtime, a few days after my birthday, I received a letter from a lawyer's office on the Rue Auber in Paris, a street northwest of the Palais Royal near the old Garnier opera. Letters from lawyers frequently bring bad news, and this was no exception. "I am writing to you in my capacity as Legal Advisor to Mrs. Alice DEBORD," the letter began, "the sole holder of the pecuniary and moral rights to all of the work of Mr. Guy DEBORD." In unadorned prose, the lawyer informed me I had violated Guy Debord's intellectual property. My eyes scanned across phrases like "exclusive rights" and "non-authorized exploitation." As I would later learn, copies of the letter were also sent to my employer and to the director of a non-profit organization where I had been an artist-in-residence.

Guy Debord, the French filmmaker and author, was already fresh on my mind. At the time, I was spending my days and nights on a laptop, writing code for a computer game. Built in collaboration with a small team of coders and artists, the computer game was a re-staging of a relatively unknown late work by Debord, a table-top strategy game called "The Game of War" that Debord had made in the 1970s. The lawyer from the Rue Auber was unambiguous. *Stop working on the game, or we will sue you for copyright violation.*

A claim of intellectual property infringement brought by the estate of Guy Debord is ironic, to say the least. This was a man who spent his entire career gleefully copying, sampling, and stealing from Hegel and Hollywood, and everything in-between. Thumbing through my dog-eared copy of *The Society of the Spectacle*, Debord's signature 1967 tract on culture and politics, I eventually found what I was looking for. Chapter eight, paragraph 207, line two, an excerpt from Debord's theory of art: "Plagiarism is necessary. Progress demands it."[1]

To resolve the matter, I indulged a momentary fantasy. I would simply respond to the lawyer with a few choice citations from Debord himself on the necessity of artistic appropriation, and that would be that. Anyhow, I had no intention of plagiarizing Debord or anyone else. Mine was a research project. I was reenacting a historical algorithm. Besides, what could be more boring than trying to "hijack" the master of *détournement* himself?

I had worked on play and games in the past. But what captivated me most about Debord's "Game of War" was not the ludic element. What captivated me was the algorithmic element. Like other games, Debord's project is defined by an algorithm of sorts (its book of rules). The game has binary conditions for winning and losing. The play board is a grid structure, not unlike a data array, or, for that matter, a bitmapped image. Players must even perform simple calculations in their heads during combat. In a certain sense, the game was already a piece of code. Re-staging the game in software was a relatively simple task. Less simple, though, were the mysteries unearthed along the way, mysteries that I would eventually explore and ultimately try to solve.

At the time, I knew I wanted to write about algorithmic culture and the history of computation. Not cybernetics in the narrow

---

1 Guy Debord, *The Society of the Spectacle*, trans. Donald Nicholson-Smith (New York: Zone, 1995), 145. These phrases from Debord were themselves derived from Lautréamont.

sense of Norbert Wiener and Gregory Bateson, but computation as a catchall for the media of multiplicity more generally. Looking at Debord's game, I saw an algorithmic artifact, and I wanted to write a history capacious enough to include this project along with other artifacts more explicitly computational. Through a series of connected episodes, this history could delve into some of the precursors of cybernetics from the 1920s, or afterward, into the artificial life experiments of the 1950s. It could talk about networks, supercomputers, and black boxes. It could bring in other formats like weaving and sculpture. It could even try to make a case—perhaps outlandish at first thought—for how nineteenth-century photography helped invent computer graphics.

Although its intent was "cease and desist," that letter from a decade ago was more of a beginning than an end. Debord's "Game of War" was merely the start of a story that continued well beyond it, into the very nature of the computable and the uncomputable. It set a whole series of things in motion for me, opening up new questions and suggesting a way forward. I had decided not to respond to the lawyer from the Rue Auber. Instead, I decided to write a book . . .

"Consider the world's diversity and worship it.
By denying its multiplicity you deny your own true nature."

Derek Jarman, *Jubilee* (1978)

Introduction

This book is about the computable and the uncomputable. No general theory—I instead narrate a series of historical episodes. These stories are drawn from the archives of computation and digital media, broadly conceived. The goal is to show how computation emerges or fails to emerge, how the digital thrives but also atrophies, how networks interconnect while also fraying and falling apart.

Such alternations—something done, something undone; something computed, something uncomputed—constitute the real history of digital machines, from cybernetics and networks to cellular automata and beyond. And, while computers have colonized the globe in recent years, they also excel at various practices of exclusion. The excluded term might be "intuition," or it might be "aesthetic experience." It might be the "flesh" or "affect." The excluded term might evoke a certain poetry, mysticism, or romanticism. Or it might simply be life, mundane and unexceptional. "Uncomputable" means all of these things, and more. The gist is that there exists a mode of being in which discrete symbols do not take hold, or at least do not hold sway. And, in the absence of such rational symbols, computation starts to drift and take on another form. Sometimes this is called the realm of "life" or "experience." Sometimes it is called the "analog" realm—yet analog computers are some of the oldest computers.

Meanwhile, the term "uncomputable" developed a series of other meanings, particularly in the twentieth century. Two of them are about limits: rational limits and practical limits. To be sure, the resistance to rationality is as old as rationality itself. Nevertheless, a rash of rational paradoxes in the early twentieth century culminated in a series of limits to rationality from within that very reason. Bertrand Russell's paradox from 1901—"the set of all sets that are not members of themselves"—seemed to impose limits on what was possible within the theory of mathematical sets. Kurt Gödel's incompleteness theories of 1931 showed that for any formal axiomatic system there will always be statements that are *true* in that system but not *provable*. Later, in 1936, Alan Turing demonstrated that it was logically impossible to calculate what sorts of machines will halt (given a certain input) and what sorts of machines will not halt. If, before, there were intuitive or poetic or biological limits to rationality, after Gödel, Turing, et al., there were also demonstrable limits to rationality from within rationality. Indeed, in a certain sense, computation in the twentieth century is defined more by the limits to computation, more by the uncomputable, than by a positive set of capacities. Or, as Beatrice Fazi wryly put it, "the founding paradox of computer science is that it is a field that is defined by what it cannot do, rather than by what it can do."[1]

Alongside the rational limit there also emerged the question of practical limit. Ask cryptographers about the "uncomputable" and they will respond: *How much computing power do you have at your disposal? Can you afford to crunch the numbers until the sun burns out?* Computability is thus also a strictly pragmatic question. Fields

---

1 M. Beatrice Fazi, *Contingent Computation: Abstraction, Experience, and Indeterminacy in Computational Aesthetics* (London: Rowman and Littlefield, 2018), 56.

like cryptography excel at generating knots and obstacles within pure rationality, obstacles that greatly impede computation, even if they are not strictly "uncomputable." Is it possible to reverse a hash function? In the abstract, yes, but practically speaking, no. At least so goes the promise of crypto security.

If these are three types of uncomputability—analog life, rational paradox, and practical limit—a fourth meaning of the term "uncomputable" comes from the indiscernable and the indeterminate. In her book *Contagious Architecture*, Luciana Parisi has written about entropy, chaos, contingency, indefiniteness, change, and what she calls patternless data.[2] For her, the uncomputable already exists; it exists in the cracks and excesses of data, in interferences and contingencies, and how these things overwhelm seemingly impervious rational systems. (Parisi was inspired, in part, by the mathematician Gregory Chaitin, who has shown that there are numbers with infinite complexity, meaning that they are, by definition, uncomputable.) Digital computation traditionally has relied on discrete symbols—relied on them being discrete and remaining that way. When symbols start to dissolve, they pose a threat to computability. When a symbol cannot be fixed, it becomes more difficult to calculate.

Or does it? Part of the story involves *incorporating* the indiscernable and the indeterminate into the very heart of computation. According to Parisi, "error, indeterminacy, randomness, and unknowns in general have become part of technoscientific knowledge and the reasoning of machines."[3] Indeed part of the history of computation is the history of the uncomputable being colonized by the computable. Claude Shannon, for instance, in 1949 defined information explicitly in terms of entropy.[4] Since then,

---

2 Luciana Parisi, *Contagious Architecture: Computation, Aesthetics, and Space* (Cambridge, MA: MIT Press, 2013).

3 Luciana Parisi, "Reprogramming Decisionism," *e-flux journal* 85 (October 2017): 1–12, 4.

4 Claude Shannon and Warren Weaver, *The Mathematical Theory of Communication* (Urbana: University of Illinois Press, 1963).

randomness and contingency have been incorporated into the body of computation, not excluded from it. 3D models are frequently textured using procedural randomness. Images are improved via anti-aliasing, essentially a form of aesthetic noise. And the empirical turn in AI has shown how contingent data is ultimately much more valuable than predictable, determinate symbols. In a sense, randomness and contingency have become fully industrial. Today the computable is closely intertwined with the uncomputable.

Beyond the uncomputable as major theme, this book also engages a minor theme, the *multiple*. In the episodes that follow, the multiple will appear as cells, units, and pixels, plus their arrangement into sets, arrays, and grids. We will see multiplicity made visible in the first pixels rendered on a computer display, in artificial life simulations, in a table-top game, and in several other media artifacts. We will explore multi-lens photography and the ability to create multiple images quickly and easily. Likewise, we will look at textiles built up through multiple strands iterating lengthwise and widthwise, the warp and weft of yarn in two dimensions mimicking the sets and arrays of mathematical formulae (and vice versa). Such formal constructions of the multiple—forging a unit, then iterating the unit in series—are at the heart of digital computation.

Indeed, the multiple has long been a topic of concern. Anxieties about copies and originals go back to Plato at least. And the modern period has its own relation to repetition and duplication: the serial novel, the multiple in art, the filmstrip, Walter Benjamin on reproduction, the post-structuralists on repetition. "Multiplicity" was already a buzzword in 1990s cyber culture. Harold Ramis even made a film about it in 1996. (It bombed.)

Here, one might distinguish between "formal" and "real" multiplicity, to adopt the Marxist argot. Things may be *formally* multiple, in that they may be duplicated or copied without much altering the integrity of the original, anxieties about the uncanny notwithstanding. Yet the sort of multiple relevant in digital computation is *real* multiplicity, that is, the always-already digital materiality of the monad, the set, the array, the molecule, the cell, or the crystal. For Euclid, arithmetical numbers were called *plêthos* [πλῆθος], typically translated as "multiple," although the nearest English cognate is "plethora."[5] Numbers, for Euclid, were real multiples: nothing more than the rote repetition of a basic unit. Digital computation thrives in such conditions of real multiplicity.

Yet other thinkers favor the multiple not for its arithmetical regularity, but in precisely the opposite sense, as a way to deviate from homogeneity and consistency. The work of Gilles Deleuze and Félix Guattari is exemplary in this regard. As they put it, multiplicity means "becoming-wolf, becoming-inhuman, deterritorialized intensities."[6] Multiplicity furnished Deleuze and Guattari with a deviation away from territory, away from the human, away from the Freudian ego, away from all manner of deterministic repetition.

A similar promise resides in the adjacent term "multitude," an old concept reinvigorated by Michael Hardt and Antonio Negri in a series of books including *Empire*, published in 2000.[7] The multitude is a "living alternative that grows within Empire," explained Hardt and Negri.[8] Composed of singularities, the multitude is not a simple array or regular grid, but rather "an open and expansive network."[9]

This reveals a basic tension. In its tessellations and permutations, the multiple seems to promise difference and variety. At the

---

5 Euclid defined arithmetical numbers in *Elements*, book 7, definitions 1 and 2. See Euclid, *Elements*, vol. 2, trans. Thomas Heath (New York: Dover, 1956), 277.

6 Gilles Deleuze and Félix Guattari, *A Thousand Plateaus*, trans. Brian Massumi (Minneapolis: University of Minnesota Press, 1987), 32.

7 Michael Hardt and Antonio Negri, *Empire* (Cambridge, MA: Harvard University Press, 2000).

8 Michael Hardt and Antonio Negri, *Multitude* (New York: Penguin, 2004), xiii.

9 Ibid., 99, xiii–xiv.

same time, the multiple requires repetition, and thus always refers back to some elemental sameness. So, does the multiple entail the blank repetition of habit?[10] Does it mean cloning? Or does the multiple disrupt and enliven, opening up new lines of flight, new modes of experience? Multiplicity, it seems, is rife with contradiction.

—

Digital media studies is currently experiencing something of a golden age. Starting more than a decade ago, Mark Marino helped inaugurate a new field of inquiry dubbed "critical code studies," a disciplinary shift evident today in scholarship from the likes of Rita Raley, Adrian MacKenzie, and Matthew Fuller.[11] At the same time a renewed interest in infrastructure has guided a number of important recent books, such as Nicole Starosielski's *The Undersea Network* and Tung-Hui Hu's *A Prehistory of the Cloud*, both devoted to the real materiality of networks.[12] Theorists like Yuk Hui have recently explored the various philosophical nuances of digitality, fueled, in Hui's case, by the tech philosophy of Bernard Stiegler and Gilbert Simondon.[13] Or consider Simone Browne's smart and timely *Dark Matters*, dealing with the technology of race, or adjacent work on opacity and queer computing from

10 On habit and brain science, see Catherine Malabou, *Morphing Intelligence: From IQ Measurement to Artificial Brains*, trans. Carolyn Shread (New York: Columbia University Press, 2019). On habit and digital media, see Wendy Hui Kyong Chun, *Updating to Remain the Same: Habitual New Media* (Cambridge, MA: MIT Press, 2016).

11 Mark C. Marino, "Critical Code Studies," *Electronic Book Review* (December 4, 2006), electronicbookreview.com.

12 See Nicole Starosielski, *The Undersea Network* (Durham, NC: Duke University Press, 2015), and Tung-Hui Hu, *A Prehistory of the Cloud* (Cambridge, MA: MIT Press, 2015).

13 See Yuk Hui, *On the Existence of Digital Objects* (Minneapolis: University of Minnesota Press, 2016).

scholars like Zach Blas, Jacob Gaboury, and Kara Keeling.[14] While feminist theory has long engaged with digital technology, the recent *Xenofeminist Manifesto* echoed particularly widely, due in no small measure to a series of staunch positions taken by the manifesto's authors on controversial topics such as alienation and posthumanism.[15] At the same time, Martine Syms's excellent "Mundane Afrofuturist Manifesto" provided a refreshing alternative to some of these "accelerationist" tendencies, stressing the mundane over the extraterrestrial. Even in the world of art criticism, computational and network aesthetics have come to the fore, exemplified by the wide dispersion of a pamphlet by the artist Seth Price, aptly titled "Dispersion," or, in a different way, by recent volumes on networks and participation from David Joselit and Claire Bishop.[16] Several of these threads are brought together in Patrick Jagoda's *Network Aesthetics*, which looked across different media formats from literature to film to games, and is focused equally on both digitality and formalism.[17]

---

14 See Simone Browne, *Dark Matters: On the Surveillance of Blackness* (Durham, NC: Duke University Press, 2015); Zach Blas and Jacob Gaboury, "Biometrics and Opacity: A Conversation," *Camera Obscura* 31, no. 2 (2016): 155–65; and Kara Keeling, "Queer OS," *Cinema Journal* 53, no. 2 (Winter 2014): 152–7.

15 Laboria Cuboniks, *The Xenofeminist Manifesto: A Politics for Alienation* (London and New York: Verso, 2018).

16 See Seth Price, *Dispersion* (self-published booklet, 2002), David Joselit, *After Art* (Princeton, NJ: Princeton University Press, 2012), and Claire Bishop, *Artificial Hells: Participatory Art and the Politics of Spectatorship* (London and New York: Verso, 2012).

17 Patrick Jagoda, *Network Aesthetics* (Chicago: University of Chicago Press, 2016). Indeed, form and formalism have returned to center stage in media and aesthetic theory, indexed if not wholly exhausted by books like Caroline Levine's *Forms: Whole, Rhythm, Hierarchy, Network* (Princeton, NJ: Princeton University Press, 2015), or Eugenie Brinkema's stunning *The Forms of the Affects* (Durham, NC: Duke University Press, 2014), the latter aiming to defend what the author calls "radical formalism." Among other sources, Jagoda himself cites Marjorie Levinson, "What Is New Formalism?," *PMLA* 122, no. 2 (2007): 558–69, along with Ellen Rooney, "Form and Contentment," *MLQ: Modern Language Quarterly* 61, no. 1 (2000): 17–40.

Meanwhile, new alternatives proliferate. I am thinking of
Homay King's discussion of "ambiguity and ambivalence" in
computational media.[18] Or Aria Dean's essay on memes and
blackness.[19] Or François Laruelle's attempt to "degrow" philosophy from within—and with it, digital computation—through his
so-called nonstandard method.[20] If the analog is about siding
with the subordinate term (real continuity, life, affect, flesh),
Laruelle's nondigital means not distinguishing between the
analog and the digital in the first place. And if encryption obfus-
cates data, Laruelle's nondigital is more a question of *compressing*
data, not hiding digital difference so much as undifferentiating
it.[21]

A number of books already cover computation since World
War II more systematically than I do, books on cybernetics by N.
Katherine Hayles and Orit Halpern, or Fred Turner's account of
"the rise of digital utopianism" toward the end of the twentieth
century.[22] Not wanting to retread material better covered by others,
I instead focus on stories not yet told, or at least not yet with
enough detail—stories of Nils Aall Barricelli, Ada K. Dietz, and
François Willème—stitching these stories together with more
canonical accounts of figures like Ada Lovelace and John von
Neumann. As a consequence, this history will be more episodic
than systematic. We will jump around a bit, guided less by a

18 Homay King, *Virtual Memory: Time-Based Art and the Dream of Digitality*
(Durham, NC: Duke University Press, 2015), 31.

19 Aria Dean, "Poor Meme, Rich Meme," *Real Life* (July 25, 2016), reallifemag.
com.

20 See François Laruelle, *Principles of Non-philosophy*, trans. Nicola Rubczak
and Anthony Paul Smith (London: Bloomsbury, 2013).

21 See Eugene Thacker, *The Pre-Cartesian Brotherhood* (Seattle: Sub Zero
Books, 1994).

22 See N. Katherine Hayles, *How We Became Posthuman: Virtual Bodies in
Cybernetics, Literature, and Informatics* (Chicago: University of Chicago Press,
1999); Orit Halpern, *Beautiful Data: A History of Vision and Reason Since 1945*
(Durham, NC: Duke University Press, 2014); and Fred Turner, *From
Counterculture to Cyberculture: Stewart Brand, the Whole Earth Network, and the
Rise of Digital Utopianism* (Chicago: University of Chicago Press, 2006).

mandate to be comprehensive than by the sometimes unpredicta-ble logic of the archive.

The book advances in loose chronological order, from the dawn of the nineteenth century up to the present day. We begin with photography and textiles, two technologies not always immedi-ately associated with computation. Section 1 looks at the practice of chronophotography, or taking multiple photographs through time, focusing in particular on the strange history of the multi-lens camera. Section 2 shows how weaving and computation have long been intimately intertwined. Section 3, set before and after World War II, outlines the first digital computer age through what the Tiqqun collective have called "the cybernetic hypothesis." Section 4 explores the question of artificial life by way of a series of early experiments in cellular automata. Section 5, on play and games, triangulates some of the political dynamics of the 1970s, including an incipient mode of asymmetrical antagonism only fully investigated in section 6 on the black box.

The research methodology for this book, while largely consist-ing of typical archival research intermixed with more synthetic theoretical claims, also entails a rather different kind of knowl-edge collection. This new method, which might be provisionally labelled "algorithmic research" or even "algorithmic reenact-ment" is gaining adherents today and will likely become more significant in the future.[23] Operating under the assumption that code has its own story to tell, I decided to reanimate some of the inert algorithms found in various archives, doing so by recoding and rebuilding them by hand. Ultimately the book is organized around three such reenactments: weaving the algebraic patterns of Ada K. Dietz from the late 1940s (for section 2); restaging the cellular automata simulations of Nils Aall Barricelli from the early 1950s (for section 4); and programming Debord's 1978

---

23   Some affinities may be found in Wolfgang Ernst's notion of "epistemological reverse engineering." Wolfgang Ernst, *Digital Memory and the Archive* (Minneapolis: University of Minnesota Press, 2013), 55.

"Game of War" to play on current software, complete with a rudimentary "Debord AI" (for section 5).

Algorithmic research means a process of discovery in which computational artifacts *are researched computationally*. Consider the work of Nils Aall Barricelli, discussed here in section 4. If one were to begin studying Barricelli, it would be natural to consult the existing publications and archives, particularly the archives at the Institute for Advanced Study in Princeton, New Jersey, where Barricelli performed his most important work. Yet these are essentially humanistic rather than computational research methods. So in addition to immersing oneself in the archival record, one might also treat Barricelli's technical research *as technical*, producing new subsidiary software as a way to engage with the archival material.

With these assumptions in mind, I decided to restage Barricelli's breakthrough 1953 experiment on my laptop (figure 19). In order to rewrite and migrate Barricelli's 1953 experiment into today's software I had to read his various white papers not simply as prose but as technical documents. Barricelli's pseudocode had to be translated, rewritten, debugged, and made executable in today's software. This process was beneficial because it afforded a more intimate knowledge of the kinds of technical claims being made by Barricelli, not simply the kinds of philosophical and cultural claims evident in his writings.

Likewise, I had hands-on engagement with the algebraic weaving patterns devised by Ada K. Dietz. While researching Dietz's various publications and news clippings, I also wove samplers of some of her designs, starting with the relatively straightforward AKD-2-3-O, and culminating with a reproduction of Dietz's more complex, eight-shaft pattern, AKD-6-2-SW (figure 12). Working on the loom—trying out different fibers, experimenting and making mistakes—afforded a kind of practical intimacy with the material beyond merely consulting and studying Dietz's book on algebraic pattern design.

A similar spirit fueled the exploration into Debord. For a variety of reasons, both practical and intellectual, Debord's late project, the Game of War, had been mostly forgotten, earning little more than a page or a footnote in some of the books on Debord. Most of his chroniclers and critics preferred to focus on Debord's core creative and intellectual output, the films and the writings, with particular emphasis given to the heyday of the Situationist International. Nevertheless, piqued by the oddity of the game, I began work on a computer-based version of Debord's game, which would ultimately be released under the title *Kriegspiel*. Programming this piece of software granted unique access into Debord's brain, access unavailable via conventional research techniques. Indeed only by rewriting and debugging Debord's code was I able to unearth a number of crucial details that affect the arguments given below in section 5, some details of which even Debord himself was unaware.

Digital research methods have been debated a great deal in recent years.[24] I will save my commentary on methodology for the afterword. Suffice it to say that I do not refuse digital methods, even as many extant examples remain unappetizing. Likewise, I do not refuse critique, and consider the choice—critique or computation—to be both forced and false. My own efforts tend to be multimodal, writing code on the one hand and writing more traditional texts on the other. Along the way, the two activities inform each other: building and coding cultivates an intimacy with the materials, while critical analysis reframes the object under inspection. My goal has never been to quarantine or subdue criticality, as some are wont to do. On the contrary, my goal has been to unify critical theory and digital media within a single project.

What are the conditions of possibility for computational media? How and when did the digital age begin? I offer here a series of episodes drawn from the long digital age, not to overturn existing

---

24 See for instance Stephen Ramsay, *Reading Machines: Toward an Algorithmic Criticism* (Champaign: University of Illinois Press, 2011), or the position offered by Nan Z. Da in her "Computational Case Against Computational Literary Studies," *Critical Inquiry* 45, no. 3 (Spring 2019): 601–39.

histories so much as to extend and reorient them. As we will see, this supplementary history started earlier than might be expected—in the nineteenth century, but one could easily go back further in time—and continues to the present day, based on sources drawn from media, culture, technology, and philosophy.

PART I.
Photography

1

Petrified Photography

In Paris in the early 1860s, a sign with large lettering appeared on the facade of a modern four-story building newly constructed in iron and glass on what was then called the Boulevard de l'Etoile, stemming northward away from the Arc de Triomphe. "Portraits— from Mechanical Sculpture," the sign touted. "Busts, Medallions, Statues."

"When a large circular cupola was first erected at 42, Blvd. de l'Etoile," one historian recounted, "constructed of metal mullions with blue and white panes of glass, it was thought to be a conservatory, a zoo for small animals in the English style, an aquarium and, only finally, a photographic studio."[1] When he visited the building's central dome in 1863, a large chamber forty feet wide and thirty feet high (figure 1), the poet Théophile Gautier likened it to "an Oriental cupola, a weightless dome of white and blue glass."[2]

---

1 Robert Sobieszek, "Sculpture as the Sum of Its Profiles: François Willème and Photosculpture in France, 1859–1868," *Art Bulletin* 62, no. 4 (December 1980): 621.

2 Théophile Gautier, *Photosculpture* (Paris: Paul Dupont, 1864), 5; this and subsequent unattributed translations are mine. Gautier's short booklet was excerpted from the *Moniteur universel* (January 4, 1864).

The author Paul de Saint-Victor, who also surveyed the premises, was impressed by the hollowness of the domed photographic studio. "Imagine a vast glass rotunda containing no instruments of any kind, no apparatus visible to the naked eye, nothing to offer any indication of the wonderful operation about to transpire."[3] Gautier advanced to the middle of the rotunda, up two steps onto a pedestal and positioned his head under a silver pendant hanging to mark the exact median of the dome. "Leaving his hat on the coatrack, he tucked his hand into the lapel of his large jacket and gazed off into the distance."[4] An operator blew a whistle and twenty-four cameras opened at once. The twenty-four apparatuses were safely hidden behind false walls occupying the perimeter of the chamber. "Each camera had a primitive shutter arrangement in front of the lens; these shutters, in turn, were all interconnected, so that a single cord could be pulled to obtain two dozen simultaneous exposures."[5] A second whistle sounded, and the exposure was complete. The entire procedure lasted less than ten seconds.

The cupola on the Boulevard de l'Etoile was not a zoo for small animals, but a studio combining the arts of photography and sculpture. Bearing the name Photosculpture de France, the studio was a new commercial endeavor initiated by the artist François Willème. Willème filed a French patent on August 14, 1860, titled "Photosculpture Process," which described a technique for producing portrait sculptures relatively quickly and cheaply.[6]

It was wonderful to think of the sun as a photographer, thought Gautier, "but the sun as a sculptor! The imagination reels in the

---

3 Paul de Saint-Victor, "Photosculpture," *La Presse* (January 15, 1866), quoted in Jean-Luc Gall, "Photo/Sculpture: L'Invention de François Willème," *Etudes photographiques* 3 (November 1997): 65.

4 Wolfgang Drost, "La photosculpture entre art industriel et artisanat: La réussite de François Willème (1830–1905)," *Gazette des Beaux-Arts* 106 (October 1985): 113.

5 Sobieszek, "Sculpture as the Sum of Its Profiles," 621.

6 François Willème, "Photosculpture Process," French patent number 46,358, August 14, 1860. See also additions filed April 6, 1861, September 9, 1863, and June 14, 1864.

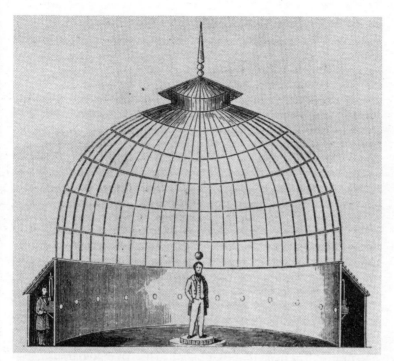

Figure 1. François Willème's reverse panopticon, a photographic studio with twenty-four cameras at the perimeter directed inward toward a central subject. Source: *The Art-Journal* (1864), 141.

face of such marvels."[7] Or as the journalist and editor Henri de Parville put it: "a sculptor and the sun will become two collaborators working together to fashion in forty-eight hours busts or statues of a hitherto unknown fidelity, of such great boldness in outline, of such admirable likeness."[8] Indeed Willème played up the magical quality of his invention, hiding the apparatus from the sitter, who likely had no idea how such a precise sculptural likeness could appear simply by bathing oneself in sunlight for ten seconds.

---

7 Gautier, *Photosculpture*, 4. For more on the complex relationship between photography and sculpture, see Bogomir Ecker et al., eds., *Lens-Based Sculpture: The Transformation of Sculpture Through Photography* (Cologne: Walter König, 2014).

8 Henri de Parville quoted in Sobieszek, "Sculpture as the Sum of Its Profiles," 622.

Seemingly magical, the sculpture in fact required several steps performed by skilled technicians. After the photographic session, craftsmen projected each of the twenty-four photographs in succession using a magic lantern.[9] A pantograph was used to trace the outline of each projected silhouette, cutting the silhouette into a clay blank. "In all probability the manual input required was very substantial."[10] Artisans turned the clay fifteen degrees on its vertical axis for each number of the twenty-four tracings, producing a rough cut of the sculpture. "It is now necessary to smooth by hand, or by a tool, all the slight roughness produced by the various cuttings, and to soften down and blend the small intervals between the outlines or profiles. This is a most delicate part of the process; for it must be understood that it requires an artist of taste and judgment to perform it satisfactorily, and to impart to the work all the finish possible."[11] The technique was pure magic to Gautier. "Each number carries its own essential line, its own characteristic detail. The mass of clay is scooped out, thinned down, and given shape. The traits of the face appear, the folds of the clothing are drawn out: reflection transformed into form."[12] The hand of the sculptor had been replaced by a mechanized technique, aided by the intermediary of photography, and ultimately by the light of the sun. *Solem quis dicere falsum audeat.*

Willème's *sculpture instantanée* was an attempt to advance a popular industrial art of sculptural portraiture for the new modern bourgeoisie, not unlike what the *carte de visite* had done in photography.[13]

---

9 "Willème almost always used a quarter-plate camera which accommodated a negative slightly less than ten and one-half centimeters high." (Sobieszek, "Sculpture as the Sum of Its Profiles," 619).

10 Philippe Sorel, "Photosculpture: The Fortunes of a Sculptural Process Based on Photography," in Françoise Reynaud et al., eds., Musée Carnavalet, *Paris in 3D: From Stereoscopy to Virtual Reality 1850–2000* (London: Booth-Clibborn, 2000): 82.

11 Anonymous, "Photo-Sculpture," *Art-Journal* (1864), 141.

12 Gautier, *Photosculpture*, 8.

13 The roots of photosculpture are complex given how many devices it combines and references. Beyond the *carte de visite* one might consider the physionotrace invented in the eighteen century by Gilles-Louis Chrétien and Edme Quénédey, following the Greek legend of Kora, who traced the profile of

"He entertained the fantasy that photosculptures, which varied in height from 35 to 55 centimeters, could be decoration pieces in the salons of the bourgeoisie, similar to daguerreotypes."[14] Willème even called his sculptural portraits *Bustes-Cartes*. As a commentator at the time put it: "They had, indeed, all the appearance of photographic productions, so correct were the forms and proportions, and so natural was the expression of countenance; they were, in fact, the very 'carte de visite' raised in solid form."[15] A fad during the years 1863 to 1868, photosculpture also produced offshoots in England and America. The technique was a hit at the 1863 photography exposition at the Palais de l'Industrie des Champs-Elysées and again at the Universal Exposition in Vienna in 1864, where Willème showed twenty-three sculptures. Willème's final success was at the Universal Exposition in Paris in 1867, after which he retired from photosculpture. His company disappeared after 1868.

"Two observations on Willème's process should be made at this point," wrote Philippe Sorel. "On the one hand, it picked up on the idea expressed by Benvenuto Cellini in the mid-sixteenth century,

---

her beloved using his shadow. The art of the physionotrace also has an important relationship to phrenology, a practice analyzed perhaps most interestingly in Hegel's *Phenomenology* in a chapter on the outtering or alienation of spirit titled "Observation of self-consciousness in its relation to its immediate actuality." G. W. F. Hegel, *The Phenomenology of Spirit*, trans. A. V. Miller (Oxford: Oxford University Press, 1977), 185–211. As Didi-Huberman reminded the reader: "When Hegel died, Niépce and Daguerre were nearing their second year of collaboration." Georges Didi-Huberman, *Invention of Hysteria: Charcot and the Photographic Iconography of the Salpêtrière*, trans. Alisa Hartz (Cambridge, MA: MIT Press, 2003), 30. Different but nevertheless also relevant is the physiotype, a pixel mesh used to take impressions of the face, developed circa 1835 by shipbuilder and inventor Pierre-Louis-Frederic Sauvage. "I had known Sauvage, in 1835, in connection with another invention called a physionotype, by means of which a mathematically correct impression could be taken of the features of any face," recalled the Prince de Joinville in his memoirs. "But as everybody made an appalling grimace before putting their face into the instrument, the result, though strictly exact, was monstrously ugly." Prince de Joinville, *Memoirs*, trans. Lady Mary Loyd (New York: Macmillan, 1895), 298.

14 Drost, "La photosculpture entre art industriel et artisanat," 124.

15 "Photo-Sculture," *Art-Journal*, 141.

and endorsed by Rodin in the late nineteenth century, that a statue results from the observation of a sum of profiles; on the other hand, it combined the two sculptural processes identified by Plato—removing material (cutting) and adding it (modelling)."[16]

Photosculpture thus has a strange relationship with chronophotography, the technique of capturing photographs through time made famous by Étienne-Jules Marey and Eadweard Muybridge. Both techniques are digital techniques—that much is clear—if we take digital to mean any mode of representation based on discrete units. Chronophotography is digital through a series of discrete photographic impressions segmented across time. Photosculpture is digital through discrete photographic impressions segmented in a spindle of space. Instead of an analysis of pictures, photosculpture relied on an analysis of profiles.

Just as one might speak of the fusion of afterimages—or "flicker fusion"—in the context of cinema, here one might speak of the fusion of sculptural sections, that is, figural silhouettes functioning as discrete dimensional samples that can be recreated into a continuous form. "Because of the law of continuity, it is not necessary to have an indefinite number of silhouettes in order to recreate the bust. A limited number will suffice, forty-eight for example."[17]

Before working in clay, Willème began his research with a prototype of a woman's head fashioned from thin slats of wood (figure 2). "This wooden head was probably shown to the Société Française de Photographie by Willème in May 1861, during the session at which he explained his new photographic process. However, the head was produced using a different technique from the one he subsequently developed and marketed. According to Willème, after taking fifty different angle shots of a statue, one

16 Sorel, "Photosculpture," 82. Sobieszek also suggests that Rodin used the technique of multiple silhouette profiles.

17 François Moigno, "Photo-sculpture: Art nouveau imaginé par M. François Willème," *Cosmos* 18 (May 17, 1861): 549–50, quoted in Sobieszek, "Sculpture as the Sum of Its Profiles," 617.

hundred strips of wood were assembled two by two so that they could be cut out according to the profiles of the photographs."[18] As in the science of psychophysics and its concept of a "just noticeable difference" in the human sensorium, Willème experimented with the width of the digital segmentation in order to achieve an optimal size. His wooden head of 1861 would have thus had a "resolution" of 3.6 degrees around the vertical axis. Later, once the technique was established using twenty-four cameras, the resolution had been degraded by a factor of four to 15 degrees.

According to Kaja Silverman, photography is "the world's primary way of revealing itself to us."[19] Yet Willème's technique reveals something profound, that there is an alternate history of photography *in which point of view has no meaning*, at least not a single point of view. The point of view, whether one or many, as in the case of montage, has so dominated how one thinks of photography, cinema, and visual culture in general that it is initially quite difficult to understand the ramifications of Willème's technique. Two things are particularly key. First, one must proliferate the number of points of view dispersed within a space—proliferated not simply to two or four but to a mathematically significant number like twenty, or a hundred, or a thousand. Second, one must conceive of the multiple points of view as temporally synchronous; in other words, one must reject the basic premise of chrono-photography, which multiplexes the image through time. Opening and closing all the camera apertures at the same moment is crucial. The resulting point of view is not "mobile," as it might be with a handheld film camera. Instead, the view is metastable, spanning all twenty-four cameras at once. Willème's mode of vision existed as the cumulative summation of twenty-four points of view fixed at the same instant in time.

---

18 Sorel, "Photosculpture," 81.

19 Kaja Silverman, *The Miracle of Analogy: or, The History of Photography, Part 1* (Stanford, CA: Stanford University Press, 2015), 10.

Figure 2. François Willème, unfinished photosculpture: portrait head of a woman, c. 1861. Source: George Eastman Museum.

In chronophotography or cinema, the multiplication of views leads to choice or synthesis. It leads, in other words, to montage or collage. An artist either montages a scene together by choosing which view to sequence at which time, or composites two or more image layers together to synthesize a new image. By contrast, Willème's mode of vision was neither choice-bound nor synthetic. It was metastable. Willème multiplied the view into a "virtual" view, a virtual camera existing synchronically across twenty-four discrete apparatuses. Willème did not choose or sequence these twenty-four streams; he did not composite them backward into a single image. He maintained the metastable view as such—the view as manipulable model.

The architecture of Willème's photographic studio (figure 1) resembled Jeremy Bentham's design of the panopticon prison, a circular structure of peripheral cells around a central focal point. Except in Willème's studio, the vectors of vision are all reversed. Instead of an eye at center, the watchful eye of the guard tower surveying the cells at the perimeter, Willème's studio revolved around the prisoner's point of view, as it were, the gazing lenses of twenty-four cameras at the perimeter all looking inward toward a single object of vision. In reversing the panopticon, Willème also reversed the normal configuration of the *camera obscura*, where light from nature passes through a single lens to make a single image. Willème multiplied the lenses from one to twenty-four, he arranged them inward rather than outward, and he synchronized them in time.[20]

For Paul de Saint-Victor, such metastases of the photographic view led not to an immaterial, omnipresent gaze but to a pure materiality, an immanent image—but a dead one. "The true mission of this useful and humble art form will be to bring sculpture into private life and to perpetuate the photographic image—by petrifying it."[21] What would it mean to petrify photography? Petrified photography is a kind of photography that has finally escaped the long shadow of the *camera obscura*. Petrified

---

20 In his canonical essay "Surveillance and Capture," Phil Agre described how "surveillance" apparatuses like photography and cinema are distinct from "capture" apparatuses like the computer. See Phil Agre, "Surveillance and Capture," *New Media Reader*, Wardrip-Fruin and Montfort, eds. (Cambridge, MA: MIT Press, 2003), 737–60.

21 Quoted in Jean-Luc Gall, "Photo/Sculpture: L'Invention de François Willème," *Etudes photographiques* 3 (November 1997): 76. The phrase "petrified photography" is Gall's.

photography converts photography into a plastic art. And in escaping the limitations of the *camera obscura*'s single aperture, photography smeared itself across a limitless grid of points, neutering the axis of time while emboldening the axes of space.

2

Dimensions Without Depth

In his monumental book *La méthode graphique*, Étienne-Jules Marey described a career's worth of work inventing a variety of writing machines and honing them for scientific research. For the most part, the book addressed the inscription of wave forms onto paper rolls. From time to time, Marey concerned himself with the clipping of these curves into quantized box shapes, and hence into digital notation. The second edition of the book was expanded to include a supplement, "The Development of the Graphical Method Through the Use of Photography," in which he reiterated the main focus of his career up to that point: "the mechanical inscription of movement using a stylus that draws on a rotating cylinder."[1]

In a lecture given at the national conservatory of arts and sciences on Sunday, January 29, 1899, at nearly seventy years old, Marey spoke in detail about the development of photography, particularly the new technique known as chronophotography

---

1 Étienne-Jules Marey, *La méthode graphique dans les sciences expérimentales et principalement en physiologie et en médecine* (Paris: G. Masson, 1885 [2nd edn.]), 1.

(taking multiple photographs through time) developed in the 1870s. It was in 1873 that his colleague at the Academy of Sciences, M. Cornu, showed the academy "four successive images of the sun taken on the same photographic plate." Then, "at about the same time" (in December 1874), Pierre-Jules-César Janssen, the astronomer and director of the Meudon Observatory, traveled to Japan to photograph the eclipse of the sun by Venus using a chronophotographic device designed to take pictures of the sky at fixed time intervals.[2] These were some of the earliest examples of chronophotography, but there would soon be others. As Marey explained, "it was only in 1878 that Muybridge, the photographer from San Francisco, began to take a large number of instant photos in very short intervals of animals in movement."[3] Marey also described his own contribution, the Photographic Gun, which was able to shoot a sequence of images in rapid succession using a single aperture and a rotating film plate, all housed in the shape of a hunting rifle.[4]

Indeed, during the period from 1873 to 1883, having already endured a series of rapid changes, photography began to split and evolve again, particularly in France but also in smaller ways in Germany and the United States.[5] A number of different futures

2 Étienne-Jules Marey, *La chronophotographie* (Paris: Gauthier-Villars, 1899), 5–6.

3 Ibid., 6.

4 Marey was not the first to marry camera and gun. See Josef Maria Eder, *Die photographische Camera und die Momentapparate* (Halle, 1892) for any number of exotic devices, such as Dr. Fol's photographic gun (587) and E. von Gothard's photographic gun (589).

5 Famous for his "Schnellseher" moving picture viewer, Ottomar Anschütz began practicing chronophotography as early as 1884, eventually using both fixed-plate and multicamera apparatuses. Like Eadweard Muybridge, he photographed horses in profile and human subjects performing various athletic movements. Like Georges Demenÿ he also made chronophotographic portraits of people speaking. "In the Summer of 1886, Ottomar Anschütz arrived in Hanover with a new and improved chronophotographic apparatus. Using the money provided by Kulturminister von Gosslar, Anschütz constructed a battery of 24 cameras with electrically linked shutters each equipped with a small

appeared for photography as a medium. One future took hold, and—the story goes—evolved into cinema and the moving picture. Another future languished in plain view, achieving partial success in certain situations.

Historians of photography, adopting somewhat onerous labels, call the first approach "moving-plate chronophotography," because the camera captures multiple images by moving the photographic plate behind a single lens. The second goes under the name "geometric chronophotography" (or fixed-plate chronophotography), because the photographic plate does not move while multiple images stack onto the same photograph like a geometric palimpsest.

It is this second approach that has so captured my attention. As with Willème's multiple lenses, geometric chronophotography multiplied the act of inscription while keeping the receptive substrate constant. As a consequence, successive inscriptions accumulate, like a palimpsest. There is something disorienting about this, but at the same time it is deeply human. "'What is the human brain, if not an immense and natural palimpsest?,'" asked Charles Baudelaire in a memorable passage. "'Such a palimpsest is my brain; such is yours too, reader. Everlasting layers of ideas, images, and feelings have fallen upon your brain as softly as light. Each succession has seemed to bury all that went before. And yet, in reality, not one has perished.'"[6]

---

electromagnet operated by an electrical metronome that allowed 24 exposures to be taken in anything from 3 seconds to as little as 0.72 second . . . Anschütz worked in Hanover with incredible energy, taking over 100 series photographs in just four weeks, sometimes making 15 separate series of 24 images a day." Deac Rossell, *Ottomar Anschütz and His Electrical Wonder* (London: Projection Box, 1997), 8–9. The sports doctor Ernst Kohlrausch also produced chronophotographic images in Germany circa 1892, likely inspired by Anschütz. The Deutsches Museum in Munich holds several such images by Kohlrausch.

6 Charles Baudelaire, *Artificial Paradises*, trans. Stacy Diamond (New York: Citadel Press, 1996), 147, quotation marks in original.

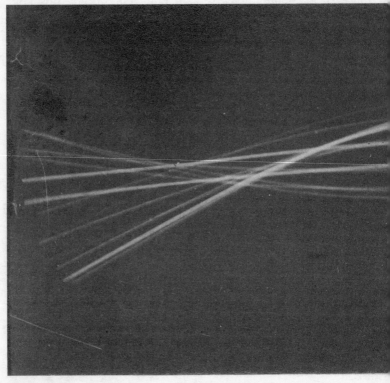

Figure 3. Étienne-Jules Marey, vibrations of a flexible rod, 1887. Source: Archives du Collège de France.

An image from 1887 of Marey vibrating a long wooden rod provides a beautiful example of geometric chronophotography (figure 3). The geometric qualities of the technique are on vivid display, as Marey's wooden stalk composes a shape by iterating a line across time, just as one might render multiple solutions to a mathematical equation on graph paper. The object draws itself in a mathematical graph of motion.[7]

---

7 For another example of the graphing ability of fixed-plate chronophotography, recall Demenÿ's work on "the generation of regular surfaces in cylinder and hyperboloid shapes, using a white wire photographed against a black background throughout the successive moments of its revolution." See

Media theorist Siegfried Zielinski described Marey's style in terms of "succession," contrasting Marey's preferences to those of Muybridge working in California:

> Muybridge, with his complex batteries of cameras, obtained successive shots of the phases of a movement as frozen moments, each on a separate photographic plate or each in one cadre. By this means, in the presentation and for the perception, he

Georges Demenÿ, *Conférences publiques sur la photographie théorique et technique* (Paris: Conservatoire national des arts et métiers, 1891), 11. Although rare, this effect resurfaces from time to time in film, perhaps most beautifully in Norman McLaren's *Pas de Deux* (1968).

accords the movement spatiality through successive juxtaposi-
tions from different perspectives. Marey, on the other hand, was
concerned with the reproduction of motion as a spatio-tempo-
ral continuum. Condensed through the lens of a single camera,
he particularly liked to melt successive images into one on a
single photographic plate or band of film.[8]

Both Muybridge and Marey experimented with many different
techniques, of course, and their resulting work cannot be said to
follow a single type at the exclusion of others. Nevertheless, Marey
favored devices with single lenses, which required him either to
iterate the image by moving the photographic plate (creating
arrays of images arranged in a strip or circle), or be satisfied with a
palimpsest of light, drawn inside a single image.

Just as a text-based palimpsest involves the layering of new
words on top of older words, so too the photographic palimpsest
heaps new light impressions on top of old, drawing onto the image
not so much a record of movement, although it is that too, but a
record of the total possibility space of a particular entity within its
own envelope of motion. The past mixes with the present by means
of a camera designed to capture successive images.

Geometric chronophotography tends to discretize pictures. The
image is segmented across two dimensions. Each small segment of
the picture claims a territory; together the individual segments
compose themselves into a whole. Consider James Ensor's 1899
painting "Self-Portrait with Masks" (figure 5), an image heavily
indebted to the kinds of collage and composite photography that
had become popular by the end of the nineteenth century. Here
the image multiplies into a series of spatial cells, which are themselves sewn together again via collage.

Indeed, if it is customary, albeit simplistic, to argue that moving-
plate chronophotography led into the cinema, then it is also

---

8 Siegfried Zielinski, *Audiovisions: Cinema and Television as Entr'actes in History*, trans. Gloria Custance (Amsterdam: Amsterdam University Press, 1999), 58.

common to suggest that geometric chronophotography fed into painting. The influence of geometric chronophotography on works such as Marcel Duchamp's *Nude Descending a Staircase* or Giacomo Balla's *Dynamism of a Dog on a Leash* has been noted by Marta Braun and other art historians.[9]

"With this tremendous development of technology, a completely new poverty has descended on mankind," lamented Walter Benjamin, responding to the recession in human experience wrought by the iron cage of modern life. "We need to remind ourselves of Ensor's magnificent paintings, in which the streets of great cities are filled with ghosts; philistines in carnival disguises roll endlessly down the streets, wearing distorted masks covered in flour and cardboard crowns on their heads. These paintings are perhaps nothing so much as the reflection of the ghastly and chaotic renaissance in which so many people have placed their hopes."[10] And, as Benjamin knew all too well, these philistines would be nowhere without a philistine aesthetic to sustain them.

So geometric chronophotography spatializes vision in segmented repetition across two dimensions, producing a kind of proto-digital repetition later regularized into the strict grid of the bitmapped image. In this sense, geometric chronophotography favors flat dimension, deemphasizing depth. But, in a different sense, these recursive palimpsests are deep as well as broad. For Benjamin's commentary was not just an allegory of the flattening of modern life, the making-superficial of a formerly deep affective self. On the contrary, Benjamin also knew that modernity performed deep surgery on the individual, constructing a complex, multilayered psyche, which ultimately collapses into the thin symptoms legible in pictures.

---

9 See in particular chapter 7, "Marey, Modern Art, and Modernism" in Marta Braun, *Picturing Time: The Work of Etienne-Jules Marey (1830–1904)* (Chicago: University of Chicago Press, 1992), 264–318. See also François Dagognet's *Etienne-Jules Marey* (New York: Zone, 1992).

10 Walter Benjamin, "Experience and Poverty," *Selected Writings, Volume 2: Part 2, 1931–1934* (Cambridge, MA: Harvard University Press, 1999), 732.

Figure 4. Albert Londe's 1891 chronophotographic camera with twelve apertures. Source: Ecole nationale supérieure des Beaux-Arts.

Recall how, in the phenomenology of Maurice Merleau-Ponty, depth is the most significant dimension because it is bound to the being of the perceiver. And if depth makes itself invisible due to foreshortening, then all the more relevant for an assessment of modern man:

> More directly than the other dimensions of space, depth forces us to reject the preconceived notion of the world and rediscover the primordial experience from which it springs: it is, so to speak, the most "existential" of all dimensions, because (and here Berkeley's argument is right) it is not impressed upon the object itself, it quite clearly belongs to the perspective and not to things. Therefore it cannot either be extracted from, or even put

Figure 5. James Ensor, "Self-Portrait with Masks," 1899.

into that perspective by consciousness. It announces a certain indissoluble link between things and myself by which I am placed in front of them.[11]

---

11 Maurice Merleau-Ponty, *Phenomenology of Perception*, trans. Colin Smith (New York: Routledge, 2004), 298.

Or consider photographic lenses: it is the telephoto lens, the lens most aggressively reliant upon the depth axis, that produces the flattest looking images. Likewise, with the recursive palimpsest, any dimensional propagation across the x and y axes is dwarfed, both technically and semiotically, by the chronological profundity of the z axis. In the end, what appears cellular is also, at the same time, deep.

3

The Parallel Image

Of course, it is cliché to explain contemporary media by revisiting the nineteenth century, rekindling the old arguments about photography and the origin of cinema, toasting those brave souls anxious about the growing technological alienation within art— Baudelaire or Benjamin (or Heidegger or Adorno), according to taste—and identifying how this or that historical detail was overlooked in the grand evolution of the image from mind and memory to the plastic and visual arts, to the automatic camera, to the moving image, and concluding with the digital.

Today, even the responses to such pat histories are themselves well rehearsed. To label nineteenth-century chronophotography "pre-cinematic" offends many historians, for not only does this reduce the specificity of real history to a mere instrumental prehistory within a process that can and must unfold in one particular way—Hollywood as destiny—it also smacks of a certain presentism within which the past is cast to play the various theatrical roles required to narrate *our s*pecial story. So Eadweard Muybridge and Étienne-Jules Marey play their respective parts because they mean something today, no matter that chronophotography was only one chapter in Marey's life's work, no matter that Marey mainly wanted to decompose movement not sew it back together again, no matter that neither of the two men can claim to have invented the technique outright, no matter that the most interesting chronophotographer was most certainly Albert Londe.

In fact, an important but often overlooked detail about Muybridge's photographic arena was that it was built around a core battery of twenty-four distinct cameras arranged in a line. Indeed, it occupied a fair amount of space. So, Muybridge's photographic "camera" was, to be precise, nothing of the sort; it was a photographic *array*, an extended series of cameras and triggers able to capture motion across a volume of space. Muybridge's practice was based on the proliferation of lenses, not simply the proliferation of photographic impressions. Furthermore, it was also common for Muybridge to record action from two or more vantage points simultaneously. For example, he might record from the side and rear angles, or from the quarter front and quarter rear angles. This typically happened diachronically in series, but it could even happen synchronically, freezing a single moment.[1]

Ever since the noble contributions of authors like Friedrich Kittler, media history has been shackled to an ignoble narrative: that the year 1900 marked the age of seriality, and that the serial image was a mechanized image firing forward in a line, like the rat-a-tat-tat of a machine gun.[2]

In many ways, Kittler was correct about the media of 1900. Nevertheless, an alternate history, parallel to the first, stands apart from the Kittlerian corpus, an alternate history with a different

1 See, for example, Illustration 24, "A Horse Rearing" in Eadweard Muybridge, *Animals in Motion* (New York: Dover, 1957), 72, or the "images of two athletes taken simultaneously from five different camera positions, 1879," reproduced in Braun, *Picturing Time*, 48.

2 This argument is presented in Friedrich Kittler, *Discourse Networks, 1800/1900*, trans. Michael Metteer and Chris Cullens (Stanford, CA: Stanford University Press, 1990), and again in Friedrich Kittler, *Gramophone, Film, Typewriter*, trans. Geoffrey Winthrop-Young and Michael Wutz (Stanford, CA: Stanford University Press, 1999), a formidable volume in its own right that Kittler nevertheless wryly disparaged as "*Discourse Networks* for kids."

origin and a different end. There is another story to tell about the evolution of chronophotography, a story that leads to some rather unexpected places: not serial but parallel, not linear but multi-plexed, not the moving image but the information model, in short, not the cinema but the computer. This is the story of the multi-lens apparatus, begun already by Willème in the 1860s, then picked up again by Londe and others in the 1880s.

On August 3, 1883, Londe presented a multi-lens device to the Société Française de Photographie, also publishing an article in *La nature* on his "photo-electric camera," a device featuring a circular set of nine apertures able to take pictures in sequence through time. Londe's apparatus, along with the photographs it produced, resembled a clock face with circular images appearing at the positions of the hours. Recall that Marey had dubbed the technique "chronophotography" only a year prior, emphasizing its affinities with clockwork.[3] Londe attached a metronome to his camera, which regulated the device through time. "The photo-electric camera created by Londe in 1883 sits at the crossroads between the two opposing devices by Janssen and Muybridge: like the former, it produces a sequence of impressions using a turning disk; like the latter, it has multiple points of view."[4] At around the same time as Londe, Marey experimented with the technique but found it tedious and quickly reverted to his own single-lens devices.[5]

---

3 Barthes noted this aspect of photography in a passing moment: "I love bells, clocks, watches—and I recall that at first photographic implements were related to techniques of cabinetmaking and the machinery of precision: cameras, in short, were clocks for seeing." See Roland Barthes, *Camera Lucida: Reflections on Photography*, trans. Richard Howard (New York: Wang and Hill, 1981), 15.

4 Denis Bernard and André Gunthert, *L'instant rêvé: Albert Londe, 1858–1917* (Nîmes: Éditions Jacqueline Chambon, 1993), 203.

5 In addition to his moving-plate and geometric chronophotographic work, Marey had "also tried a multiple-lens camera, in which the lenses were uncovered one at a time, sequentially exposing the single plate behind them. Muybridge had sent Marey sketches of such an instrument on 17 July 1882, but Marey was already familiar with the multiple-lens camera used by his friend Albert Londe. [. . .] Only one image—that of Marey throwing a stone—remains from Marey's own version of Londe's camera, constructed in winter 1883 [. . .] With this camera, the

While the multi-lens camera has important roots in stereoscopy, and in devices designed for *carte de visite* photographs or
smaller medallion portraits, Londe's nine-lens photoelectric
camera represented an important threshold in the history of optical media because of how it assembled an array of lenses within a
single apparatus.[6] Like a clock, the device could likely advance
regardless of a fixed beginning or end position, and thus the operator would be required to keep track of the starting position and
stop the clock manually to avoid double exposures.

Londe worked under Jean-Martin Charcot at the Salpêtrière
Hospital in Paris and used his camera there. "Photography decom-
poses movement," he wrote. "So what better field of study for it than
medicine! If some sick people are unable to move, there are others
afflicted with energetic movement! I'm referring here to those individuals suffering from illnesses of the nervous system, such as
hysteric-epileptics, epileptics proper, etc."[7] Londe domesticated and
medicalized the chronophotographic apparatus by moving it
indoors. No more of Muybridge's horses, no more of Marey's open
air tracks. Londe's subjects were in beds, many of them women
coaxed into familiarity with the camera by way of an electric relay
line that Londe would use to actuate the camera remotely, allowing
the apparatus to sit at a safe remove from doctor and patient.

"Londe, it seems, was interested in photographing the 'leading
ladies' of hysteria," wrote Joan Copjec, "for he brought to Charcot

---

biggest difficulty was making sure the light entered each of the lenses only once.
As insurance, he needed a second shutter that opened for the duration of the disk
rotation and then immediately closed. The way this second shutter operated and
its speed caused a 'violent shock' that, he wrote, 'certainly will compromise the
life of the instrument.'" Braun, *Picturing Time*, 85, 91.

6 Among other exotic devices, Josef Eder documented a nine aperture
"Medallion Camera," as well as Gorde's six-cel grid camera called the "Vélographe,"
in which an objective is placed over a plate and each cel is exposed individually.
See Josef Eder, *Die Photographische Camera und die Momentapparate* (Halle,
Saxony-Anhalt: Wilhelm Knapp, 1892), 449, 452.

7 Albert Londe, "La photographie en médecine: appareil photo-électrique,"
La nature 535 (September 1, 1883): 215.

three of the most famous, Louise Glaiz, Alphonsine Bar, and Blanche Wittmann. These women had the special talent of responding well to hypnotic suggestion and on this account they were used by hospitals, exchanged from one to the other throughout France for medical and legal experimentation."[8]

Londe continued working with multi-lens cameras, migrating to a twelve-lens apparatus in 1891 (figure 4). This new camera arranged its lenses in a two-dimensional array, rather than the circular design of the previous device. Subsequent to Muybridge's multi-lens battery, and a little-known "Type-16" camera-projector made by Augustin Le Prince in 1886, Londe's grid camera of 1891 is one of the most important photographic devices of the period because of how it proliferated the number of photographic eyes. "Just as there is no limit to the size of the device, the number of apertures isn't limited either," Londe explained. "In this way one could have any number of pictures. It is simply a question of apertures."[9] Instead of simply expanding through time, Londe also expanded the camera eye dimensionally across space. His device refused the monocular singularity of vision, dominant since the invention of renaissance perspective, in favor of a matrix of multiple sensors.

Yet in Marey's assessment, Londe's device was an inferior design. As evidence, Marey cited the fact that each of the twelve apertures captured the object from a slightly different vantage point, what in photography is called the parallax effect. Even if the difference in vantage point is minimal, the distortion in perspective created by multiple apertures was too great for Marey, a man for whom

---

8 Joan Copjec, "Flavit et Dissipati Sunt," *October* 18 (Autumn 1981): 24. On the complex interconnections between Charcot, Londe, Marey, and Freud, see also Mary Ann Doane, "Temporality, Storage, Legibility: Freud, Marey, and the Cinema," *The Emergence of Cinematic Time: Modernity, Contingency, the Archive* (Cambridge, MA: Harvard University Press, 2002), and Thomas Elsaesser "Freud as Media Theorist: Mystic Writing-pads and the Matter of Memory," *Screen* 50, no. 1 (2009): 100–13.

9 Londe, "La photographie en médecine," 217.

scientific precision was always paramount. But Londe was a scientist too; from Londe's perspective it was Marey's approach that was inferior. Where Marey wanted fusion between images, Londe required difference from one image to the next. The parallax effect was thus not a liability for Londe. Furthermore, Londe was not seduced by Marey's capturing of time, "which consists in obtaining the largest possible number of images per second."[10] Since a metronome governed Londe's camera, time could be both consistent within a given tempo but also elastic across slow and fast speeds. Indeed, the movement of some hospital patients was rapid, requiring a quick shutter speed, but for others it was slower.

The use of more than one aperture had, of course, already been widely adopted at the time, particularly during the period 1850–1880, thanks to the popularity of the stereoscope. The two-channel stereoscope was indeed a revolution in visuality, yet it remains a curiosity in the history of media: enormously popular, yet adrift in the family tree of optical representation. "Stereographic space is perspectival space raised to a higher power," wrote Rosalind Krauss. "Organized as a kind of tunnel vision, the experience of deep recession is insistent and inescapable."[11] Jonathan Crary

10 Albert Londe, *La photographie médicale* (Paris: Gauthier-Villars et fils, 1893), 107.

11 Rosalind Krauss, "Photography's Discursive Spaces," in *The Originality of the Avant-Garde and Other Modernist Myths* (Cambridge, MA: MIT Press, 1985), 136–37. Baudelaire mentioned the stereoscope along with various scientific toys—"of which I have neither good nor bad to say"—in his essay "A Philosophy of Toys." See Charles Baudelaire, *The Painter of Modern Life and Other Essays*, trans. Jonathan Mayne (New York: Phaidon, 1995), 202. A tidbit from Thomas Mann, writing in 1924 about Europe at the turn of the twentieth century, is also irresistible: "The majority of the patients stood about chatting in little groups. Two green folding tables had been set up for devotees of games—dominoes at the one, bridge at the other, although only young people were playing cards . . . In the first social room there were also a few optical gadgets for their amusement: the first, a stereoscopic viewer, through the lenses of which you stared at photographs you inserted into it—a Venetian gondolier for example, in all his bloodless and rigid substantiality; the second, a long, tubelike kaleidoscope that you put up to one eye, and by turning a little ring with one hand, you could conjure up a magical

The Parallel Image   41

generally agreed with this sentiment, noting that the stereoscope ushered in a newfound awkwardness of seeing, just as much as it heightened realism via depth and dimensionality:

> In such images the depth is essentially different from anything in painting or photography. We are given an insistent sense of "in front of" and "in back of" that seems to organize the image as a sequence of receding planes. And in fact the fundamental organization of the stereoscopic image is *planar . . .* Thus stereoscopic relief or depth has no unifying logic or order. If perspective implied a homogeneous and potentially metric space, the stereoscope discloses a fundamentally disunified and aggregate field of disjunct elements.[12]

This disjunct is precisely what kept Marey away from multi-lens cameras. Yet the disjunct—once reaffirmed as a precisely calibrated set of differentials—would eventually become an asset to vision rather than a liability.

The *carte de visite* of André-Adolphe-Eugène Disdéri is the missing link between Londe and the stereoscope. As "photographer to the Emperor" and popularizer of the small portrait card (*carte de visite*), Disdéri had perfected a technique of printing multiple portrait pictures onto a single photographic substrate, thereby increasing the number of images produced by a single apparatus.[13] To capture multiple images, Disdéri did not move the

---

fluctuation of colorful stars and arabesques; and finally, a little rotating drum in which you place a strip of cinematographic film and then looked through an opening on one side to watch a miller wrestle with a chimney sweep, a schoolmaster paddle a pupil, a tightrope-walker do somersaults, or a farmer and his wife dance a rustic waltz." Thomas Mann, *The Magic Mountain,* trans. John Woods (New York: Knopf, 1995), 98.

12 Jonathan Crary, *Techniques of the Observer: On Vision and Modernity in the Nineteenth Century* (Cambridge, MA: MIT Press, 1990), 125.

13 Along with Louis de Loménie, Disdéri was also a prominent figure in the publication of the *Galerie des Contemporains*, featuring pictures of contemporary life and portraits of well-known people. The *Galerie* was published twice a week

photographic plate as Marey and others would later, but instead used multiple lenses. "Another very useful development," he wrote of his custom-made camera, "is the ability to take several images at the same time on the same glass."[14] He began with a two-lens "camera designed to take stereoscopic images," then stacked two such cameras one on top of the other, resulting in a device with four lenses arranged in a two by two square.[15] Yet, instead of opening the lenses in sets of two, as the stereoscopic camera did to capture binocular vision, Disdéri modified his camera so that each of the four lenses could be opened at different times. This freed up all four lenses to function independently. The stereoscope was locked into the rubric of binocular vision, yet Disdéri's device was unlocked, able to write in parallel using a number of distinct optical channels, first four then more.[16]

Disdéri's photography was a photography of scenes, not a photography of movement. Each of Disdéri's photographs was part of a parallel collection of images, scattered in time, but not part of a regularized, temporal sequence. Disdéri's system was not

---

and collected four times a year into volumes. Immodestly describing himself in publicity material as the "Titian of the genre," Disdéri promised to deliver portraits of all the "crowned heads, princes, generals, grand dignitaries, illustrations drawn from literature, the arts, the clergy, the magistracy, moguls from the world of finance and diplomacy, the best that nature has to offer. [. . .] With the *Galerie des Contemporains* one is never alone; be it on the road or in the country, riding by train or tucked away in an ocean liner, in the shade or at the fireside, you'll never be far away from the celebrities of the nineteenth century." See André-Adolphe-Eugène Disdéri, "Galerie des Contemporains," December 1861, AD-1822 (184), box 4, supplement, 2–3, 6, La Bibliothèque nationale, Richelieu, Estampes et photographie, Paris.

14 André-Adolphe-Eugène Disdéri, *L'art de la photographie* (Paris: J. Claye, 1862), 99.

15 Ibid., 104.

16 Which was Muybridge's trick too, although in slightly different formation. "Twelve magnificent Scoville cameras were ordered from New York, and their double lenses for taking stereoscopic pictures were ordered from Dallmeyer of London. Swift-action shutters were constructed . . . to fire the cameras." See Robert Hass, *Muybridge: Man in Motion* (Berkeley: University of California Press, 1976), 109–10.

"pre-cinematic," in that sense, and could never be. Instead, Disdéri recorded a subject across its many aspects, its many dimensions. Like Disdéri and Willème before him, Londe proliferated his lenses in a spatial array, deemphasizing time while emboldening space.

All this begins to reveal the photographic *array*, an ordered arrangement of discrete elements. For Marey, the array was immediately visible as repeated inscriptions on the photographic plate. For Willème, the array was built up from a multiplicity of discrete lenses arranged in space. Like Willème, Londe also literalized the array in the photographic apparatus itself, using a grid of lenses that anticipated the sensor arrays in today's digital cameras.

4

Photographic Modeling

If Londe neglected to model the world with his multi-lens device (merely photographing it), a slightly different technique, owing perhaps more to Muybridge and Willème than to Londe, was revealed in the early 1890s in Germany. Christian Wilhelm Braune and a student thirty years his junior, Otto Fischer, developed a technique for capturing the motion of a body and modeling it in three dimensions. Where photographers like Disdéri, Londe, and Le Prince took small steps in this direction, unknowingly to be sure, Braune and Fischer took a giant leap into the realm of parallel optical dimensionality.

Braune and Fischer used multiple cameras arranged in an arc around the test subject, similar to Willème's reverse panopticon. Pointed inward, the cameras could fire together, capturing a single moment from multiple sides. The cameras also took photographs in sequence, generating a synchronized stream of images from multiple points of view. By integrating both the parallelity of Willème with the seriality of Muybridge and Marey, Braune and Fischer were able to pinpoint the movements of a test subject in both space and time. Today we refer to this as "motion capture."

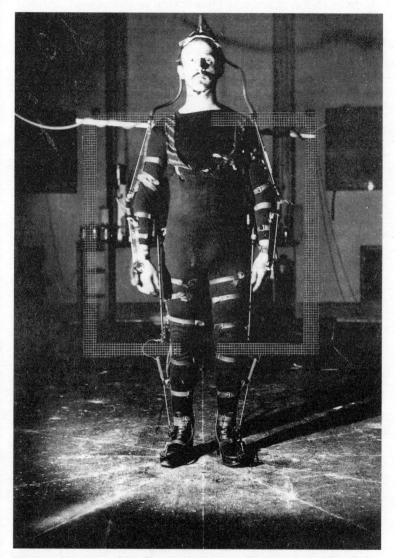

Figure 6. Braune and Fischer, test subject wearing the chronophotographic suit used for the documentation and analysis of human locomotion. Source: Wilhelm Braune and Otto Fischer, *Der Gang des Menschen* (1895).

Like a cyborg, Braune and Fischer's test subject wore an exoskeleton of electrical wires and glass light bulbs called Geissler tubes (figure 6). Similar to neon, Geissler tubes emit light when electrified. The test subject would perform a series of movements, the tubes would flash, and four different cameras arranged in a semicircle around the subject would capture the event.

"Braune and Fischer's experimental design sought to solve a problem associated with Marey's method," wrote Siegfried Zielinski.

The Geissler tubes in Braune and Fischer's experiment ran parallel to the rigid parts of the limbs and were held in place by leather straps. In all, there were eleven tubes. The advantage of this experimental design was that, since the Geissler tubes used induction current, they could produce short flashes of light in quick succession . . . [so] it was possible to take photographs in which the individual limbs appeared as separate lines.[1]

In fact, Braune and Fischer's goal was not simply to produce a photographic image, chronographic or otherwise. Their goal was to record precise mathematical coordinates in three-dimensional x-y-z space for the shoulders, knees, and other parts of the body in motion. Since Braune and Fischer deployed a multi-lens technique, and since all cameras fired together, the resulting photographs could be measured and correlated with each other, similar to the use of stereometric cameras in photogrammetry. What began as chronophotography thus evolved into a form of dimensional modeling.

To achieve the desired level of precision, Braune and Fischer would inspect the resulting chronophotographs under a microscope, measuring the precise positions of the arm, leg, and torso to

---

1 Siegfried Zielinski, *Deep Time of the Media: Toward an Archeology of Hearing and Seeing by Technical Means* (Cambridge, MA: MIT Press, 2006), 248.

several decimal points of accuracy. Relying on registration marks
that appear in each image and by correlating each measurement
across all four cameras, extremely precise spatial coordinates could
be triangulated along three-dimensional axes. They were able to
generate x-y-z vertex coordinates for specific points. For Braune
and Fischer, the ultimate prize was thus the data; the photographs
themselves were mostly incidental. The two scientists published
their vertex coordinates in long tables of numbers, which not
surprisingly resemble the kinds of three-dimensional graphics
formats that would be invented decades later for architectural
drafting and computer modeling.

While incidental by-products, Braune and Fischer's photographs
were nevertheless complex. Ostensibly a genre of geometric
chronophotography, the images also have a primitive "heads-up
display" consisting of a mesh square and other registration marks
superimposed over the image. Such nondiegetic technical supports
were common across all kinds of chronophotography: Muybridge
frequently used a gridded backdrop; Marey put clocks and check-
erboard hash marks in his images to help with registration. As
nondiegetic technical supports, such details shifted the image
away from traditional photographic representation and toward a
more informatic and computational usage.

But photography was only the means to an end. Braune and
Fischer made novel use of their heaps of data. Just as Willème
had used photography as a way to produce sculpture, Braune
and Fischer used photography to build models (figure 7).
Inspired perhaps by Marey's bronze sculpture of a pigeon in
flight, Braune and Fischer restaged their scores of vertex coordinates into actual three-dimensional models of human locomotion. If Marey's metier was geometric chronophotography,
Braune and Fischer added dimensionality to the mix and
produced something quite different, geometric *chrono-models*.
What resulted was a diffuse, omniscient gaze engulfing a
precisely modeled object world. The model could be spun
around, manipulated at will.

Figure 7. Braune and Fischer, model of human locomotion. Source: Cinémathèque française.

In a sense, Braune and Fischer performed three-dimensional modeling in the 1890s akin to the computer graphics of several decades later.[2] Consider the celebrated "bullet time" sequences from *The Matrix* (directed by the Wachowskis, 1999).[3] A certain

---

2 For more on the evolution of modeled objects in computer graphics, see Jacob Gaboury, *Image Objects* (Cambridge, MA: MIT Press, 2021).

3 As James Hodge has pointed out to me, others had been experimenting with this mode of vision well before it ended up in Hollywood. In the early 1980s

mythology has grown up around this technique, yet there is nothing particularly high-tech about it. The ability to freeze and rotate a scene within the stream of time is possible with normal cameras. All that is required is a battery of apparatuses arranged along an arc, along with the technical wherewithal to trigger them at exactly the same instant. The individual photographs can then be spliced together into a movie strip to achieve the effect. Thus, nothing technological would have prevented bullet time from appearing a hundred years before the Wachowskis. Indeed, Willème's arc of twenty-four cameras resembles the kinds of photographic stages used to record "bullet time." And, while Braune and Fischer used only a handful of cameras, the effect was similar.

Yet by 1900, Kittler's symbolic year, this kind of "bullet time" went into hibernation, and time bullets took over instead. Marey's photographic gun shot multiple images of the same scene from the same point of view, only divided into separate photographs and extended through time. Each "bullet" was an individual photograph, and, as a series, the bullets resembled what would later become the cinematic filmstrip. Marey's time bullets settled time, regularizing it into a fixed frequency.

By 1900, time had become the natural infrastructure of cinematic animation, while spatial representation and visual expression had become variables.[4] The cinema mechanized time, thereby perverting it, and instead elevated the value of worlds. Indeed,

---

Tim Macmillan developed what he calls a "time-slice" camera, which he would eventually use in a video projection titled "Dead Horse" that exhibited at the London Electronic Arts Gallery in 1998.

4 A number of articles narrate the mid-twentieth-century passage from a traditional photographic image rooted in perspectival, Renaissance techniques to a computer-enhanced photographic image oriented around the techniques of volumetric capture, multiple points of view, and world simulation. See in particular Lisa Cartwright and Brian Goldfarb, "Radiography, Cinematography and the Decline of the Lens," in *Incorporations*, ed. Jonathan Crary and Sanford Kwinter (New York: Zone, 1992): 190–201.

Gilles Deleuze would later speak of "time cinema" as a kind of art cinema.[5]

But with bullet time—whether in the 1890s or the 1990s—time had become a variable, and space was suspended in synchrony. Volumetric representation became a natural infrastructure of the medium. Willème's photosculpture or Braune and Fischer's chrono-models were thus forerunners to today's computer modeling. By multiplexing vision, as in Muybridge's multiple synchronic images or in Londe's grid cameras, a new pathway emerged. These approaches deployed multiple lenses in order to animate the camera by making it metastable and virtual. By modeling the spatial coordinates of the test subject, it became possible to translate the movement (of the camera) into spatial dimensionality, and in doing so, translate photography into sculpture.

    5 See in particular volume 2 and the end of volume 1 of his *Cinema* books (Deleuze, *Cinema 1*, and Gilles Deleuze, *Cinema 2: The Time-Image*, trans. Hugh Tomlinson and Robert Galeta [Minneapolis: University of Minnesota Press, 1989]). Deleuze's book on Francis Bacon is also interesting here, since, as is well documented, Bacon was cognizant of Muybridge and even incorporated the chronophotographic aesthetic into his paintings, including the nondiegetic registration marks and the rounded ring as a kind of photographic stage. See Gilles Deleuze, *Francis Bacon: The Logic of Sensation* (Minneapolis: University of Minnesota Press, 2003).

5

Our Best Machines Are
Made of Sunshine

How did the computer learn to see? The most common response is that the computer learned to see from the movies, that is, from the twentieth century's most highly evolved technology of vision. But where did the cinema get that ability from? From nineteenth-century still photography of course, which apparently got it from the venerable *camera obscura*, which, in turn, gained the faculty from the sun itself. As an origin myth, the story has the benefit of being neat and tidy, perhaps too tidy, a bit like the old story of how Prometheus transferred the technology of illumination from divine nature to mortal man. An engaging tale, it nevertheless bears the distinct disadvantage of being untrue, at least in part.

How did the computer learn to see? As I have been suggesting thus far, a better answer is to say that the computer learned to see not from cinema or even from photography but from adjacent fields like sculpture or architecture, specifically the tradition of architectural modeling, that special mode of sculpture devoted not to the integral object but to complexities of the built environment.[1]

---

1 Taking a different approach, a number of scholars have preferred to stress the essential *continuity* between the cinema and the computer. See, in particular,

Not architecture in the classical sense of temples and monuments, or caves and campfires (as Reyner Banham once put it), but rather that the computer sees the world through a kind of virtualization of space.

Part of this alternative conception—the notion that the computer sees more like a sculptor or a model maker—has to do with a particular contract made between perception and the objects of perception. The photographic version of the contract, if it were drawn as a diagram, would resemble a cone splayed outward from an origin point, like a horn. Something of great importance occupies the spot at the tip of the horn, something important like a lens or an aperture or an eyeball or a subject. Starting at the focal point, photographic vision fans out into the world, locating objects in proximal relation to the origin. Because of its putative resemblance to human vision, what with its rich focal point (the eye, the mind) and conical purview (the human gaze), the photographic diagram has indeed been quite influential, playing an outsize role in philosophy and culture.

Yet the human eye is too rich. Physiologically too rich, the eye has accumulated an excess of perceptual power. It looms over the other senses, disciplining them and claiming their territory for its own. Pity the eye, for its very success is a kind of handicap. Like the glutton who can no longer experience pleasure, the eye is so ravenously successful at raw perception that it obstructs and stunts the other senses. We are those fiddler crabs whose single claw, oversized and asymmetrical, lords over an atrophied body.

Gilles Deleuze and Félix Guattari used the term "deterritorialized" to describe the face. Their claim was counterintuitive at first, given how the face is home to a number of fragile and complex

---

Lev Manovich, "The Automation of Sight: From Photography to Computer Vision," in *Electronic Culture* (New York: Aperture, 1996), 229–39; Friedrich Kittler, "Computer Graphics: A Semi-Technical Introduction," trans. Sara Ogger, *Grey Room* 2 (Winter 2001): 30–45; and Anne Friedberg, *The Virtual Window: From Alberti to Microsoft* (Cambridge, MA: MIT Press, 2006).

organs, the eyes above all. But Deleuze and Guattari saw the face as deterritorialized because of the sheer amount of stuff that passes through it every day, stuff both material and immaterial. More promiscuous than the skin or the genitals or any other part of the body, the face allows for high throughput of air, food, and water, plus immeasurable amounts of sensational riches, from words and ideas to caresses and kisses.

Yet computational media has finally impoverished the eye, thereby hastening the dissolution of the face. Indeed, computational vision is also conical, but inverted, more like a funnel with the tip facing away. Here the perceiving subject is not focused into a dense, rich point at the center but diffuses itself outward toward the edge of the space (as in Willème's work). The object, by contrast, lies at the point of the funnel, receiving all the many inputs issued to it from the perimeter. Thus, if the photographic eye is, as it were, *convex*, like the prow of a ship jutting out into the world from the middle, then the computational eye is *concave*, flanking and encompassing the world from the fringe.

In other words, architecture, modeling, and all those art forms where the complexities of system and dimension are more important than the integrity of the object or a particular point of view, share a special condition, not so much a problem to be solved but a state of affairs waiting to be explored. The condition is simple: assume that objects and worlds will be viewable and manipulable from all sides in multiple dimensions. Industrial designers encounter this condition frequently; non-Brechtian theatrical producers consider it less. Architects, all the time; photographers, almost never. Plato, sure; Husserl, probably not. And, it turns out, computer modelers encounter this condition as well. It is a basic part of what they do every day.

Computational vision takes it as a given that objects and worlds can and will be viewable from all sides. Indeed, the point should be made more forcefully. Computational vision takes it as a given that *point of view is not necessary for seeing*. The issue is not simply that vision has become abstract, not simply that vision has been unloosed from its subjective mooring, two feats already accomplished during the Renaissance if not earlier. The crux of the issue is that seeing no longer requires a *point*. Indeed, if we persist in granting the *camera obscura* pride of place within such a genealogy, the narrative will always return to the same point; luckily those other arts (chief among them architecture, modeling, and sculpture) exist to demonstrate the utility of pointlessness.

"Our best machines are made of sunshine," wrote Donna Haraway, "they are all light and clean because they are nothing but signals, electromagnetic waves, a section of a spectrum."[2] In a superficial sense, Haraway was wrong of course; computers are not made of sunshine, and in fact computers are not optical devices in the strict technical sense, favoring abstract mathematical values over illuminated visuality.[3] Yet, in another sense, Haraway captured the essence of computation. Computers are made of sunshine because they include things like fiber optic cables and photon switches. They are made of sunshine in a looser sense too because they consist of energy moving through matter. Furthermore, the discipline of computer modeling strives to simulate the behavior of light using mathematical equations, and thus is a kind of "sunshine simulator." In other words, computers still use light, even if they abjure the commands of the *camera obscura*.

To accomplish the simulation of sunshine, a raft of Renaissance techniques were imported wholesale into computer graphics, from vanishing-point perspective to the radiosity of light. Media theorists like Friedrich Kittler have chronicled the complicated origins of computer graphics, granting admittance to the

---

2 Donna Haraway, *Manifestly Haraway* (Minneapolis: University of Minnesota Press, 2016), 13.

3 Whether computers are optical media is a point of some debate. Compare for instance Friedrich Kittler's conclusions to the negative in *Optical Media: Berlin Lectures 1999*, trans. Anthony Enns (Cambridge: Polity, 2010) with the more positive account provided in Bernard Dionysius Geoghegan, "An Ecology of Operations: Vigilance, Radar, and the Birth of the Computer Screen," *Representations* 147 (Summer 2019): 59–95.

modern optical sciences, but also including strange antecedents like radar, which assigns addresses to dots, and indeed text and literature itself, which provides some explanation for the wordiness of source code.[4] (While the proper art-historical narrative has yet to be written about aesthetic biases inherent to computer graphics, suffice it to say that the computer tends to be more classical than experimental in its assumptions about how light moves through space, with a lot of Jacques-Louis David or M.C. Escher and very little Odilon Redon or James Turrell.) In fact, the history of computer graphics is largely a history of *rendering*, that is, the process of projecting a volumetric space onto a flat rectangle.

The abstraction of vision is quite old, to be sure, from outlandish narratives in Plato's cosmological dialogue *Timaeus* to the development of the science of optics under Kepler, Descartes, Newton, and other moderns. In literature, free indirect discourse allowed for the abstraction of subjectivity from a specific human witness—a James Boswell or a Dr. Watson—to a free-floating mode of observation. (According to Pasolini, such free-floating observation was subsequently imported wholesale into the cinema.[5]) The concept of neutral vision has also played a role in the development of empiricism and the objective sciences, along with, in a different way, political theories about blind justice and the indifference of the machines of state. Point of view has also long been a problem in painting, the most ready if not cliché example being cubism.

Still, none of these approaches discards the eye entirely. These various techniques merely modify the quality of the eye, allowing it to be fluid rather than fixed, objective rather than subjective, or neutral rather than motivated. What would it mean to see

---

4 See for instance Friedrich Kittler, "Computer Graphics: A Semi Technical Introduction," *Grey Room* 2 (Winter 2001): 30–45.

5 See Pier Paolo Pasolini, *Heretical Empiricism*, trans. Ben Lawton and Louise K. Barnett (Washington, DC: New Academia, 2005).

something in all ways from all sides at all times? Not merely abstractly, not merely objectively, not merely neutrally, but actually? An "ethical" visuality will be its proper moniker, for the ethical is that mode in which all points and positions dissolve in favor of a single, generic claim: "all is love"; or, here, "there is no point of view." Photography says *here is a view*, but computer vision says there is no point of view because *here are all of them*.

Historically, there have been two basic ways to obtain such ethical vision, either via the multiplicity of vision (the schizophrenic route), or via the virtualization of vision (the gnostic route). And if the cinema is a schizophrenic machine with its jump cuts and multiple cameras and parallel montage, the computer is most certainly a gnostic one, promising immediate knowledge of all things at all times from all places. There is some irony here, as any art form in which seeing does not require point of view will experience a newfound freedom to reduplicate points and views to infinity. Visuality does not vanish. On the contrary, visuality goes metastable, appearing at any place and any time under the aegis of the "virtual camera."

After all, vision is just a variable for the computer, a variable like anything else. And the typical elevations and sections inherited from architectural drafting are now as fungible as any other kind of input. Such unbridled freedom itself breeds a secondary form of regularization in which the infinity of possible views reduces to a short list of common ones. Thus architecture, the art of space and volume, is also the profession that has most efficiently disciplined vision into elevation, section, and plan. But regularity need not be shunned out of mere reflex. The apparent rigidity of the Euclidean coordinate system in fact furnishes much needed structure to this aesthetic mode that, as we have said, has no point of view (because it has all of them).

The result is less a meditation on light than an experiment within media systems, an experiment in which nothing is revealed, except the novel revelation that light might not be revelatory after all. Instead, the computer's revelation comes in the form of a reduplication: multiply the points of view, distribute them in space, and favor parallel capture over diachronic series. The photographic multiple is thus the start of a story but by no means a sufficient end. In order to understand computation more fully, we will need to explore multiplicity in other media formats, including textiles, games, calculating machines, cellular automata, and beyond.

PART II.
Weaving

6

Spider Work

Clytemnestra was lost by music. For it is said that when her husband, the general Agamemnon, left his Clytemnestra behind in search of glory at Troy, he stipulated that a Dorian musician—and no other—should remain behind in his wife's chambers as a sort of prophylactic against any potential seduction. With Agamemnon abroad, Aegisthus came as a suitor to the lonely queen. At first the Dorian kept Aegisthus at bay through his song. Yet once Aegisthus discovered that the martial spirit of the music was conspiring to keep Clytemnestra true, Aegisthus slit the bard's throat and claimed his prize, the queen no longer chastened by the Dorian mode.[1]

If Clytemnestra was lost by music, Agamemnon was lost by webs and networks. In fact, the tragedy *Agamemnon* by Aeschylus contains some of the oldest depictions of networks, and hence some of the oldest examples of media systems in Western literature. In his play Aeschylus depicted two different types of networks.

---

1 The story is recounted in Jacques Ozanam and Jean Etienne Montucla, *Recreations in Mathematics and Natural Philosophy*, vol. 2, trans. Charles Hutton (London: Longman, Hurst, Rees, Orme, and Brown, 1814), 360.

The first was an actual communications network, which was described in detail but remained off stage. The second was a mesh-work of traps, which while visible and present was but a symbol of larger machinations.

The actual communications network was a chain of fire beacons, spanning a few hundred miles, which carried the message of the fall of Troy back to Argos, and thus warned of the victor Agamemnon's imminent homecoming. "Ida first launched his blazing beam; thence to this place / Beacon lit beacon in relays of flame" (lines 281–3), Clytemnestra explained, describing each of the dozen nodes in the overland communications chain.[2] "They blazed in turn, kindling their pile of withered heath, / And passed the signal on" (294–5).

But later, upon the return of Agamemnon to his hearth, a second net was deployed, this one a "vast voluminous net" (1382) used by Clytemnestra—now in league with Aegisthus—to ensnare her husband and bring about his ruin. This voluminous net, later decried by the chorus as a "foul spider's web" (1492) found form in a symbol: the sea of purple textile created by Clytemnestra and her weavers to adorn the threshold of the house, and upon which Agamemnon was eventually convinced to tread against his better judgment. With that silken step Agamemnon was, as Aegisthus gloated in the final lines of the play, "tangled in a net the avenging Furies wove" (1580) and his fate at Clytemnestra's bloody hands was all but sealed.

Sensing that her wait was nearly over, the coy betrayer enticed Agamemnon with mock concern for his many rumored battle scars:

Why, if my lord received as many wounds as Rumour,
Plying from Troy to Argos, gave him, he is a net,
All holes! (866–8)

---

2 Parenthetical citations refer to line numbers from the Greek text. The translation is from Aeschylus, *The Oresteian Trilogy*, trans. Philip Vellacott (New York: Penguin, 1956).

Indeed, the image of the hero as netting, with his wounds representing the holes coming between each strand of the net, eventually materialized as his body was perforated three times in the play's final scenes. Before it was recounted by Clytemnestra, the murder, and the weaponized net necessary for its consummation, was predicted first by Cassandra:

> There, there! O terror! What is this new sight?
> A hunting-net, Death's weapon of attack!
> And she who hunts is she who shared his bed. (1114–16)

Webs and nets thus oscillate here between two related but incompatible formal structures. On one side, the chain of triumph; on the other, the web of ruin. In *Agamemnon* the chain of triumph is linear, efficient, and functional. It is contagious and additive as it moves. The lighting of one hilltop beacon does not dim or dilute the previous node but in fact compounds it. The chain of triumph is communicative and telepresent. It is directional. It follows a chain of command. It is constitutive of reality rather than destructive of it. And perhaps most evocative: the chain of triumph is made of pure energy. It is Iris and Hermes combined.

On the other hand, the web of ruin is none of these things. The divine referent is not Iris or Hermes, but the Furies. Less concerned with connectivity, the web of ruin brings with it a flood of insatiable persecution. Here the net is not a tonic, tethering together distant elements, but a solvent set on dissolving those ties. It is commonly characterized as a swarm, or a pack of animals, and is always unknowable in quality and innumerable in form. It is a nonlinear mesh, not a linear chain, designed to ensnare and delimit. Hence the web of ruin can always be deployed against the most intractable of opponents. So, while the first network of fire beacons runs in advance of the second, it is the second that undoes the first. Only Clytemnestra's net can trap Ilium's conqueror, eviscerating the house of Atreus.

In *Agamemnon*, the first play of Aeschylus's Orestes trilogy, the Furies are only mentioned in passing. But in the third play, *The Eumenides*, the Furies return to saturate the narrative so fully that they are personified in an actual character, the chorus, but a character that can only be represented by a multiplicity of physical bodies. What were three in Virgil, these numerically variable divinities are twelve in Aeschylus (in Euripides they are fifteen). In tragedy, the chorus is generally a signifier for the social community. It is not a synonym for "the masses" or "the people" but simply the social "group." This makes *The Eumenides* unusual, for what were stern, scolding elders in *Agamemnon* and clamoring female maidservants in the second play, *The Libation Bearers*, have in the third play devolved into a personification of vengeance itself, but in a nonhuman, which is to say divine, form. This is no longer the "group" but the swarm.

The web of ruin, symbolized in the first two plays by Clytemnestra's various textiles—her weaponized nets and the purple sea of fabric, but also the tentacles of fabric forming the robe used to subdue Agamemnon like a straightjacket, what Orestes in *The Libation Bearers* calls "a trap, not of iron, but of thread" (493)—this web of ruin is no longer a symbol in the third and final play, but an actual incarnation of networked presence itself. In short, the Furies are the web of ruin personified. Hermes (as the chain of triumph) appears in *The Eumenides* too, if only for an instant. He shepherds Orestes in his travel link from Delphi to Athens. So, while Athena and the concept of justice certainly dominate the final play, the Furies indicate the lingering threat of networked forms of being, if not also networked vengeance.

The concordance between textiles and spider webs is noted also in Ovid with the story of Arachne, the haughty weaver maiden whom Athena transforms into a spider: "her hair and then her eyes and ears fell off, and all her body sank. And at her sides, her slender fingers clung to her as legs. The rest is belly; but from this,

Arachne spins out a thread; again, she practices her weaver's art, as once she fashioned webs."[3]

Arachne reappears in Dante as an allegorical figure for the poet himself, undone at the hands of his own artistic creation.[4] The thread used to weave the pictorial textile becomes a noose with which Arachne tries to hang herself in defiance of the goddess. But the noose becomes a web again, referring back to the "spinning" of the artist, be it tales or tapestries.

If Clytemnestra used her textiles as weapons, Penelope also had a tactical relationship with the loom and her weaving. As Liddell and Scott describe it, Penelope was called by her name because of the *pēnē* [πήνη], the web that she wove.[5] Or, more accurately, unwove, as Penelope alternated between weaving and unweaving as a way to manage and subdue her male suitors.

Penelope's loom did not resemble modern draw looms, but rather stood up vertically, an upright frame where the warp yarns draped downward, held taut by weights at the bottom. Ancient Greek weavers could create a shed by pulling warp threads outward, and the weft was likely beaten upward from below, as opposed to the pulled beat of the typical hand loom. As Penelope wove, the fabric would have hung down vertically from the beam, like laundry.

The beam also furnishes a clue. For Penelope's husband, Odysseus, was himself guiding a beam, only far away from home, his beam the mast of a ship, hers the mast of the loom. (The Greek *histós* [ἱστός] can mean both the mast of a ship, as well as the beam

---

3 Ovid, *Metamorphoses*, trans. Allen Bandelbaum (New York: Harcourt, 1993), 183. On Arachne, see also Nancy Miller's "Arachnologies: The Woman, the Text, and the Critic" in *Subject to Change: Reading Feminist Writing* (New York: Columbia University Press, 1988), 77–101.

4 See Dante, *Inferno*, canto 17 and *Purgatorio*, canto 12.

5 Henry George Liddell and Robert Scott, *Greek-English Lexicon* (Oxford: Clarendon Press, 1929), 559, with πήνη in the plural meaning "web" and in the singular meaning the specific weft threads passing crosswise to form the weave. Still, some might object to this kind of etymological divination around names. Does the *aristos* in Aristotle's name make him "the most excellent"?

of the loom on which the warps are tied.) As classicist Marie-
Louise Nosch put it, "The protagonist couple of the Odyssey,
Odysseus and Penelope, each manipulate two large instruments all
along the narrative thread: the ship and the loom."[6] And if
Odysseus was in part defined by his mast—piloting it across the
sea, being lashed to a mast before the Sirens, driving a beam
through the eye of the Cyclops—Penelope too with her mast,
Penelope the Weft Weaver who knew when to weave and when to
unweave.

The web of ruin is thus also the ruin of the web, deciding to
dissolve ties, if that be advantageous. For, while Penelope was
synthesizing her weave by day, she was analyzing it by night,
following the literal meaning of analyzing as "unloosening" or
"unraveling." And if weaving has always been a digital technology—as many will want to claim and I would certainly agree—
Penelope indicates, with Clytemnestra as well, that the most digital act might not be that of sewing, or knitting, or synthesizing, or
constructing, or erecting, but rather of unraveling, unloosening,
deconstructing if not also destroying.

"Weaving . . . is perhaps less a contribution to civilization than
its terminal decline," wrote Sadie Plant on this kind of tactical
usage of textiles.[7] And, by the modern period, the textile industry
with its power looms, spinning machines, and knitting machines
became the site of "networked vengeance," both the subduing and
exploitation of women (along with men and child workers), as well
as resistance to it. Perhaps this is why textiles and weavers play
such an important role in Marx's *Capital*, from his elementary

---

6 Marie-Louise Nosch, "The Loom and the Ship in Ancient Greece: Shared
Knowledge, Shared Terminology, Cross-crafts, or Cognitive Maritime-textile
Archaeology?," in Henriette Harich-Schwarzbauer, ed., *Texts and Textiles in the
Ancient World: Materiality—Representation—Episteme—Metapoetics* (Oxford:
Oxbow, 2015), 109. See also Reyes Bertolín, "The Mast and the Loom: Signifiers
of Separation and Authority," *Phoenix* 62, no. 1/2 (Spring/Summer, 2008): 92–108.

7 Sadie Plant, "The Future Looms: Weaving Women and Cybernetics," *Body
& Society* 1, nos. 3–4 (1995): 56.

examples involving "our old friend the linen weaver" with his twenty yards of linen being exchanged for one coat, to Marx's extended investigations into the experience of textile labor during the working day, how it corrupts the life world of spinners, knitters, and weavers, driving them to starvation and despair.[8] "World history offers no spectacle more frightful than the gradual extinction of the English hand-loom weavers," wrote Marx.[9] Of particular importance was the gendered division of labor. Marx quoted the social reformer Lord Ashley, who had testified that a certain manufacturer "employed females exclusively at his power-looms," preferring married over unmarried women, since, according to the shop owner, married women were "attentive, docile ... compelled to use their utmost exertions to procure the necessaries of life."[10]

New inventions such as mechanical knitting machines (known as "frames" or "stocking frames"), or the automated draw-boy loom patented by Joseph Marie Jacquard in 1805, put new pressures on labor, and incited new kinds of resistance to the machines. "Jacquard's invention was an efficient means of economizing on labour" wrote textile historian Agnes Geijer. "One can therefore readily understand how the many poor silk weavers of Lyons (*les canuts*), feared for their livelihoods. Serious rioting broke out on Jacquard's return to Lyons, the new loom was publicly burned and Jacquard himself had to leave the city."[11]

"Not twelve hours elapsed without some fresh act of violence," testified Lord Byron in 1812, after touring the knitting mills of Nottinghamshire. "On the day I left the county I was informed that forty frames had been broken the preceding evening, as usual,

---

8 Karl Marx, *Capital: A Critique of Political Economy*, vol. 1, trans. Ben Fowkes (New York: Penguin, 1976), 199.

9 Ibid., 557.

10 Lord Ashley quoted in Marx, *Capital*, 526 n. 60.

11 Agnes Geijer, *A History of Textile Art* (Totowa, NJ: Sotheby Parke Bernet, 1979), 106.

without resistance and without detection."[12] Himself somewhat seduced by the motivations of the frame breakers, Byron noted the hardship and plight of those knitters and weavers newly unemployed by the machine. Yet industrialization offended Byron's aesthetic sensibilities most of all, for the new mechanized fabrics and garments were "inferior in quality," he proclaimed. And this machine-made textile, an impoverished garment for an impoverished body, "was called, in the cant of the trade, by the name of 'Spider-work.'"[13]

---

12 From a February 27, 1812, speech by Lord Byron in the House of Lords, quoted in Humphrey Jennings, *Pandaemonium: The Coming of the Machine as Seen by Contemporary Observers, 1660–1886* (New York: Free Press, 1985), 131.

13 Ibid., 132.

7

The Crumb Machine

Weaving is quite old, as we have seen. It is also international, with the Chinese silk industry exerting great influence historically, along with the tapestries and rugs of central and southern Asia, and the many dyes and textiles sourced through colonial networks and the exploitation of minerals, plants, and people. Much reverence is reserved for Andean weavers in the area of Peru, whose skill was unmatched. For instance, Anni Albers, the protégé weaver of the Bauhaus, who would help insinuate weaving into the rarified confines of modern art, dedicated her influential book *On Weaving*, the culminating statement of her life's work, to "my great teachers, the weavers of ancient Peru."[1]

As to when and how weaving became enmeshed with computation, the explanation is both startlingly obvious and stubbornly elusive. Since 1953 at least, with the publication of B. V. Bowden's *Faster Than Thought*, pride of place has been given to one Ada Augusta, Countess of Lovelace (a.k.a. Ada Lovelace, daughter of the aforementioned Lord Byron), and her pivotal role in the

---

1 Anni Albers, *On Weaving* (Princeton, NJ: Princeton University Press, 2017), v.

development of calculating machines.[2] For it was Lovelace who understood the power of the Jacquard punched cards, which Charles Babbage had grafted onto his calculating "Engine" in three places. And it was Lovelace who wrote the most sophisticated gloss of Babbage's Engine, and who itemized a sequence of operations that one might execute on that machine, thereby writing a kind of "software." By 1977 computer scientist Herman Goldstine would, without hesitation, refer to Lovelace as "the world's first programmer."[3]

Yet here I will ape the argument of Ellen Harlizius-Klück, that although it is common to trace computation back to Babbage and Lovelace, and through them to the Jacquard loom with its punched cards and automated draw-boy, the narrative of "Jacquard as origin" belies the fact that weaving has always been a digital art, and thus Jacquard or Lovelace are not the beginning of a story so much as its culmination.[4] And, if Jacquard did not make weaving computational—surely it was that already—Jacquard did in fact *compress* the digitality of weaving. Since, instead of dancing atop multiple treadles, the Jacquard loom reduced the weaver "to an operator who had to step on a single treadle repeatedly."[5] And so, with Jacquard, the multiple devolves back down to the one.

---

2 See B. V. Bowden, ed., *Faster Than Thought: A Symposium on Digital Computing Machines* (London: Sir Isaac Pitman & Sons: 1953), where Ada Lovelace adorns the frontispiece and is discussed throughout. Alan Turing had already mentioned Ada Lovelace a few years earlier in his influential 1950 essay, "Computing Machinery and Intelligence," *Mind* 59, no. 236 (October 1950): 433–60.

3 Herman H. Goldstine "A Brief History of the Computer," *Proceedings of the American Philosophical Society* 121, no. 5 (October 17, 1977): 341. Doris Langley Moore had just published the first major biography of Lovelace, titled *Ada, Countess of Lovelace: Byron's Legitimate Daughter* (New York: Harper and Row, 1977).

4 See Ellen Harlizius-Klück, "Weaving as Binary Art and the Algebra of Patterns," *Textile* 15, no. 2 (2017): 176–97.

5 Ibid., 179. On compression, see Jason LaRiviere's forthcoming book project *Lossy Elegance: The Politics and Poetics of Compression*. Lovelace was also invested in a form of compression. Many of her famous notes on the Analytical Engine were concerned with using cycles and repetition to reduce the number of operations and hence the number of cards. See Ada Lovelace, "Notes by the Translator," in Robin Hammerman and Andrew L. Russell, *Ada's Legacy* (New York: ACM Books, 2016), 57–105.

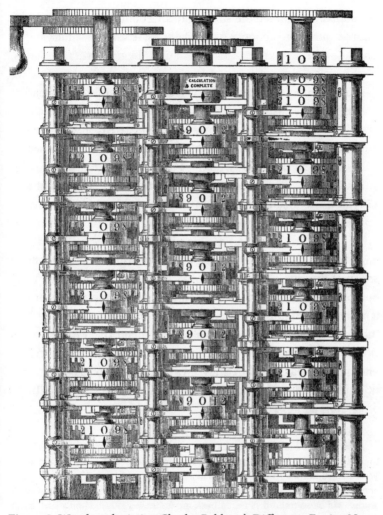

Figure 8. Woodcut depicting Charles Babbage's Difference Engine No. 1. Source: Charles Babbage, *Passages from the Life of a Philosopher* (1864), frontispiece.

That is one shortcoming. And here is another: Babbage's machine never even existed, except on paper. The so-called invention of the computer was thus also the invention of vaporware, the promise of a device to come that does not yet exist. In fact, "the mechanisms forming the historical line culminating in the one from Jacquard are all more or less failures," Harlizius-Klück stated dryly,

> stored in collections devoted to tinkering mechanisms of inventors like Vaucanson's duck or his androids. On the other hand, we have the cheap, self-made, working and therefore outwearing mechanisms with untranslatable names invented and used by nameless regional weavers for weaving strange-named fabrics like *Kölsch* or *Schachwitz*. Such tools do not enter the collections of national museums as long as they are in use, and afterwards they hardly ever survive.[6]

Instead of Babbage, Jacquard, or Vaucanson, shall we not instead praise the many nameless weavers who stored energy in their bodies and stored patterns in their fingertips? *Worn out* and forgotten, they are still nevertheless *worn*. We wear their handiwork to this day, textile as media, and media as memory. Perhaps this is why Albers considered weaving a bona fide form of writing, naming her weavings with titles drawn from the world of language, titles like "Code," "Memo," "Haiku," "Epitaph," "Ancient Writing," or "Pictographic."[7]

---

6 Harlizius-Klück, "Weaving as Binary Art and the Algebra of Patterns," 192. In addressing the charge that his defecating duck was a hoax or a failure, Vaucanson admitted: "I don't pretend to pass this off as perfect digestion, capable of making nutritious particles for the blood needed to nourish the animal. I hope no one will be so unkind as to reproach me on these grounds. I only pretend to imitate this action in three ways: (1) to swallow the corn, (2) to macerate, stew or dissolve it, (3) and to make it come out in a sensibly changed state." Jacques Vaucanson, "Lettre de M. Vaucanson, à M. l'Abbé D. Fontaine," *Le mécanisme du flûteur automate* (Paris: Jacques Guerin, 1738), 19.

7 For more on language and textuality in Albers, see T'ai Smith, *Bauhaus Weaving Theory: From Feminine Craft to Mode of Design* (Minneapolis: University of Minnesota Press, 2014), 146–51. Shannon Mattern and Taeyoon Choi discussed computing and weaving by way of Albers in their dialog "Woven Circuits," in Laura Forlano, Molly Wright Steenson, and Mike Ananny, eds., *Bauhaus Futures* (Cambridge, MA: MIT Press, 2019): 215–23.

Let us then praise the nameless artisan who built the Crumb Machine (*Bröselmaschine*). As Heinz Zemanek recounted the story, "Professor Adolf Adam has discovered in a weaving museum in Upper Austria near the three-country corner of Germany, Bohemia, and Austria a weaver's programming device built in 1740, but in all probability invented between 1680 and 1690."[8] Housed today at the Museum of Weaving in Haslach, Austria, the Crumb Machine predates the Jacquard system by many years, but uses a similar technique. Wooden pegs or "crumbs" are encoded on a conveyor belt, not unlike a musical score for a player piano or music box. The pegs rub against an array of wooden fingers, displacing the fingers in a given pattern, engaging certain heddles while leaving others at rest. The weaver actuates a lever, which opens the warp shed in accordance with the engaged heddles. As different patterns of crumbs move through the head of the loom, different patterns are woven into the fabric.

What were crumbs at the start of the eighteenth century became holes by the end of it. The Jacquard weaving system had a number of important antecedents in other industrial devices along the way, including machines made by Basile Bouchon and Jean Philippe Falcon. It was Bouchon in 1725,

who had the idea of eliminating the hodgepodge of cords and knots, replacing it with an assortment of needles and hooks, which would be depressed or released by virtue of holes punched in a long paper band . . . This idea was soon modified by Falcon around the year 1734, who replaced the paper with rectangular, punched cards, laced together in series as we see them today.[9]

---

8 Heinz Zemanek, "Central European Prehistory of Computing," in *A History of Computing in the Twentieth Century*, N. Metropolis et al., eds. (New York: Academic Press, 1980), 589. See also Adolf Adam, *Von himmlischen Uhrwerk zur statistischen Fabrik* (Vienna: Munk, 1973), 139.

9 Paul Eymard, *Historique du métier Jacquard* (Lyon: Imprimerie de Barret, 1863), 4.

Jacquard did not invent a new loom so much as rediscover and recombine existing techniques into a new system. In fact, much of the loom remained essentially untouched from the old hand looms; only the mechanism for raising and lowering warp threads was modified.

Large looms would employ a primary weaver at the front, but frequently also an assistant, the so-called "draw-boy," who would scramble up to a perch on top of the loom, drawing up the loom's many strings like a puppeteer. But what were two weavers working on the same loom soon became one, as Jacquard (like others before him) sought to eliminate the draw-boy, replacing him with an automated set of brains and fingers. The Jacquard system was first and foremost a supplementary machine grafted on to the existing loom. The automatic draw-boy added a new control mechanism overhead. But migrating to the draw-boy also meant that certain existing features of the loom could be discarded, such as multiple lamms and foot treadles, typically in favor of a single treadle for on and off positions: engage the draw-boy, disengage the draw-boy.

Older automated looms, like the silk looms of Philippe de Lasalle, had rigged up various mechanical apparatuses to achieve a similar result, but Jacquard's new automated draw-boy appealed to those seeking greater efficiency and elegance in the industrial process:

The old loom took up considerable space due to the volume of the paddles and the semples. It couldn't be moved without disturbing the rigging. The Jacquard loom, with an elegant and useful design, lends itself to any arrangement without the least inconvenience. The old loom was weighed down with pulley systems, paddles, and semples, etc. The new one is totally freed of this paraphernalia.[10]

10 François-Marie Fortis, *Éloge historique de Jacquard* (Paris: Imprimerie de Béthune et Plon, 1840), 72.

As with the Crumb Machine, the essence of the draw-boy was a mechanism by which an encoded substrate—whether pegs on a belt or cards punched with holes—could be "read" in sequence, actuating the raising and lowering of heddles to create specific weaving sheds. Here matter comes in contact with information. Of course, it was prone to failure. Writing in the mid nineteenth century, Paul Eymard recounted his memory of the machine, particularly how difficult it was to get the encoded cards to engage correctly:

> It is true that incorporating the carriage was a difficult task: It struck too hard or too softly; sometimes it arrived too late, sometimes it arrived too early, would bounce and do damage to the cards . . . [M]ounted on four castors, the carriage would easily juggle left or right a small amount, enough to keep the cards from landing flush. What's more, it made an enormous racket. I remember how Mr. Dutilleu and my father, both manufacturers back in that period, would speak of it: each time the cylinder turned they would close their eyes like it was an explosion.[11]

Yet Jacquard had the personal blessing of Napoleon, along with a commission from the Society for the Promotion of National Industry, and with the help of new money coming in, Jacquard had built fifteen of his looms by 1805, and twenty-six by May 1807.

The Jacquard looms moved across the English Channel as well, and Babbage likely encountered them in 1823 when he toured factories in England and Scotland: "Babbage had been making the most detailed study of industry," wrote biographer Anthony Hyman, "touring the country to visit factories, inspecting every machine, every industrial process he could discover."[12] Biographer

---

11 Eymard, *Historique du métier Jacquard*, 13.
12 Anthony Hyman, *Charles Babbage: Pioneer of the Computer* (Princeton, NJ: Princeton University Press, 1982), 103. Babbage's research on factories and manufacturing went into his book *On the Economy of Machinery and Manufactures* (London: Charles Knight, Pall Mall East, 1832), which influenced political

Betty Toole states that Babbage adopted his punch card system from Jacquard. At the same time, Ada Lovelace and her mother, Lady Byron, also recognized the utility of the loom as a kind of proto-computer.[13] In 1834 the pair "embarked on a tour of the industrial heartland of northern England, visiting many factories and seeing with their own eyes the immense potential of machinery. They saw a Jacquard loom in action, and Lady Byron even drew a picture of a punched card used to control the loom's operation."[14]

While equating computer to loom is a seductive way to rethink media history, it is clear that Babbage's own metaphor was *engine*, not loom or some other device, thereby associating his machine with the steam engine, the railroad locomotive, and the various mechanical engines of the early nineteenth century. Both Babbage and Lovelace spoke of "the Engine," never "the Loom."[15] At the same time, Babbage borrowed organizational and architectural terminology from textile factories, two terms in particular, *store* and *mill*. In Babbage's machines, the store was something like the memory or storage, the place where numbers could be held in reserve, following the analogy of yarn held on shelves in a factory's storehouse. The mill was what would today be called a central processing unit (CPU), the mechanism for carrying out numerical

---

economy from John Stuart Mill to Karl Marx. Indeed, Marx cited Babbage half a dozen times in *Capital*, although it seems he preferred Andrew Ure's *The Philosophy of Manufactures* (1835).

13 Betty A. Toole, *Ada, The Enchantress of Numbers* (Mill Valley, CA: Strawberry Press, 1992), 196, 252.

14 James Essinger, *Ada's Algorithm: How Lord Byron's Daughter Ada Lovelace Launched the Digital Age* (Brooklyn, NY: Melville House, 2014), 121. Lady Byron's drawing of the card is reproduced in Christopher Hollings, et al., *Ada Lovelace: The Making of a Computer Scientist* (Oxford: Bodleian Library, 2018), 42.

15 One-to-one comparisons between Jacquard looms and computers—evident in pop biographers like James Essinger but also Sadie Plant (as well as me here)—is admittedly metaphorical, since the Analytical Engine was a calculator not a computer and the operations of Babbage's engine were quite different from those of the Jacquard loom. For criticism of the loom-computer comparison, see Martin Davis and Virginia Davis, "Mistaken Ancestry: The Jacquard and the Computer," *Textile* 3, no. 1 (2005): 76–87.

operations, just as a millstone would grind grain or a shuttle and reed would weave yarn.[16]

Lovelace also pushed the loom analogy, referencing Jacquard a few times in her famous "Notes," as in the following passage, the most frequently quoted line penned by Lovelace:

> The distinctive characteristic of the Analytical Engine . . . is the introduction into it of the principle which Jacquard devised for regulating, by means of punched cards, the most complicated patterns in the fabrication of brocaded stuffs . . . We may say most aptly that the Analytical Engine *weaves algebraical patterns* just as the Jacquard-loom weaves flowers and leaves.[17]

To weave algebraical patterns—Babbage was enamored by a small 20 x 14-inch silk weaving in his possession (figure 9), which he would display to visitors at his home. The weaving was in fact a finely wrought portrait of Jacquard, a sort of display piece to demonstrate the kind of realistic detail furnished by Jacquard's system. Owing more to the traditions of painting or lithography than weaving, or if textiles then the pictorial tradition of tapestry weaving, the portrait was machine woven in silk yarn, requiring a staggering 24,000 punched cards for its production.[18] The portrait depicts an old man dressed in fine clothes, sitting in an ornate, well-upholstered chair. Workshop paraphernalia appear around him: chisels, compass, vice, bottles, rolls of plans in a drawer. Jacquard is holding calipers over a stack of punched cards; he seems to be measuring or comparing sizes. Also present are various weaving implements, including a reed and shuttle, along with festoons of fabric, and a scale model of Jacquard's automated draw-boy.

---

16 For more on the analogy between engine and factory, see Seb Franklin, *Control: Digitality as Cultural Logic* (Cambridge, MA: MIT Press, 2015), 21, and Simon Schaffer, "Babbage's Intelligence: Calculating Engines and the Factory System," *Critical Inquiry* 21, no. 1 (Autumn 1994): 203–27.

17 Lovelace, "Note A," in Hammerman and Russell, *Ada's Legacy*, 63.

18 Lovelace, "Note F," in Hammerman and Russell, *Ada's Legacy*, 92.

Figure 9. Didier-Petit & Co., "À la mémoire de J. M. Jacquard" (detail), 1839. Source: Library of Congress Prints and Photographs Division, Washington, DC, USA.

Babbage had one of the silk portraits already but he wanted a second. On a trip to Turin in Northern Italy in 1840, he stopped along the route in Lyon to spend a few days at the textile mill of one Didier-Petit and Co. of Quai de Retz, no. 34, where the silk portrait had been made. "I was especially anxious to see the loom in which that admirable specimen of fine art, the portrait of Jacquard, was woven," he recalled later in his autobiography. "I passed many hours in watching its progress."[19]

Babbage's 1840 trip to Turin would prove historic, since it put in motion a series of events culminating in Lovelace's "Notes" a few years later. In Turin Babbage had convinced the Italian mathematician Luigi Federico Menabrea to draft a text describing his yet unbuilt Analytical Engine. After the publication (in French) of Menabrea's text, Lovelace proposed to translate Menabrea's text into English, which she did, while also glossing it (and, through it, Babbage's engine) by means of a series of extensive endnotes. These notes included interesting commentary on the design and use of Babbage's engine such as the technique of running backwards in repetition to create loops of operations, as well as the famous "Note G," in which Lovelace described a sequence of specific operations on Babbage's engine—essentially an algorithm—by which to compute Bernoulli numbers. (Bernoulli numbers are a sequence of rational numbers important in analysis and number theory.)

The textual chain is nothing if not intricate. If Lovelace wrote the world's first "software," she did so in an endnote, to a translation, of an article, about a machine—a machine that did not yet exist! I suspect that this magnifies rather than diminishes the significance of Lovelace's efforts.

Sadie Plant and others have commented on how Lovelace's contributions to Babbage's engine were largely para-textual, and thus emblematic of women's work more generally. Here was Lovelace, acting as a kind of female secretary, drafting auxiliary

19 Charles Babbage, *Passages from the Life of a Philosopher* (New Brunswick, NJ: Rutgers University Press, 1994), 228–9.

endnotes for a man's hardware.[20] Yet Lovelace's seeming marginality, upon closer inspection, reveals a whole series of interesting insights. I will merely highlight one of them, the technique of *backing*.

Admiring Jacquard's system, Lovelace nevertheless determined that Jacquard's use of punch cards "was not found . . . to be sufficiently powerful for all the . . . varied and complicated processes as those required in order to fulfil the purposes of an Analytical Engine."[21] Seeing this shortcoming, Lovelace's solution was labeled "backing," that is, rotating the Jacquard prism backward to access previous cards in the pattern sequence. "The prism then resumes its *forward* rotation, and thus brings the card or set of cards in question into play a second time."[22] In this way, sequences of cards could be repeated, creating multiple iterations and loops. In the parlance of today's computer science, Lovelace's "backing" would be called a control structure.[23]

Lovelace even suggested that this "backing" technique could be reintroduced into Jacquard looms to great advantage: "By the introduction of the system of *backing* into the Jacquard-loom itself, patterns which should possess symmetry, and follow regular laws of any extent, might be woven by means of comparatively few cards."[24] In essence she was thinking about how the cards represent snippets of operations that could, like patterns or phrases of text, be taken out of context, looped and repeated, an activity that weavers already understood intuitively.

---

20 See in particular Sadie Plant, "The Future Looms: Weaving Women and Cybernetics," *Body & Society* 1, nos. 3-4 (1995): 63–4.

21 Lovelace, "Note C," in Hammerman and Russell, *Ada's Legacy*, 75.

22 Ibid., 76.

23 Lovelace's "backing" is also, in a sense, the origin of the "go to" statement, where flow control moves to a specific operation. These sorts of jumps, while greatly enabling computing, also lead to complications, as described in Edgar Dijkstra's influential paper "Go To Statement Considered Harmful," *Communications of the ACM* 11, no. 3 (March 1968): 147–8. See also Wendy Hui Kyong Chun, *Programmed Visions: Software and Memory* (Cambridge, MA: MIT Press, 2011), 36.

24 Lovelace, "Note C," in Hammerman and Russell, *Ada's Legacy*, 75.

The centerpiece of Lovelace's celebrated "Note G" was a table of instructions. And Lovelace used the principle of backing (looping) there to practical effect. "The table is what computer scientists would now call an 'execution trace,'" wrote one historian, meaning it documented the state of the machine as it changed through a series of performed operations.[25] An execution trace, it also resembled what weavers call the treadling sequence of draft notation.

"The draft notation is something like an image of practice," wrote art historian T'ai Smith. "It tells us not how the textile will *look* so much as . . . the technical operation through which it is made . . . It is something of an algorithmic code-as-image."[26] Lovelace was, in a sense, writing draft notation, treadling the Engine, just as a weaver would treadle a loom. And her notation reveals the essence of algorithms: one part encoded pattern (from the textile loom), and another part kinetic motion (from the steam engine).

25 Hollings, *Ada Lovelace*, 79.
26 Smith, *Bauhaus Weaving Theory*, 149.

8

Regular Irregularity

From one Ada to another, leap forward one hundred years from London circa 1840 to Detroit, Michigan, in the early 1940s. There Ms. Ada K. Dietz, a school teacher on the verge of retirement, soon to turn sixty years old, no children and never married, decided to change her life and begin again. On the suggestion of her close friend Ruth E. Foster, Dietz enrolled in a weaving class offered at Wayne University (today called Wayne State University), to study textile art under the tutelage of Nellie Sargent Johnson, a veteran weaver and prolific author and publisher on the subject. Quickly excelling at the craft, Dietz would soon leave her life behind, the job she held at Eastern High School since 1912, the school from which she herself had graduated in 1908, her Sigma Theta sorority sisters from the University of Michigan, her women's leagues and bridge games, trading in the Midwest for sunny California. Once out West, in close collaboration with Foster, Dietz would go on to create her own approach to designing draft patterns for textiles, an unusual technique based on translating simple algebraic expressions into two-dimensional patterns of interlaced warp and weft.[1]

---

1 For more on the generative possibilities of rethinking craft and design history in the context of computation (and weaving), see Daniela K. Rosner,

A number of colorful stories help fill out the life of Ada Dietz. Born October 7, 1888, the daughter of a cigar manufacturer, Dietz seemed to have had a comfortable upbringing in the lively Detroit of the turn of the century. Keen on science, she studied plant ecology at the University of Michigan, where, while traipsing through the bogs around Douglas Lake, she discovered "a mosquito bearing on its head two small yellow masses that looked like pollen," demonstrating the insect's role in the pollination of orchids and earning Dietz a commendation in *Science* magazine.[2] Upon graduation, Dietz went to work almost immediately as a teacher, first at Central High School in the spring of 1912, where she played center on the faculty basketball team, before switching to her alma mater Eastern High School in the fall of 1912. Hired at Eastern as an assistant physical geography teacher, Dietz had to work out of what was formerly a teacher's lounge, the room recently having been converted into classrooms in order to handle excess student enrollment. Dietz would eventually become a teacher of biological sciences and mathematics, and also serve as a school counselor, teaching at Eastern for thirty years. She directed the high school orchestra during graduation ceremonies, was head of the "dancing committee" at the school carnival, and in her free time was devoted to any number of women's groups and society shindigs.

Basketball, orchestra, bridge, biology—Dietz had yet more experiences ahead of her, sparked by her friendship with Ruth Foster. Both spinsters, both school teachers, Foster and Dietz had become friends by at least 1941 and possibly earlier. A complementary pair—Foster taught art, while Dietz taught math—Foster was living in California, where she taught at Polytechnic High School in Long Beach, California. An interest in textiles had led

---

Critical Fabulations: Reworking the Methods and Margins of Design (Cambridge, MA: MIT Press, 2018).

2 John Smith Dexter, "Mosquitos Pollinating Orchids," *Science* 37, no. 962 (June 6, 1913): 867. For a humorous take on this incident, see also Leonard Keene Hirshberg, "Those Suffragette Mosquitoes Are the Deadly Malaria Fiends," *Philadelphia Inquirer* (August 5, 1913), 8.

Foster to study weaving at Wayne University as well as at the Cranbrook Academy of Art in Bloomfield Hills, Michigan, twenty miles north of Detroit. By the mid 1940s, Foster had convinced Dietz to take up weaving as well, and, more importantly, had convinced her to retire from teaching in Detroit and come to live with Foster in her "pleasant bungalow" in Long Beach.[3]

"In a sunlit hobby room opening on a charming patio, a mathematician and an artist happily combine their talents to produce textiles of originality and beauty," was how one journalist described Foster (the artist) and Dietz (the mathematician) in their California weaving studio. "In their cheery hobby room with its walls tinted in a delicate shade of green, where looms of many sizes occupy the floor spaces, there are drawers filled almost to overflowing with yarns and threads in a riot of shades and colors like Joseph's coat."[4]

Dietz and Foster decided to go in together as artisans and collaborators. Under the informal trademark "Hobby Looms," they began to weave together, "Miss Dietz drafting mathematically and Miss Foster grasping the picture it presents and translating it."[5] They divided up the various steps of the weaving process. Foster "planned many of the colorings and textures," while Dietz being more left-brained tackled the analytical and technical aspects of drafting the weave.[6] Along with some small table looms, one of which was nicknamed "Mary Jane," they had a large countermarch loom—likely the four-shaft Leclerc Fanny loom or a similar model—which they affectionately christened "Brunhilda," after the Valkyrie queen from Norse mythology. They also had a small Heinz terrier named Pickles.

3 Lilian Haislip, "They Weave by Algebra," *Long Beach Press-Telegram* (November 28, 1948), 64.

4 Ibid.

5 Margaret Warren, "Algebra Creeps into Warp and Weft of Modern Weaving," *Christian Science Monitor* (June 30, 1949), 12.

6 Lou Tate in Ada K. Dietz, *Algebraic Expressions in Handwoven Textiles* (Louisville, KY: Little Loomhouse, 1949), 3.

These two intrepid weavers set out on a series of long road trips between 1946 and 1952, along the way developing a unique series of textile designs at the intersection of weaving and computation. The crucial breakthrough seems to have arrived at the end of a multiday drive from Long Beach, California, up to Banff, Canada. Dietz and Foster "were driving north to study at the Banff School of Fine Arts in Canada under Mrs. Ethel Henderson and Mrs. Mary E. Sandin."[7] And it was in the summer of 1946, "in the clear cool air of Alberta, that Miss Dietz conceived the idea of using algebra as a basis for patterns."[8]

Most weavers rely on tacit knowledge of basic patterns like point twills or overshot techniques, or might refer to draft books for documentation on more complex weaves. At the same time, a weaver might wish to experiment with new patterns, changing the arrangement of threads through the loom's harnesses, the vertical frames used to raise and lower warp threads, as well as the sequence in which the harnesses are moved, called a treadling sequence. Dietz began to focus on these kinds of threading patterns. In the three most basic weaves, plain weave, twill, and satin, the warp threads running lengthwise through the loom are raised and lowered in small repeated patterns, while the crossing thread, the weft, is passed back and forth using a shuttle. In these basic weaves, the threading patterns are also rather straightforward: warp yarns are threaded through the loom harnesses in regular succession. I suspect it was this regularity that piqued Dietz's interest—or perhaps the somewhat arbitrary nature of the regularity—since she began to develop new ways to generate patterns. Instead of a simple 1-2-3-4 threading pattern, then back again to 1-2-3-4, and repeating width-wise across the textile, Dietz began to spin out more complicated phrases of integers, repeating not after 4 threads but after 16, or 240, and ultimately 504 threads.

---

7 "Two Weavers in a Trailer," *Handweaver & Craftsman* 4, no. 2 (Spring 1953): 20.

8 Warren, "Algebra Creeps into Warp and Weft of Modern Weaving," 12.

Dietz found her pattern generator in algebra, in that very thing she had taught for so many years in Detroit. From her past experience as a teacher, Dietz knew how common polynomial expressions like $(x + y)^2$ were in fact a means of expressing patterns between numbers. If she could simply expand the expression in long form, and if she could translate the resulting pattern to the loom, she would, in effect, have devised her own pattern generator, a kind of algorithmic draft pattern for weaving. What's more, her technique, if it were successful, would not simply furnish one or two new patterns, but a seemingly unlimited number of weaving drafts, based on the many combinatorial possibilities of algebraic expressions, from squares to cubes, from two variables to three, and beyond.

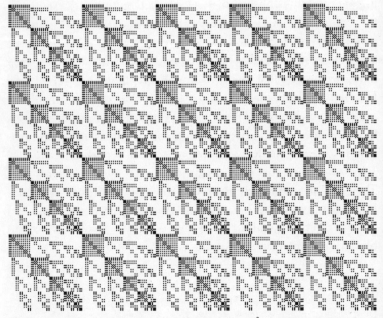

Figure 10. The polynomial $(a + b + c + d + e + f)^2$ rendered using Ada K. Dietz's technique. Source: Ralph E. Griswold, "Design Inspirations from Multivariate Polynomials, Part 1" (2001).

By early summer 1947, Dietz had woven eight samples based on rendering a series of different formulae (figure 10). She wrote to her former teacher, Nellie Sargent Johnson, to describe the technique. "First I tried the 'Cube of a Binomial,'" she explained to Johnson. "When woven I found the proportions were pleasing, and I liked its regular irregularity."[9]

In fact, it was an even more complex design from the square of a polynomial in six variables expressed as the formula $(a + b + c + d + e + f)^2$ that would eventually furnish Dietz the "regular irregularity" she so desired. In 1948, Dietz and Foster sent three entries to the summer country fair held at the Little Loomhouse in Louisville, Kentucky, where they took blue ribbons for their textiles. The director of the Little Loomhouse, Lou Tate, was so taken by the new weavings that she asked Dietz to assemble an exhibition and to begin work on a booklet explaining the various drafts and weavings, eventually published in 1949 by the Little Loomhouse under the title *Algebraic Expressions in Handwoven Textiles*.[10] (The pamphlet is attributed to "Ada K. Dietz," however Ruth Foster is acknowledged as a collaborator, and much of the text itself seems to have been compiled and written by Tate and others at the Loomhouse, based on notes and diagrams provided by Dietz.)

Buoyed by interest in their work, Dietz and Foster hit the road to share their wares. They "motored to Louisville this summer [1948] to see the Little Loomhouse . . . From there they went on a 10,000-mile tour that took them as far north as Toronto, Canada. They went wherever they heard that somebody was doing interesting things in weaving."[11]

Back home in California, they continued weaving, assembling a "traveling exhibit of more than 30 handwoven textiles,"

9 Ada Dietz quoted in Nellie Sargent Johnson, "Algebraic Formulae for Draft Writing," *Handweaving News* (July 1947), 1.

10 "Two Weavers in a Trailer," 22.

11 Lilian Haislip, "They Weave by Algebra," *Long Beach Press-Telegram* (November 28, 1948), 64.

many of them based on Dietz's algorithmic designs.[12] By late 1951 or early 1952, they embarked on another big trip. "They bought a trailer, locked the doors of the Long Beach studio, and started out to see what was going on in handweaving elsewhere."[13]

First stop again was the Little Loomhouse in Louisville, "where plans for the future of the exhibition of 'Algebraic Expressions in Handwoven Textiles' were discussed."[14] This was followed by nine weeks back home in Detroit, including a "visit to Mrs. Alpaugh's lake shore home, designed by Frank Lloyd Wright," before subsequent stops in Rochester and Saranac Lake in New York state.[15] Continuing on to Bangor, Maine, they left the trailer stateside before crossing over to Canada to visit the Leclerc loom factory in L'Islet Station, Quebec. The Leclerc factory was "just then being rebuilt after a disastrous fire" on February 9, 1951.[16] Continuing eastward, they sampled the weavings of New Brunswick and Nova Scotia, before returning back southward to Boston, down the Eastern Seaboard for three months in Florida, eventually returning home via Houston and San Antonio. During this year-long odyssey, they visited homes of friends, women's groups, and weaving clubs. They parked their trailer in RV parks, took Pickles out for walks, and set out their looms and textiles on display to make for an easy conversation starter.

The two had quickly outgrown their old weaving studio in Long Beach. They decided to knock out a wall to enlarge the space, and to fill it with better natural light. "Now this sky-lighted, window and French-door lighted room, combining workmanlike air with an artistic flair, is the heart of the house."[17] And if mathematics

---

12 "Weavers Back from Exhibit," *Long Beach Press-Telegram* (November 12, 1950), 47.

13 "Two Weavers in a Trailer," 22.

14 Ibid.

15 Ibid.

16 Ibid.

17 Haislip, "They Weave by Algebra," 64.

shares something with weaving, it certainly also has a special relationship with music, and when "Miss Dietz goes to work . . . the result is something like a bar of music, and from it she 'plays' a 'tune', a melody of color and design on her big loom she calls Brunhilda."[18]

18 Ibid.

9

Algebraic Weaving

"The idea is too new, too exciting, too varied, too unexplored to tie down," wrote master weaver Lou Tate on the draft patterns devised by Ada Dietz in the late 1940s.[1] They were also tedious and obtuse, with even one of Dietz's simplest mathematical expressions expanding out to the rather inscrutable pattern:

$$xxxxx \; y \; xx \; y \; xx \; y \; x \; yy \; x \; yy \; x \; yyyyy$$

The trouble with pattern is that it needs a rationale. Why is one pattern used in place of another? Sometimes the answer is found in practice and use, what this or that pattern will generate in terms of its drape or its texture. Sometimes it is simply a matter of taste, when someone prefers one pattern over another. But often, pattern is more or less arbitrary, as there are any number of ways to weave a twill, and in any case patterns come and go with the passing fashion.

---

1 Lou Tate in Ada K. Dietz, *Algebraic Expressions in Handwoven Textiles* (Louisville, KY: Little Loomhouse, 1949), 3.

By her own admission, what Dietz sought was "a reason for writing a draft in a definite way."[2] She wanted "the most definite basis from which to work."[3] And Dietz found her definite basis in the geometric patterns generated by simple algebraic formulae such as the cube of a binomial, $(x + y)^3$, or the square of a trinomial, $(x + y + z)^2$. Having taught the binomial theorem to hundreds of high school students over her long teaching career, Dietz put the theorem to work in her weaving as well. Using the binomial theorem, Dietz wrote out the expansions of various algebraic expressions. For instance, the squared binomial $(x + y)^2$ expands to the equivalent expression $x^2 + 2xy + y^2$. Then, departing from algebraic rules, Dietz migrated this pattern further into a strict alternation between the two variables, so $x^2 + 2xy + y^2$ became *xx xy xy yy*, or when fused together, *xxxyxyyy*.

Dietz's technique was, in fact, half algebra and half creative patterning. "Although the procedure described [by Dietz] is not mathematically sound," the computer scientist and weaving enthusiast Ralph Griswold noted, "it is unambiguous if somewhat arbitrary."[4] Griswold referred to these sorts of pattern strings as "Dietz Polynomials," calculating that a rather large Dietz Polynomial with 9 variables raised to a power of 6 would generate a pattern 3,188,646 characters long, which, using Dietz's normal loom dressing technique and a yarn sett of 30 ends per inch, could weave a nonrepeating fabric pattern over three miles wide!

Dietz's experiments using algebra to generate threading patterns, along with detailed instructions for the home weaver, were ultimately collected in her rather remarkable 1949 pamphlet *Algebraic Expressions in Handwoven Textiles*. An unusual publication in several ways, one might comment first on its cover, a block

---

2 Ada Dietz quoted in Margaret Warren, "Algebra Creeps into Warp and Weft of Modern Weaving," *Christian Science Monitor* (June 30, 1949), 12.

3 Dietz, *Algebraic Expressions in Handwoven Textiles*, 2.

4 Ralph Griswold, "Design Inspirations from Multivariate Polynomials, Part 1," www2.cs.arizona.edu/patterns/weaving/webdocs/gre_pol1.pdf (accessed January 14, 2020), 1.

Figure 11. Ada K. Dietz, *Algebraic Expressions in Handwoven Textiles* (Louisville, KY: Little Loomhouse, 1949), cover block print by Ruth Foster.

print by Dietz's collaborator Ruth Foster (figure 11). A bold heading rendered in arts-and-crafts lettering announces the title and author. At the bottom right appears the brand of "Hobby Looms," the two women's collaborative moniker. Butterflies and leaves adorn a cascade of algebraic expressions—at Dietz's preference, two-, three-, four-, and five-term polynomials—which seem to float down from the great beyond, slotting into the side of three simple hand looms, like input for a computer. Off to the right side of each loom spills a ribbon of fabric, decorated in geometric patterns reminiscent of Bauhaus weavers like Gunta Stölzl. The orientation here is all wrong, of course, but no matter: patterns, if they come from anywhere, might come from above, as in the Jacquard draw-boy, or below, from the feet in a treadling sequence, and fabric when it is woven doesn't spill out rightward from the loom but moves frontward toward the weaver, collecting on a roll near one's knees. Nevertheless, this is a compelling illustration, and it sums up the project well. Equations go in, and fabric comes out.

At the same time, Foster's illustration bears an uncanny resemblance to the computing machine defined by Alan Turing in 1936. (This is not surprising, given how the computer is, in some senses but not in others, already a remediation of the textile loom.) In both devices, a scrolling medium passes through a central processing mechanism that manipulates the scroll according to mathematical rules.

"Insofar as weaving reproduces a binary logic (the alternate interlacing of warp and weft threads)," observed T'ai Smith, "woven patterns and structures are essentially manipulations of algebraic equations."[5] Having generated her basis patterns (for example, the squared binomial pattern *xxxyxyyy*), Dietz would then pivot to the loom to map the pattern onto the various mechanisms involved in weaving. Today's computer artists are familiar with the notion of a "data conversion," where a data source (of whatever kind) is interpreted as the input for some kind of visualization. Sometimes the data source matters a great deal, as when bodies are scanned or when labor is extracted. Other times, the source of the data matters less than the pattern or behavior it transcribes; a stochastic input, for instance, might trigger certain behaviors in a game or simulation.

---

5 T'ai Smith, "Textile, A Diagonal Abstraction," *Glass Bead*, glass-bead.org/article/textile-diagonal-abstraction, 1.

Dietz did something similar in the late 1940s on her loom. She took the various algebraic patterns as input and mapped them onto how the warp yarns were threaded through the harnesses of the loom. (Although the patterns could also be interpreted in different ways, in, say, the alternations of the colors of warp yarns.) For instance, Dietz might define x to mean "one yarn through harness A and another yarn through harness B," while y might indicate "yarns through harnesses C and D." Preceding in this manner, Dietz would dress her loom following whatever x or y threading the pattern dictated. Instead of a simple twill threading repeating after four or eight threads, Dietz's threading patterns were a bit more complex, in the case of the simple squared binomial repeating after 16 warp ends, and much longer in some of her more sophisticated weavings.

Dietz experimented with all sorts of different equations in the late 1940s. She also tried different styles of weaving, preferring most frequently overshot weave, crackle weave, and summer-and-winter weave. Many of her patterns could be woven in different ways, and she documented several of the combinations in the 1949 pamphlet. Each textile was assigned a special code of the form "AKD-3-2-O" or "AKD-3-3-PW." The prefix referred to Dietz's initials, followed by the number of variables in the polynomial and the power of the equation. Thus "3-2" meant a trinomial raised to the second power, and "3-3" meant a trinomial raised to the third power. The final letter indicated the type of weave, "O" for overshot, "PW" for plain weave, and so on.

Of the initial set of samples woven using this technique, many viewers were entranced by one in particular, Dietz's most sophisticated textile, a six-term polynomial to the second power dubbed "AKD-6-2-SW" (figure 12) and defined using the expression $(a + b + c + d + e + f)^2$. "It was the 'panel on a six-term polynomial in summer and winter weave' that claimed everyone's attention," wrote one observer.[6]

---

6 Warren, "Algebra Creeps into Warp and Weft of Modern Weaving," 12.

While she frequently worked on a four-harness loom, here Dietz needed to incorporate more variables. To accommodate the six unknowns, she switched to a larger loom with eight harnesses. She also elected to weave in the "summer-and-winter" technique, which relies on a basic 8-thread block (4 pattern picks plus 4 tabby picks) and builds up patterns by diverting these blocks toward the front or the back of the fabric, effectively turning them on or off like a block of "pixels." If a contrasting colored yarn is used in the pattern weft, it becomes possible to draw simple graphical and even pictorial patterns. Dietz dressed her loom with 504 warp threads in this nonrepeating pattern. "Rarely did Miss Dietz use the same weft as the warp for her background yarn," observed Lana Schneider, who had Dietz's techniques handed down to her through a mutual acquaintance and wove her own Dietz samples. "More frequently, she used yarn that contrasted with the pattern yarn, often with added texture in a very fine thread."[7] For AKD-6-2-SW, Dietz selected a soft yellow pattern color, which contrasted well with the navy blue yarns used for the warp and tabby weft.

"Like a cubist's dream!" was one viewer's reaction to AKD-6-2-SW, although the art historians would likely disagree.[8] Nevertheless the weaving is striking in its composition. The pattern orients around the diagonal axis, an artifact stemming from how Dietz treadled the weave following the same pattern as the threading, allowing the weft to mirror the warp. At the edge of the textile, a broad border pattern wraps the composition on all four sides. At the center the pattern becomes almost fractal, with blocks increasing proportionately in size along the diagonal, spinning off tendrils

---

7 Lana Schneider, "Algebraic Expressions of Handwoven Textiles," fiberarts. org. See also Lana Schneider, "Algebraic Expressions: Designs for Weaving," *Handwoven* (January/February 1998): 48–51. I thank Lana Schneider in particular for helping me understand Ada Dietz's biography as well as her various weaving techniques.

8 Drusilla Hatch, "Peaceful Patterns," *Los Angeles Times* (January 11, 1948), D11.

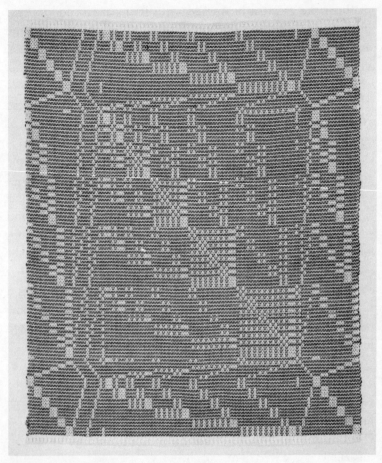

Figure 12. Ada K. Dietz, "AKD-6-2-SW," c. 1947 (reproduction 2020).

in their wake. Overall, the weaving is beguiling if not also slightly disorienting. A woven textile, nevertheless this fabric does not resemble the many commonplace twills or even more complex overshot or lace weaves. Is this a pictorial tapestry, and if so, a picture of what?

The answer might simply be pattern itself, or some snippet of mathematical space rendered visible. "As patterns grew and the possibilities opened up," Dietz wrote in 1949, "I found that mathematics gave the beautiful space divisions, proportions, and individuality of pattern which the artist strives to achieve."[9] Dietz was in effect spatializing math and, in so doing, rendering math visible as alternations of colors in two dimensions.

9 Dietz, *Algebraic Expressions in Handwoven Textiles*, 2.

10

Webs Rewoven

Both Ada Lovelace and Ada Dietz excelled at mathematics, and both women linked calculation to weaving in different ways, Lovelace back to the Jacquard punched card, Dietz via algebraic draft patterns. Still, the relation between women and computational media is complicated. The role of women in math and computation is frequently understated, and much of the history of computers has been an attempt to diminish or reframe women's contributions.

"There are only two females in the history of math, Sofia Kovalevskaya and Emmy Noether: the former wasn't a mathematician, the latter wasn't a woman."[1] Or so goes the infamous quip attributed to Hermann Weyl, and emblematic of the conventional

---

1 This aphorism attributed to Weyl is quoted in Sara N. Hottinger, *Inventing the Mathematician: Gender, Race, and Our Cultural Understanding of Mathematics* (Albany, NY: State University of New York Press, 2016), 15. A number of books deal with women in mathematics, among them Talithia Williams, *Power in Numbers: The Rebel Women of Mathematics* (New York: Race Point Publishing, 2018), and Lynn M. Osen, *Women in Mathematics* (Cambridge, MA: MIT Press, 1974), who addresses the problem of "glamorizing the exceptional case" (164).

wisdom on women in math: there *weren't any*, and, anyway, *they weren't*.

Weyl's joke is obfuscating and incorrect; it is also cruel. The joke does the work that jokes are supposed to do, in that it twists the screw one rotation further, forcing those denigrated by the comment to overcompensate in an attempt to invalidate it: *Didn't Weyl admire Noether, she whom he eulogized so movingly after her death? Doesn't he remember Kovalevskaya's work on differential equations?*[2] To try to undo the joke is to be snared by it a second time, which doesn't mean one shouldn't try.

The same biases seen in math—evident also in philosophy and related fields like logic—were incorporated into computer science at an early stage, despite the legacy of historical figures like Lovelace. (Dietz is mostly unknown outside a small group of weavers.) A liminal logic is at work, marginalizing women while still including them. Computer historians have shown how women have always been a part of computing, even if the histories tend to diminish their roles. Wendy Hui Kyong Chun, for instance, has written on the kind of programming work performed by women, often deemed auxiliary or secretarial, and the way in which commanding a machine was interwoven with the notion of commanding a "girl."[3] Historians like Mar Hicks have shown how women were marginalized within postwar computing, their jobs re-assigned to men.[4] And the cyberfeminist movement, itself

---

2 Weyl's memorial address in appreciation of Emmy Noether appears in Hermann Weyl, *Levels of Infinity: Selected Writings on Mathematics and Philosophy* (Mineola, NY: Dover, 2012), 49–66. Among her many accomplishments, Kovalevskaya ran away to France to join the Paris Commune, and also wrote a novel titled *Nihilist Girl*, trans. Natasha Kolchevska and Mary Zirin (New York: MLA, 2001).

3 See Wendy Hui Kyong Chun, "On Software, or the Persistence of Visual Knowledge," *Grey Room* 18 (Winter 2004): 26–51. See also Jennifer S. Light, "When Computers Were Women," *Technology and Culture* 40, no. 3 (1999): 455–83.

4 Mar Hicks, *Programmed Inequality: How Britain Discarded Women Technologists and Lost Its Edge in Computing* (Cambridge, MA: MIT Press, 2018).

complex and multilayered, has long shown the complicated inter-
relation between women and machines, not just looms, but the
typewriter, the telephone switch, the automaton, and the robot.[5]

"The existence of cheap, female labor is absolutely taken for
granted as a precondition of digital media's existence," wrote Lisa
Nakamura.[6] She was commenting on the particular experience of
indigenous labor, in this case Navajo women working at the
Fairchild semiconductor plant in Shiprock, New Mexico. But
Nakamura's observation might also apply more generally. Still, this
was not just any kind of labor. In hiring Navajo women, the
Fairchild bosses were appealing to a racialized notion about weaving and textiles, that these indigenous women possessed a special
kind of weaving know-how uniquely applicable to the circuitboard
industry, with its intricate filaments and complex microstruc-
tures.[7] A 1969 Fairchild brochure "features a large photograph of
a rectangular brown, black, and white rug, woven in a geometric

---

Laine Nooney addresses a similar question in the adjacent field of computer
games in her essay "A Pedestal, A Table, A Love Letter: Archaeologies of Gender
in Video Game History," *Game Studies* 13, no. 2 (December 2013), gamestudies.
org.

5 Among many works dealing with cyberfeminism broadly conceived, see in
particular Donna Haraway, "A Cyborg Manifesto: Science, Technology, and
Socialist-Feminism in the Late Twentieth Century," in *Simians, Cyborgs and
Women: The Reinvention of Nature* (New York: Routledge, 1991), 149–82; Radhika
Gajjala and Yeon Ju Oh, eds., *Cyberfeminism 2.0* (New York: Peter Lang, 2012);
and Laboria Cuboniks, *The Xenofeminist Manifesto: A Politics for Alienation*
(London and New York: Verso, 2018).

6 Lisa Nakamura, "Indigenous Circuits: Navajo Women and the Racialization
of Early Electronic Manufacture," *American Quarterly* 66, no. 4 (December 2014):
936.

7 For more on computers and racialization see Ruha Benjamin, *Race after
Technology: Abolitionist Tools for the New Jim Code* (Cambridge: Polity, 2019). On
the role of African Americans in the computer and software industry, see
Charlton McIlwain, *Black Software: The Internet & Racial Justice, from the AfroNet
to Black Lives Matter* (Oxford: Oxford University Press, 2019). On the roots of
racialization in mainframe computing, see Tara McPherson, "U.S. Operating
Systems at Mid-Century: The Intertwining of Race and UNIX," in *Race after the
Internet*, ed. Lisa Nakamura and Peter A. Chow-White (New York: Routledge,
2012), 21–37.

pattern composed of connecting and intersecting right angles."[8] Through this, wrote Nakamura, the industry was "depicting electronics manufacture as a high-tech version of blanket weaving performed by willing and skillful indigenous women."[9]

Women and textiles are always "in the fray," as Julia Bryan-Wilson elegantly put it, " 'in the fray' of heated disputes, controversies, and disagreements, and . . . at the center of arguments about the materiality of gendered labor."[10] The fray might be cultural and political—fray as social scrum—or it might be a question of medium and substrate, since yarns will fray at their edges, and knits will unravel when they are pulled (or even when they're not pulled). "I use *fray* in several senses," explained Bryan-Wilson, "the material wearing out of textiles, the undoing of threads, the pulling apart of fibers through strain and repeated use. Edges—or borders—are more prone to fraying, as they are subject to more friction."[11]

These kinds of alternations—something woven something unwoven, something computed something uncomputed, a story told a story left untold—pervade the history of texts and textiles, just as they punctuate the history of computers and cybernetics. Indeed, computing has always been something of a convenient fantasy, a fantasy about ignoring one side (the unraveling, the glitch), in favor of the other (pure number, frictionless function). If it's not Fairchild's fantasy about exploiting indigenous knowledge, then it is the fantasy that software exists in some immaterial realm untethered from the machines that run it—the machines but also the people, and the animals, and the plants, and the minerals, and the elements, and on and on.[12]

---

8 Nakamura, "Indigenous Circuits," 926.

9 Ibid., 931.

10 Julia Bryan-Wilson, *Fray: Art and Textile Politics* (Chicago: University of Chicago Press, 2017), 4.

11 Ibid.

12 On the elemental in media, see in particular Nicole Starosielski, "The Elements of Media Studies," *Media+Environment* 1, no. 1 (2019): 1–6, and John

In one sense Clytemnestra's "web of ruin" evokes a classic
misogynous stereotype. Here is Clytemnestra, who uses her feminine snares—threads and deceptions—to betray and kill her
husband. Yet, in another sense, the web of ruin is bona fide feminist technics. "The loom is a fatal innovation," wrote Sadie Plant.
And if men fear feminized webs and tendrils it is because "misog-
yny and technophobia are equally displays of man's fear of the
matrix."[13] In other words the "web of ruin" is less a negative moral
judgment about the dangers of the female as it is a positive description of a different kind of organization, the insinuation of a
"ruin"—a skipped thread or a glitch in the pattern, wayward fingers
or sleepy eyes—within an existing system of organization.[14] So the
web of ruin is really a ruin of the web.[15] And, as with the example
of Penelope, the meshwork might be unwoven by night just as it is
rewoven during the day. Alternations of doing and undoing are
not so much moral as they are practical (or tactical). Or as my
knitter friend likes to put it: *less damning, more darning.*

—

In the summer of 1998 artist Nina Katchadourian created a series
of works called "Mended Spiderwebs." To make the work, she
looked for broken spiderwebs around her house, and if the webs
had holes or missing patches, she would repair the webs using a
fine, red thread. Sometimes the thread had to be stiffened with

Durham Peters, *The Marvelous Clouds: Toward a Philosophy of Elemental Media*
(Chicago: University of Chicago Press, 2015).

13 Sadie Plant, "The Future Looms: Weaving Women and Cybernetics," *Body
& Society* 1, nos. 3–4 (1995): 56, 62.

14 On glitch aesthetics more generally, see Carolyn L. Kane, *High-Tech Trash:
Glitch, Noise, and Aesthetic Failure* (Oakland: University of California Press,
2019). On degraded images as "poor images" see Hito Steyerl, *The Wretched of the
Screen* (Berlin: Sternberg Press, 2013).

15 To be sure, just as the ruin of the web might threaten existing power, it also
installs a new sort of power in the wake of the patriarch, what I have previously
explored under the heading "protocol."

starch to hold its shape. If it wouldn't attach to the naturally sticky web, Katchadourian would adhere her micro threads with glue. Too much repair thread would make the webs sag, so it was best to keep a light touch. Piecemeal and patchy, the rewoven webs consisted partially of the original gossamer spider's silk, and partially of the more vivid embroidery thread.

Yet the customs of the spider follow their own logic. "My repairs were always rejected by the spider and discarded," Katchadourian admitted, "usually during the course of the night, even in webs which looked abandoned."[16] Katchadourian's "repairs" were thus their own sort of alien event intruding into spiderland, like a twig or leaf damaging the web as it falls. And if one repair was rejected, it was replaced by the spider's own reweaving, a first reconstruction removed, before the beginning of the second.

16 Nina Katchadourian, "The Mended Spiderweb" series, ninakatchadourian. com.

PART III.
The Digital

11

From One to Two

In the year 1948, a sliver of computer memory was a bit, and a bit
was a pixel, and a pixel was a dot, and a dot was a keystroke. Like
the old techniques of textile weavers, memory had become an
image again, just as images were deployed as memory devices. A
threshold was being transgressed, the threshold between the
analog and the digital.

In July of that year, John von Neumann and his team at the
Institute for Advanced Study (IAS) in Princeton, New Jersey, were
working on a complicated device with a simple name, the
Electronic Computer Project (ECP). While not the first of its
breed, von Neumann's machine was important in the development
of computers in the mid twentieth century because of the way in
which it solved certain problems of computer design and because
of the number of copies its successful design later spawned.

The engineers at the institute had built a primitive hard drive
for the machine by spinning magnetic wire up and around two
large bicycle wheels (figure 13). An engine drove a belt that spun
the wheels. As it spun, magnetic signals could be loaded and
unloaded from the wire. The hard drive fit into a cluster of other
devices including a keyboard, a storage unit, and even a printer.

Figure 13. High-speed mechanical wire drive used at the Institute for Advanced Study. Source: Bigelow et al., "Interim Progress Report on the Physical Realization of an Electronic Computing Instrument," (January 1, 1947), 36A, Electronic Computer Project records, Series I – Box 5. From the Shelby White and Leon Levy Archives Center of the Institute for Advanced Study, Princeton, NJ, USA.

The team drafted diagrams to indicate which part of the machine could send information back and forth to which other part of the machine. The keyboard was a master device, able to issue information to almost every other node. The printer, on the other hand, was a receiver only. The punched-tape storage unit could send information to the large, bicycle-wheel magnetic-wire storage unit. And the "shifting register" could receive information, manipulate the data, and send information back out again.

The bicycle-wheel hard drive with its metal wire was essentially an analog device. The wheels exhibited an elegant curvature, a frequent indicator of analogicity. Yet the device was analog not because of its shape, but because it stored magnetic signals in continuous variation. The signal on the wire was a continuous signal, with the intensity of the signal rising or falling continuously through time (figure 14). Continuous signals are excellent for storing waves, sound waves for instance. But continuous signals are not very good at storing symbolic information, information like letters, numbers, words, and sentences. Von Neumann's machine was a digital machine; it manipulated discrete symbols, not continuous signals. For the hard drive, the trick was to convert continuously varying waveforms into discrete on-and-off positions.

How to make the jump? How to leap from a noisy, continuous, irregular analogical signal to a clean, discrete, symbolic signal? Pulled directly from the magnetic wire, the signal was curved and messy. Sometimes it curved down and up, like a parabola. Sometimes it rose up from the bottom, pausing, then up again (resembling an elongated S). Out of these basic formal differences, von Neumann and his team constructed an entire alphabet.

The first step was to filter the signal, clipping the extremes and focusing on the mid-range. Sometimes the signal curved in from the top. Sometimes it came up from the bottom. Still messy and irregular, the filtered signal nevertheless began to gain greater coherence. Flickering like a candle, the signal faded in and out with a rhythmic precision.

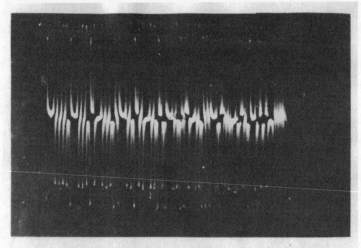

PHOTOGRAPH 4-a
OSCILLOGRAM OF WORD REPRODUCED DIRECTLY FROM MAGNETIC WIRE

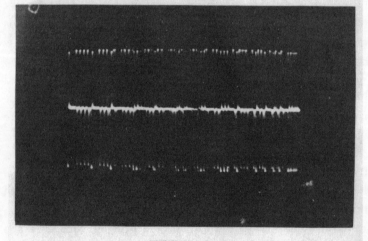

PHOTOGRAPH 4-b
OSCILLOGRAM OF WORD AFTER LIMITING

Figure 14. Oscillogram of word reproduced from magnetic wire, before and after limiting. Source: Bigelow et al., "Third Interim Progress Report on the Physical Realization of an Electronic Computing Instrument" (January 1, 1948), 37, Electronic Computer Project records, Series I – Box 7. From the Shelby White and Leon Levy Archives Center of the Institute for Advanced Study, Princeton, NJ, USA.

In other words, the bicycle wheel contained a lot of information, digital information. The key was to decode it. A flair down (or up) corresponded to a particular mark. A sequence of such marks—down or up—would be sufficient to encode letters or numbers. The series of five flickers down-down-down-down-up, corresponded to a single mark, the number 1. The number 4, by contrast, took the binary sequence down-down-up-down-down. Although the analog signal began as messy, continuous, and blurry, once clipped and rationalized it functioned as a series of discrete numbers.

What is the digital? On the wheel's magnetic wire, digital simply indicated the difference between up or down. The digital was nothing more than that. The up-or-down flickers corresponded to numbers like 0 or 1. But these 0s and 1s themselves were not so important. What was important was that there were two of them, that there was a difference between them: *up or down*. Digital information is thus constructed from the most minimally noticed amount of difference, what Gustav Fechner once described as the "just-noticed difference," or what Gregory Bateson called "the difference that makes a difference." The digital requires some form of generic difference, difference of whatever kind.

More generally, the digital means that *the one has divided into two*, that something continuous has been differentiated. Thus, the digital indicates twoness, the "making of the two," but also beyond the two, to the three, the four, and the multiple. The digital means distinction or making-discrete. The digital happens wherever separation and distinction form the essential substrate of the medium. "Two is the smallest unit of Being," wrote Kaja Silverman. "It is also only through this interlocking that we ourselves exist."[1] Here, on the magnetic wire, twoness was fabricated from the difference between magnetic intensities.

---

1 Kaja Silverman, *The Miracle of Analogy: or, The History of Photography, Part 1* (Stanford, CA: Stanford University Press, 2015), 11. Silverman's topic is analogy, yet even analogy entails an elemental digital encounter, the encounter of the two.

So, the natural numbers (1, 2, 3, and so on) are aptly labeled "digital" because they are separate and distinct, but the arc of a bird in flight is not, because it is smooth and continuous. A filmstrip is correctly called "digital" because it contains distinct breaks between frames, but the photographic frames themselves are not, because they record continuously variable chromatic intensities. Or, here on the bicycle wheel, the encoded numbers are digital, even if the underlying analog signal is only masquerading as such.

Scientists had realized that any medium could be a digital medium, provided it was able to register difference. In those years, Tom Kilburn and Freddie Williams, working at Manchester University in the United Kingdom, had figured out a way to use an oscilloscope not simply as a visual display but also as a storage device. When painted with a certain chemical, the glass surface of the oscilloscope's tube would retain a ghost image for a fraction of a second. Refresh the signal within that latency interval, and the image would remain. Using a raster grid of 1024 dots arranged in a 32 by 32 square, what was once a display device was now also a storage device. What was once an image to the eye was now also an image in memory. Their device was dubbed the Williams Tube.[2]

In 1948, a bit was a pixel, and a pixel was a dot, and a dot was a sliver of memory. What was once a messy, continuous signal now functioned as a series of dots on the cathode-ray tube display (or CRT), the dots themselves corresponding to simple numbers. Consistency was essential for this device, as for the digital more generally. But the analog machine will seek its revenge, and the dots would not always perform as expected. The Williams Tubes were known to malfunction, the grid pattern corrupted by failing

---

2 Such uses of cathode-ray tubes during this period were by no means the most significant uses of the device. See in particular Susan Murray's discussion of television in *Bright Signals: A History of Color Television* (Durham, NC: Duke University Press, 2018).

dots. Engineers would test each screen with what they termed "intensive sparking" in order to measure the amount of stress each digital dot could endure. Each dot was measured, and their various flaws were recorded on a spectrum from zero to one.

With these tubes on hand, von Neumann's team in Princeton used simple quadratic equations to draw letters to the screen. The equation $y = x$ appeared as a diagonal line. The equation $y = 2x$ also rendered a diagonal line, only now a bit steeper. More complicated equations created elegant curves, arches that began to resemble the crest of the letter A, along with other letter forms. By snipping together different equations, these dots of computer memory, these pixels on an oscilloscope, could reveal a written alphabet and, eventually, construct words (figure 15).

Anticipating the gravity of their discovery, the team at the Institute for Advanced Study did what any responsible scientists would do. They made a doodle. The scientists used this new pixel font to spell out their name (I-A-S), followed by the name of the Electronic Computer Project itself (E-C-P). The modern pixel thus appears first as a series of letters, practically nonsense—E-C-P-I-A-S. The whole affair was "a whim," the scientists wrote in the summer of 1948, to demonstrate "the use of this equipment to plot not graphs but letters."[3] It was, by some estimations, the first electronic digital bitmap display.

The names were reduced to letter abbreviations, just as each letter is displayed using a fixed grid of sample points turned on or off. And the pixels were created not from a raster-based display system, but from its opposite, an oscilloscope that draws its image analogically using continuously variable x and y coordinates. How wonderful that the modern pixel appeared first on the oscilloscope, a device invented for displaying continuous curves and

---

3 Julian H. Bigelow et al. "Fourth Interim Progress Report on the Physical Realization of an Electronic Computing Instrument," 1 July 1948. Records of the ECP, Courtesy of the Archives of the Institute for Advanced Study, Princeton, New Jersey.

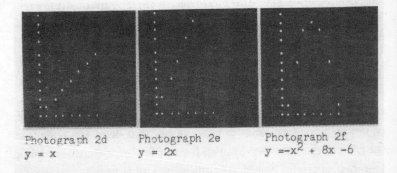

Photograph 2d
y = x

Photograph 2e
y = 2x

Photograph 2f
y =-x^2 + 8x -6

Photograph 2c
Oscillographic Production of Letters

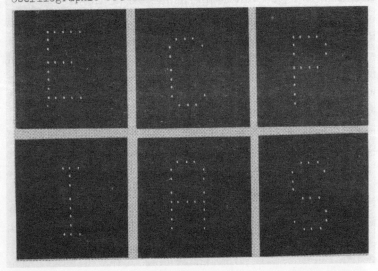

Figure 15. Oscillographic production of letters. Source: Bigelow et al., "Fourth Interim Progress Report on the Physical Realization of an Electronic Computing Instrument" (July 1, 1948), II-8g, Electronic Computer Project records, Series I – Box 7. From the Shelby White and Leon Levy Archives Center of the Institute for Advanced Study, Princeton, NJ, USA.

lines. This analog hardware facilitated a new digital aesthetic because the 1948 pixel was a fabrication of information, not a fact of hardware. The 1948 pixel was a remnant not of the raster grid, but of signal voltages made discrete. In other words, the first modern pixel was a simulated pixel. Could there be any other kind?

Does this mean that the future is digital and the past is analog? Absolutely not, since these are techniques that recur throughout history. There is nothing particularly modern about the digital. In fact, the digital died an early death in the continuous calculus of Newton and Leibniz, and the curvilinear revolution of the Baroque that came with it, both thoroughly modern inventions. And the digital has suffered a thousand blows since, from the swirling vortex of nineteenth-century thermodynamics to the chaos theory of recent decades.

The switch from analog computing to digital computing in the middle twentieth century is but a single battle in the multimillennial skirmish within human culture between the unary and the binary, proportion and distinction, curves and jumps, integration and division—in short, over when and how the one divides into two. If a medium could be made to register the "two" of discrete difference, it could be put to use in digital computation.

12
The Cybernetic Hypothesis

"If I were to choose a patron saint for cybernetics out of the history of science, I should have to choose Leibniz,"[1] wrote Norbert Wiener, the MIT mathematician and defense researcher. Indeed, in the early modern period, Leibniz described a unique arrangement of system and agent that would later influence cybernetics and network science. Leibniz, with his *Monadology*, described a smooth, universal network of "monads," each of which was singular but also contained within it a mirror of the totality. A few years earlier, in his *Ethics*, Spinoza had also constructed an agent-system model, this time forged from a universal substance, from whose infinite attributes thought and extension emerge to form the human body. For Spinoza, the affections of the body superimposed onto substance a type of distributed network of relations and counter-relations, a theory further developed by the French philosopher Gilles Deleuze.

---

1 Norbert Wiener, *Cybernetics, or Control and Communication in the Animal and the Machine* (Cambridge, MA: MIT Press, 1965), 12. For quick immersion into some of these conversations, see Leif Weatherby, "The Cybernetic Humanities," *Los Angeles Review of Books* (January 2, 2017), lareviewofbooks.org.

In the twentieth century, Ludwig von Bertalanffy, with the science of general systems theory, and Wiener, with the science of cybernetics, helped describe open versus closed systems, how subsystems are nested within systems, and how communication and control pass from one part of a system to another. In roughly the same period Claude Shannon and Warren Weaver put forth their information theory, which defined communication not solely in terms of semantics but in terms of the relative integrity of symbolic patterns and the amount of unpredictability contained in the languages used to construct those patterns. In mathematics, graph theory was also a key influence. Graph theory provided a vocabulary for understanding networks (renamed "graphs") as groups of nodes and links.

Cybernetic systems are essentially communication networks in which information may pass between system components, affecting their ongoing states. Wiener's influential 1948 book *Cybernetics, or Control and Communication in the Animal and the Machine* looked across disciplines—from electrical engineering to neurophysiology—and suggested that human, animal, and mechanical systems were united in their ability to handle input and output data in the ongoing management of the system.

A central aspect of such cybernetic systems was the role of feedback, which implied a degree of self-reflexivity to any web of relationships.[2] Information, for Wiener, was a statistical choice from among the "noise" of the surrounding world, and as such it implied an apparatus with the ability to instantiate the very act of choice or selection.[3] Wiener referred to this ability as "control by

---

2 Wiener described feedback in the following way: "It has long been clear to me that the modern ultra-rapid computing machine was in principle an ideal central nervous system to an apparatus for automatic control . . . With the aid of strain gauges or similar agencies to read the performance of these motor organs and to report, to 'feed back,' to the central control system as an artificial kinesthetic sense, we are already in a position to construct artificial machines of almost any degree of elaborateness of performance" (ibid., 27).

3 As Wiener elaborated, "Just as the amount of information in a system is a measure of its degree of organization, so the entropy of a system is a measure of

informative feedback." Like Aeschylus's chain of triumph, networks in Wiener tended to be efficient and directed. They were machinic in nature, and acted to better interoperate complex aggregations of bodies and technologies into functional, systemic wholes. In fact, Wiener formed the term "cybernetic" from the Greek word *kubernetes* [κυβερνήτης] or "steersman," while also making reference to the nineteenth-century writings of Clerk Maxwell on "governors," which Wiener suggested was a Latin corruption of the same Greek term.

While Wiener was doing cybernetic military research on anti-aircraft ballistics, his colleague Claude Shannon was doing tele-communications research for Bell Labs. Much of Shannon's work with Warren Weaver is acknowledged as the foundation for modern telecommunications networks and can be said to have paved the way for the idea of the ARPAnet in the late 1960s. Shannon's work, while much less interdisciplinary than Wiener's, resonated with cybernetics in its effort to define "information" as the key component of communications technologies (indeed, Wiener cited Shannon's work directly). Shannon and Weaver's information theory emphasized the quantitative view of information, even at the expense of considering quality or content. "Information must not be confused with meaning," Weaver advised. "In fact, two messages, one of which is heavily loaded with meaning and the other which is pure nonsense, can be exactly equivalent, from the present viewpoint, as regards information."[4]

Such a hard-nosed technical view can still be seen today in the internet's implementation of packet-switching, in which chunks of data are fragmented and routed to destination addresses. While analysis of data packets on the internet can be interpreted to reveal

---

its degree of disorganization; and the one is simply the negative of the other" (ibid., 11).

4 Claude Shannon and Warren Weaver, *The Mathematical Theory of Communication* (Urbana and Chicago: University of Illinois Press, 1963), 8.

content, the technical functioning has as its implicit priority the delivery of quantity x from point a to point b, regardless of semantic content.

If both cybernetics (Wiener) and information theory (Shannon) implied a quantitative, statistical view of information networks, a third approach, contemporaneous with cybernetics and information theory, offered a slight alternative. Perhaps because he trained as a biologist, Ludwig von Bertalanffy's "general systems theory" differed significantly from the view of Wiener or Shannon. Wiener viewed human, animal, and mechanical systems together from an electrical engineering perspective, while Shannon viewed human users as separate from the communications technologies they used. By contrast, von Bertalanffy's work stressed the view of human or technological systems from a biological standpoint. In doing so, he elaborated theoretical distinctions between open and closed systems and showed how subsystems are always nested within larger systems (a model that would be adopted wholesale in the layered construction of internet protocols). As he stated,

> The organism is not a static system closed to the outside and always containing the identical components; it is an open system in a quasi-steady state, maintained constant in its mass relations in a continuous change of component material and energies, in which material continually enters from, and leaves into, the outside environment.[5]

This view has several consequences. One is that while von Bertalanffy did have a definition of "information," information played a much smaller role in the overall regulation of the system than other factors. While information is central to any living network, it is nothing without an overall logic for defining

---

5 Ludwig von Bertalanffy, *General Systems Theory: Foundations, Development, Application* (New York: George Braziller, 1976), 121.

information and utilizing it as a resource for systems management. In other words, the logics for the handling of information are just as important as the idea of information itself.

Another consequence is that von Bertalanffy's systems theory, in its organicist outlook, provided a means of understanding "information" in biological terms, rather than those of engineering or communications. This is not to suggest that systems theory was in any way more accurate or successful a theory than those of Wiener or Shannon. But what the genealogies of cybernetics, information theory, and systems theory do show is that "information," and an informatic worldview, displayed an ambivalent relation to the material world. On the one hand, information was seen as being abstract, quantitative, and reducible to a calculus of management and regulation—this is the disembodied, immaterial notion of "information" referred to above. On the other hand, cybernetics, information theory, and systems theory all showed how information was immanently material, configured into military technology, communications media, and even biological systems.

Taking a page from the French collective Tiqqun, one might label this historical phenomenon the *cybernetic hypothesis*.[6] Such a hypothesis refers to a specific epistemological regime in which systems or networks combine both human and nonhuman agents in mutual communication and command. Along with the many related fields that parallel cybernetics—network sciences like ecology, systems theory, and graph theory; the sciences of economic decision such as game theory and rational choice theory; information science and signal processing; behaviorism, cognitivism, and the post-Freudian sciences of the subject—the cybernetic hypothesis has come to dominate the production and regulation of society and culture.[7] Indeed, the

6 Tiqqun, "L'Hypothèse cybernétique," *Tiqqun* 2 (2001): 40–83.

7 A number of accounts have helped fill out this history, including Fred Turner, *From Counterculture to Cyberculture: Stewart Brand, the Whole Earth*

Tiqqun group viewed the cybernetic hypothesis as the most prevalent new form of social management involving both human and nonhuman assets. "At the end of the twentieth century the image of steering, that is to say management, has become the primary metaphor to describe not only politics but all of human activity as well."[8]

By labeling it a hypothesis, Tiqqun meant to stress the provisional nature of cybernetics and the computational and media society it entails. They meant that cybernetics was a technological proposal and thus, like any experimental hypothesis, subject to ratification or indeed refutation. Like Tiqqun, I also wish to historicize this computational universe, describing it less as a form of collective fate than as a series of specific shifts in the foundations of knowledge and culture.

The cybernetic hypothesis may be defined broadly or narrowly. As we have seen, cybernetics in the narrow sense came from the work of Wiener and his important research in the years immediately following World War II.[9] Yet in a more general sense, cybernetics refers to any kind of regulatory system in which human and nonhuman agents are connected in networks of control and communication. Because of this, cybernetics is often credited with inaugurating a particular historical relationship between subject and world. Specifically, cybernetics refashions the world as a *system* and refashions the subject as an *agent*.

A system is an aggregation of things brought together to form a complex whole. Cybernetics aims to view the world as one or more systems. The systems may be arranged and linked laterally or stacked orthogonally as system, subsystem, and super system. Here, I will assume a network model for systems, meaning an

---

Network, and the Rise of Digital Utopianism (Chicago: University of Chicago Press, 2008), and Bernard Dionysius Geoghegan, "From Information Theory to French Theory: Jakobson, Lévi-Strauss, and the Cybernetic Apparatus," *Critical Inquiry* 38 (2011): 96–126.

  8 Tiqqun, "L'Hypothèse cybernétique," 44.
  9 Norbert Wiener's landmark text *Cybernetics* was first published in 1948.

architecture of nodes and links in which interaction and communication may pass from one point in the system to another. Indeed, an important characteristic of cybernetic systems is an internal message loop in which messages originating within the system also affect the operation of the system. This results in dynamic change, and as a result systems use feedback in order to mitigate imbalance and pursue homeostasis.

Given their overall complexity, cybernetic systems also require a high level of control. Thus, such systems require a subsidiary mechanism for overall organization and management. Given these qualities, systems also tend to be algorithmic, which is to say operational or executable rather than static or descriptive, in that they prescribe a set of possible behaviors and then facilitate the step-by-step execution of those behaviors according to dynamic variables originating from within the system.

An agent is an entity capable of carrying out an action. Cybernetics assumes that an agent may be either animal or machine, human or nonhuman. Thus, an aircraft pilot may be an agent, but so too are the dials and controls in the cockpit, since they carry out the actions of collecting and distributing vital information such as altitude and speed. Together the pilot and the aircraft form a cybernetic system.

Agents in such systems are assumed to be autonomous to themselves and arranged on "equal footing" vis-à-vis the system as a whole. What this means is that, while agents may be wildly different in their relative size and power, each agent is endowed with the power of local decision according to the variables and functions within its own local scope. Thus, while the pilot and instruments are not equal in power or type, they interoperate as equal peers to the extent that each may accommodate inputs and outputs and each may influence the outcome of the overall system.

Agents are thus understood as more or less autonomous and equal at the level of their systematicity. In fact, agents are nothing more than subsystems within the super system. Given the existence of multiple agents, systems also display the quality of self-organization, meaning that no external metaphysics defines or dictates the behavior of the system. Systems are thus self-determining and rely on a high degree of reflexivity and self-referentiality in order to work properly.

This kind of agent infrastructure produces a few important results, the first pertaining to the agents themselves, and the second to the kind of messages flowing between them.

First, while cybernetic systems do not require digital message encoding per se (analog signals work just fine in a thermostat, for example), such systems are digital at the level of infrastructure due to a necessarily atomistic architecture. Like the lines and boxes on a flow chart, discrete entities are separated by communications links. This is sometimes called an object-oriented infrastructure because it describes a system of objects (of whatever kind) that perform functions and may connect or communicate with each other via interfaces.

Second, it is necessary to consider the messages themselves that propagate through cybernetic systems, not simply the agents that send them. Cybernetic systems are understood in terms of the sending, receiving, and processing of information. And such information is by definition highly encoded, so that messages may propagate and interface with agents in predictable ways. At the same time, such information is often uncoupled from a human observer, given that information may be gathered, processed, and re-sent by instruments regardless of human intervention. Thus, just like the agents within the system, information also gains a relative autonomy when deployed within a cybernetic environment because it may directly affect certain outcomes without the intervention of a human actor.

Of the many consequences of the cybernetic hypothesis, I focus here on one, the creation of a *regular, discrete framework*. This framework may take different forms. As with Londe, it might take the form of a grid of lenses. It might look like Dietz's threading patterns, with their discrete alternations of warp and weft. Or, as we will see later with Barricelli and Debord, it might appear as complex arrays of creatures and soldiers. In the cybernetic hypothesis, all entities are reduced to cells that function like black boxes, peers of agents interacting in parallel.

13

Latticework

In 1922, via a "numeric process," the English mathematician Lewis Richardson proposed a massive chess game to span the continents, a system to predict weather via a cellular space of distributed meteorological sensors measuring atmospheric pressure and momentum (figure 16). He used the term "lattice" to describe it, borrowing a word from crystallography. Later, John von Neumann would learn of Richardson's work, developing it into a full-fledged spatial model for computation:

> We take a piece of paper ruled in large squares, like a chessboard, and let it represent a map. The lines forming the squares are taken as meridians and parallels of longitude—an unusual thing in map projection. Next, we lay down the convention that all numbers written inside a square relate to the latitude and longitude of its center. The longitude of the centres of the squares is written down at the top of the table, and the latitude along the left-hand margin ... It is seen that pressure and momentum alternate in a pattern, which is such that, if a chessboard had been used, the pressures would all appear on

the red squares, and the momenta all on the white ones, or vice versa.[1]

Richardson's computational framework extended horizontally like a game board, but it extended vertically too, rising through four distinct atmospheric layers.[2]

In his writing, Richardson used the language of complex and nonlinear systems, borrowed in particular from thermodynamics. Richardson wrote of eddy movements, laminar stresses, air viscosity, turbulence, heat flows, and conductivity. There is a whole section on "heterogeneity," a term that would eventually become fashionable in critical and cultural theory. Indeed, using terminology also seen later in the work of Deleuze and Guattari, Richardson spoke in terms of the "molecular" level and the "molar" level. He discussed the complexity of interactions between layers and the turbulence that results. Then, with a wink, he added a little rhyme to help remember it all: "big whirls have little whirls that feed on their velocity, and little whirls have lesser whirls and so on to viscosity."[3]

Merely overlaying a grid on a map was not the ultimate attraction of Richardson's system. In fact, the grid was not primarily a spatial technology for him. His crystalline grid was world-bound

---

1 Lewis Richardson, *Weather Prediction by Numerical Process* (Cambridge: Cambridge University Press, 1922), 5. It is uncanny how frequently chess in particular and games in general come up in the history of computational media. The gamic logic seems to permeate this discourse at a very low level; chess figures in the work of John von Neumann, Claude Shannon, Gilles Deleuze and Félix Guattari, Jean Baudrillard, Guy Debord, and many others.

2 "It is desirable to have one conventional dividing surface at or near the natural boundary between the stratosphere and troposphere . . . Secondly, that to represent the convergence of currents at the bottom of a cyclone and the divergence at the top, the troposphere must be divided into at least two layers. Thirdly, that the lowest kilometre is distinguished from all the others by the disturbance due to the ground. Thus it appears desirable to divide the atmosphere into not less than 4 layers." Richardson, *Weather Prediction by Numerical Process*, 16–17.

3 Ibid., 66.

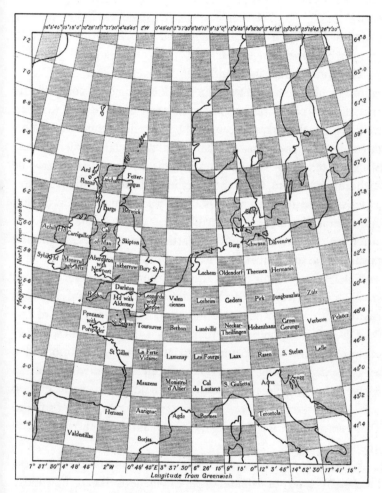

Figure 16. "An arrangement of meteorological stations designed to fit with the chief mechanical properties of the atmosphere . . . Pressure to be observed at the centre of each shaded chequer, velocity at the centre of each white chequer." Source: Lewis Richardson, *Weather Prediction by Numerical Process* (1922), frontispiece (detail).

but it also existed in an abstract geometric realm, oblivious to national borders or geographic features. Richardson's grid was a latticework for parallel calculation; each square was represented by a number that fed into an integrated algorithm for modeling atmospheric phenomena.[4]

As the cyberneticists would later discover, these sorts of "crystalline spaces" benefited from the black boxing of each individual crystal. This phenomenon was evident in Richardson's work as well. With each square represented by a single number located on the map at the coordinates of its center, the square was effectively black boxed. No sub-square information was necessary in Richardson's system. Once the lower bounds of the grid's granularity were determined, each cell essentially became an atom—uncuttable, impenetrable, and invisible. The cell's functionality was purely an outward relation to the lattice as a whole, never inward toward some sort of real microcosm or interiority.

Richardson used the phrase "definite portions" to describe these small atomic envelopes. "In hydrodynamics or aerodynamics it is customary to speak of the motions of 'definite portions' of the fluid, portions which may be marked by a dot of milk in water or of smoke in air . . . It is customary to ignore the fact that molecules are constantly passing in and out of the element called 'definite.'"[5] Richardson's "definite portions" were thus not objects in the proper sense of the term, but more like drops of water or puffs of smoke. They existed as localizable zones of flux, as thresholds or intensities.

After designing his climate model, Richardson proposed to test the system by way of pen and paper calculations. "Let us now illustrate and test the proposals of the foregoing chapters," he wrote, "by applying them to a definite case supplied by Nature and measured

4 For more on Richardson and the computational infrastructure of clouds and weather, see Seb Franklin, "Cloud Control, or The Network as Medium," *Cultural Politics* 8, no. 3 (2012): 443–64.

5 Richardson, *Weather Prediction by Numerical Process*, 66.

in one of the most complete sets of observations on record."[6] Given an empirically measurable set of weather data, Richardson's goal was to reproduce the same data in the structure of the lattice, or, in his words, to enact a "lattice-reproducing process."

> The initial data are arranged in a pattern which, by borrowing a term from crystallography, we may call a "space-lattice." Wherever in the lattice a pressure was given, there the numerical process must yield a pressure. And so for all the other meteorological elements. Such a numerical process will be referred to as a "lattice-reproducing process."[7]

Richardson's "process" was a kind of writing system for algorithmic machines. Multiple cells expressed themselves in parallel based on a set of complex nonlinear computations. If his matrix corresponded to actually observed measurements, then the model was successful.

At the same time, Richardson understood that the lattice would be internally complex, that it would be bringing together heterogenous zones and heterogenous elements. Such variations were described by Richardson as changes in the "density" of the lattice. Just as an open ocean or a remote wilderness would likely have fewer meteorological sensors, the grid in those zones would necessarily be spaced wider apart. Yet a heavily populated part of the land mass might have a surplus of sensors and therefore a tightly interwoven grid. Richardson developed a technique for dealing with unequal density resolutions that by necessity must be "interfaced" or integrated into the same overall map. He called these interfaces "joints."

> On parts of the oceans, near the poles, and within the desert tracts of land there are no people to provide observations or to

---

6 Ibid., 181.
7 Ibid., 156.

> appreciate forecasts . . . There are other portions of the globe,
> especially the seas, where some rough sort of forecast might be
> possible and desirable if it could be carried out with a much
> opener network than that in use where population is dense. But
> the two networks must be united on the computing forms in
> such a way that air, represented by numbers, can flow across the
> joint.[8]

Joints bridge the low-resolution zones of the wilderness or the
open ocean and the high-resolution zones of cultivated areas and
land masses. This same technique is evident in today's digital
networks, where high-volume "backbone" cables are joined, via
switches and routers, to low-volume "capillary" channels.

He even went so far as to work out the numbers for an optimal
interface between wilderness and cultivation. "It is seen that the
ninefold reduction gives a neater joint than the fourfold, in the
sense that the latter involves more interpolations."[9] Ninefold
rather than fourfold, the ratio itself does not particularly matter.
Either way, Richardson was trying to avoid, as he put it, "a violent
change in the lattice" between the wild and the civilized.[10] And, in
so doing, he articulated, in embryonic form, the facility with which
complex systems accommodate and manage heterogeneous
elements. If individual cells or agents were granted autonomy, then
their relative differences might pose a threat to the system overall.
Richardson's latticework was thus a sort of real-time management
apparatus, a way to account for both the "wild" and the "cultivated"
within a single technology.

---

8 Ibid., 153.
9 Ibid.
10 Ibid., 155.

14

A Regular Discrete Framework

In early 1940, Warren Weaver and John von Neumann exchanged letters discussing a hypothetical invention that would use film photography to organize an archive of mathematical articles. The goal of the device was "the coding of mathematical literature and the application of a photographic high speed selection process to hunt out all of the mathematical literature bearing on a certain topic."[1] While it was never built, Weaver envisioned the device in the following manner:

> Suppose that someone has photographed, on very long strips of movie film, *abstracts* of all the mathematical articles which have appeared since, say, 1900. Each abstract might require one exposure of "frame" of the film; and in the margin of the film there would be recorded a complex code symbol which, according to some flexible system, characterizes the nature of the article. A research mathematician might be interested in locating

---

1 Warren Weaver, letter to John von Neumann, March 29, 1940, box 7, John von Neumann Papers, Manuscript Division, Library of Congress, Washington, DC.

all the articles which treat (or indirectly bear on) some certain topic. He appeals to the library or other organization which has the above-mentioned film record. This film is placed in a machine, the operator adjusts the machine so that it will select only those abstracts which (making use of the code symbols) treat of or bear on the topic in question.[2]

Weaver's device to encode and retrieve written articles, which he mailed simultaneously to a number of colleagues in addition to von Neumann, predates by five years a similar device proposed by Vannevar Bush in a famous *Atlantic Monthly* article from 1945.[3] Weaver envisioned, in essence, a sort of primitive database of information tagged with metadata, which could be queried using a search engine.

The film is run through this machine with extreme rapidity (1,000 frames or abstracts a second, say) and the machine automatically photographs these desired abstracts and passes the others by. Thus in an incredibly brief time each individual abstract is, so to speak, examined for its possible interest to this particular mathematician and problem, and the ones really of interest are photographed and delivered to the person making the inquiry. With this complete list of abstracts in his

2 Warren Weaver, letter to John von Neumann, January 31, 1940, box 7, John von Neumann Papers, Manuscript Division, Library of Congress, Washington, DC.

3 See the "memex" device described in Vannevar Bush, "As We May Think," *Atlantic Monthly* (July 1945). One might also compare Weaver's device to the so-called Zuse palimpsest, the film stock used by Konrad Zuse to encode binary data for his Z3 computer, completed in 1941. Zuse: "During the war I couldn't get ordinary commercial punched-tape machines, which were then already in use in the telephone business for 5-track punched tape. I built my own punching and reading devices and used normal filmstrips—[Helmut] Schreyer's idea. They were punched with a simple manual keypunch." Konrad Zuse, *The Computer— My Life* (Berlin: Springer-Verlag, 1984), 63. Of course, Zuse's filmstrips had no real relationship to photography or cinema; the image on the filmstrip was unimportant, a mere trace of the medium's former life.

possession, it is presumed that he would look them up, if he is located near a suitably extensive library, or would make further use of film procedures by sending to some central bureau for photographic copies of the articles.[4]

Such microfiche databases had been proposed before, perhaps most vividly by Paul Otlet around the turn of the twentieth century. Otlet, the Belgian lawyer and inventor of the universal decimal classification system (which he hoped would alleviate some of the shortcomings of Dewey's system), was an innovator in the area of library and archival science. A utopian and global thinker, Otlet organized the International Institute of Bibliography in 1895, which aimed to synthesize all the different systems that existed for classifying the printed word. "By 1900 there were some 17 million cards organized along the lines of Melvil Dewey's system ... By 1908 Otlet had floated the notion of a international central library, with support of some 200 organizations. By 1910 he had held the first meeting of the World Congress on Bibliography."[5]

Around that same period, circa 1906–1907, Otlet developed, with Robert Goldschmidt, a "projected book" called the *bibliophote*, a coinage combining the terms "biblio" (book) and photography.[6] As in Weaver's subsequent proposal, Otlet's bibliophote was a system for photographing books and then reproducing them via projection. The technique of microphotography was already known at the time, and in fact had been used during the siege of Paris in 1870, when thousands of letters were reproduced in miniature on film and sent via carrier pigeon, as depicted in a famous painting hanging in the Musée Carnavalet in Paris. Otlet's

4 Warren Weaver, letter to John von Neumann, January 31, 1940, box 7, John von Neumann Papers, Manuscript Division, Library of Congress, Washington, DC.

5 Bill Katz, *Cuneiform to Computer: A History of Reference Sources* (London: Scarecrow Press, 1998), 326-7.

6 Françoise Levie, *L'Homme qui voulait classer le monde: Paul Otlet et le Mundaneum* (Bruxelles: Les Impressions Nouvelles, 2006), 107.

innovation was evident in the scale of his ambition, as he sought to unify the totality of all human knowledge, which would be photographed and filed and made easy to access. With the bibliophote as building block and as a culmination of his life's work, having enlisted Le Corbusier as chief architect and Nobel peace prize laureate Henri La Fontaine as collaborator, Otlet launched an ambitious initiative in 1910 called the Mundaneum, which, although never realized, was designed as a home for all the world's knowledge, classified and archived inside a massive library facility to be located on the shores of Lake Geneva. "Humanity has arrived today at the stage of globalization," he proclaimed.[7]

In 1940, both Weaver and von Neumann were influenced by a new paradigm for information machines recently proposed by Alan Turing, in which data was encoded on a long strip of tape and fed through a central processing machine.[8] "What is an automaton in the Post-Turing sense?" asked the mathematician and computer scientist Herman Goldstine. "It is one of the proverbial 'black boxes' which has a finite number of states which we may number 1, 2, . . ., n. . . . The change [in state] takes place by an interaction with the world outside the automaton which is considered as being a tape."[9] For Weaver, the "tape" came in the form of movie film. But while the strips of film were linear in nature, the user of such a device would be able to follow threads through the archive in a nonlinear fashion. "He proceeds to follow this thread wherever it leads him," wrote Weaver in a follow up note to von Neumann. "This thread frequently cuts across all pre-existing lines of subject classification."[10]

---

7 Paul Otlet and Le Corbusier, *Mundaneum* (Brussels: Union des Associations Internationales, 1928), 2.

8 See Alan Turing, "On Computable Numbers, with an Application to the *Entscheidungsproblem*," *Proceedings of the London Mathematical Society* 42 (1937): 230–65.

9 Herman Goldstine, *The Computer from Pascal to von Neumann* (Princeton, NJ: Princeton University Press, 1972), 274.

10 Warren Weaver, letter to John von Neumann, March 29, 1940, box 7, John von Neumann Papers, Manuscript Division, Library of Congress, Washington, DC.

Weaver's proposal was much more modest in scale than Otlet's, and at the same time more immediately realizable. Contrary to the conventions of cinematic film production, which gave the illusion of movement by fusing successive frames together in linear sequence, Weaver's proposal leveraged the inherently digital nature of film's discrete framework of successive frames to assemble a miniature archive that could be processed rapidly by computer. Yet there was to be no mediatic continuity between each cell in Weaver's film; continuity was to be achieved in other ways, via the recombination of cellular units into codified sequences and patterns. It was, shall we say, a kind of structural film *avant la lettre*.

Recall the key features of Weaver's device: a database built from a cellular array consisting of one frame per text; a frame rate that was an order of magnitude more rapid than cinematic projection; symbolic codes for addressing and classifying each entry in the cellular array; associative browsing of subject themes; photography for storage; and rephotography for retrieval.

The use of rephotography for retrieval might sound odd, yet in the 1940s there were essentially no printers in existence, at least not in the modern sense. A common technique for "printing" on early computers was to take a photograph of the computer's oscilloscope screen, assuming it had a screen at all, and then to develop and print the photograph. So Weaver's suggestion that the "search results" would be rephotographed is in step with the media conventions of the time.

Weaver proposed using film celluloid, but this was no film in the conventional sense. Would the film run slower than the cinema, or perhaps much faster? The question of speed was up for grabs. Weaver proposed 1,000 frames per second, but this number is arbitrary and would have been limited only by the available reading and parsing hardware. With the computer, speed, like its cousin time, became a technical variable like any other. Speed and time began to float apart from the machine, uncoupled from the medium at the lowest levels.

Weaver's "complex code symbols" were also notable. His system would have worked much like Hollerith's tabulator and sorter, or Babbage's Jacquard cards, with binary holes designating different classification headings. All photographic cells marked with an appropriate dot in the "nonlinear differential equations" box would be rephotographed and returned in response to a query of that nature, and so on, just as Hollerith's punch cards contained boxes for the different census categories. The logic of classification was also a logic of selection.

Putting all this together, Weaver proposed a device that would make it more efficient to locate material in the archive, that would facilitate the researcher in his or her inferences, that would open up inductive and associative pathways through information, that would in fact be disruptive of existing classification systems, placing the individual intellect at the heart of the informatic system.

He fretted over a few things. Would mathematicians actually want to use it? How could a coding scheme be fine-grained enough to describe all the nuances of each article accurately? Could stored articles be made forward compatible, for example if the coding schema needed to be updated? A solution was found in the coding scheme itself. Use "at least 12" symbols, he advised von Neumann, because such combinatory latitude would certainly afford "a complete functional characterization" of the text in question.[11]

Only twelve symbols to characterize the essence of a text? I suspect not. Symbol systems seem so impoverished when compared to the richness of thought and experience. Shouldn't our language be as detailed and complex as the world? "Consider the world's diversity and worship it," Ariel advised in Derek Jarman's *Jubilee* (1978). "By denying its multiplicity you deny your own true nature."

---

11 Warren Weaver, letter to John von Neumann, January 31, 1940, box 7, John von Neumann Papers, Manuscript Division, Library of Congress, Washington, DC.

Weaver's multimedia hybrid, which combined text, film, and code, is nevertheless quite an unusual artifact. That it should be considered a forerunner to hypertext and today's computer is clear. What it says about film is also remarkable, for film with its flicker was already digital to begin with, even if classic Hollywood is remembered as "analog media." Weaver understood that the discrete regular nature of the photographic cells could be repurposed as individual entries in a computer database. And as with Willème or Londe before him, the camera was integrated as one element in a larger digital machine.

PART IV.
Computable Creatures

15

Experiments in Bionumeric Evolution

By the early 1950s, John von Neumann's Electronic Computer Project (ECP) had gained an international reputation. Having learned of the machine, Nils Aall Barricelli, the Italian-Norwegian mathematician who helped invent the field of artificial life, traveled from Europe to Princeton, New Jersey, to gain access to von Neumann's number cruncher.[1] Barricelli had already succeeded in creating numeric organisms based on principles gleaned from Darwin's theory of evolution. Although they existed as purely mathematical values, Barricelli had used graph paper to generate a universe populated by small creatures that could live, die, propagate, and mutate.

In the twentieth century, having been dominant for over one hundred years, the grand Kantian gambit—which Éric Alliez economically defined as "the making explicit of the relationship between the subject and the object in a theory of

---

1 Born and raised in Rome, Barricelli got his middle name Aall from his mother, who was Norwegian. A vocal critic of Mussolini in the early years of World War II, Barricelli would eventually relocate to Norway with his sister and his mother in 1936, finding a new home in the Department of Mathematics at the University of Oslo. Barricelli never married.

knowledge"—began to slip away, replaced by a new, more materially immanent and process-oriented philosophy.[2] Figures like Henri Bergson and Alfred North Whitehead aimed to circumvent Kant's framework. Later, philosophers like Gilles Deleuze and Catherine Malabou also took up the mantle, helping to dissolve the anthropocentrism of the subject–object split, replacing it with a smooth milieu of material entities constantly changing and transforming.

The influence of scientific discovery on such figures is well known. Whitehead frequently cited quantum physics. Deleuze had his Riemann surfaces and Malabou her neuroscience. As we have seen, the science of cybernetics was also influential, and it too conceived of the world as a material system, constantly signaling and balancing itself through control and communication. Largely overlooked by the canonical histories of cybernetics, Barricelli staged a number of important and unusual experiments during the spring and early summer of 1953, work that culminated in his most important publication "Experiments in Bionumeric Evolution Executed by the Electronic Computer at Princeton, N.J."[3]

---

2 Éric Alliez, "What Is—Or What Is Not—Contemporary French Philosophy, Today?," trans. Andrew Goffey, *Radical Philosophy* 161 (May/June 2010): 13.

3 Nils Aall Barricelli, "Experiments in Bionumeric Evolution Executed by the Electronic Computer at Princeton, N. J." (August 1953). Records of the ECP, Box 4, folder 45 (with additional blueprints in Map Box 1), Institute for Advanced Study, Princeton, NJ (hereafter cited as IAS Archives). A former student of Barricelli, Simen Gaure, described Barricelli as "balanc[ing] on a thin line between being truly original and being a crank" (quoted in George Dyson, *Darwin Among The Machines: The Evolution of Global Intelligence* [New York: Basic Books, 1998], 129). Despite being acknowledged as a pioneer Barricelli has received scant coverage in the literature and is almost entirely unknown outside of the small community of artificial life researchers. The main exception is Dyson, who devoted a chapter to Barricelli in *Darwin Among The Machines* and has lectured on Barricelli as part of his research into the history of the Electronic Computer Project at the Institute for Advanced Study.

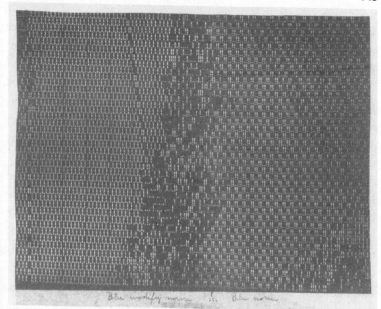

Figure 17. Detail from Nils Aall Barricelli's 1953 demonstration of bionumeric evolution showing both chaotic and stable gene clusters. The relatively chaotic center region depicts processes of mutation and disorganization. Texture fields on the right and left represent different bionumeric organisms. Source: Nils Barricelli, "blueprints" Figure 1d (detail), Electronic Computer Project records, Series I – Oversize. From the Shelby White and Leon Levy Archives Center of the Institute for Advanced Study, Princeton, NJ, USA.

Inspired by cybernetics, Barricelli created a universe of genes able to rearrange themselves to form more complex symbioses with other genetic entities (figure 17). Mimicking the homeostatic nature of biological ecosystems, Barricelli sought in his artificial life experiments to strike a balance between two dangerous extremes, each threatening to block the development of living organisms: on the one hand, the eradication of heterogeneous forces brought on by the overreaching greediness of a single monoculture; on the other hand, the suffocation of heterogeneous forces brought on by the collapse of organic structures into pure randomness. Life exists in the balance, he realized: the balance between unpredictable chaos and repetitive sameness, between pure randomness and absolute monoculture.

Barricelli's work thus revealed two important aspects of cybernetic systems: first, what Whitehead referred to several years earlier as the twin virtues of *intensity and survival*; second, the general development during the twentieth century of a model for *parallel causality*, that is, a theory of causality evident in systems with a large number of causal agents operating in parallel rather than in series.

—

"I was born in Rome 24 January 1912," Barricelli wrote in late 1951 on a Fulbright application that would eventually bring him to the United States.

> In 1932 I passed the Italian Artium examination (classical line), and in 1936 the Italian graduation in Mathematical and physical sciences. In 1936 I settled in Norway where I have been working with scientific researches in theoretical statistics and stationary time series . . ., mathematical theory of evolution . . ., tensorcalculus and [the] theory of relativity . . ., [and the] mathematical theory of evolution . . . Since 1947 I have been Assistant Professor at the University of Oslo.[4]

But Barricelli's official biography contained a curious gap. As a young student pursuing his doctorate, he purportedly furnished to his doctoral committee after the war in 1946 a dissertation topping out at 500 pages. A document this long fell well outside the accepted standards for dissertation length in his field. His doctoral committee responded, sensibly, by asking Barricelli to trim his

---

4 "Application for United States Government Travel Grant for Citizens of Norway," Barricelli member file, "Members," Box 7, IAS Archives.

dissertation to the acceptable length: 50 pages maximum. No, Barricelli replied; it was 500 pages or nothing. In the end, he chose nothing, forfeiting his doctoral degree in the home stretch.[5]

Barricelli gained a reputation for independence, fueled perhaps by his refusal to associate himself too closely with any specific research university for any length of time, moving throughout his professional career from the University of Rome, to the Mathematics Institute at the University of Oslo, to the Institute for Advanced Study in Princeton, to Vanderbilt University's Department of Biology, to the University of Washington's Department of Genetics, among other institutions, before ultimately settling down as an unsalaried researcher at the University of Oslo for twenty years to complete his career. He was also keen to swim against the current, sometimes meeting with success (as with his influential 1953 experiments on bionumeric evolution), sometimes belying a stubbornness that flew in the face of established scientific discourse (as with his vain attempts later in life to upend Kurt Gödel's incompleteness theorems), and sometimes admitting a simple affection for anachronism (as with his insistence on using computer punch cards long after his colleagues had abandoned them).[6]

"Nils Aall Barricelli was, to my knowledge, the first person to actually run artificial evolution experiments on computers,"

---

5 The anecdote is from Tor Gulliksen's obituary of Barricelli, recounted during an interview with Gulliksen in Oslo on March 11, 2009. Barricelli's doctoral committee included the esteemed mathematician Thoralf Skolem and the Nobel laureate Ragnar Frisch, as well as Herman Wold, who, as Olav Bjerkholt of the University of Oslo recounted to me, ultimately approved the dissertation prior to Barricelli's withdrawal.

6 "He insisted on using punch cards, even when everybody had computer screens. He gave two reasons for this: when you sit in front of a screen your ability to think clearly declines because you're distracted by irrelevancies, and when you store your data on magnetic media you can't be sure they're there permanently, you actually don't know where they are at all." Simen Gaure, quoted in Dyson, *Darwin Among the Machines*, 120.

claimed computer scientist Tim Taylor.[7] But Barricelli's experiments, and how he gained access to a computer on which to run them, are not well known. Barricelli had been working on translating Darwin's theory of evolution into a more strictly mathematical model, and prior to gaining access to the newly invented electronic computers of the time he had been doing his calculations longhand using pencil and paper.

Barricelli realized his experiments could be carried out more effectively and extensively with the assistance of an electronic computer, then a novelty. One reason was the advent of random-access memory, and, thanks to the adoption of the Williams Tube, von Neumann's ECP boasted one of the first real uses of random-access memory in a computer. The engineers in Princeton acquired forty Williams Tubes, arranging them side by side. Since it resembled the pistons of an automobile engine, the scientists would informally refer to their computer memory as a "V40."

The memory tubes in the ECP could accommodate 1024 words total, with each word being forty "letters" (bits) long. Yet the forty tubes were arranged in parallel rather than in series, meaning that the user need not wait to receive each word letter by letter—first letter, second letter, up to the fortieth letter. With all forty tubes working in synchrony, each word of memory could pop out all at once (or be written back to memory all at once). "When we stored forty bits in forty tubes, a word of forty bits could be removed or written all in parallel," recalled Arthur Burks in his oral history of the ECP.[8]

The inventors of the tube, Frederic Williams and Tom Kilburn, described the method of reading and writing to the tube memory in the following way: "Information may be extracted from any line by exploring it with an electron beam, a process known as 'reading'

---

7 Tim Taylor, *From Artificial Evolution to Artificial Life*, PhD Thesis, University of Edinburgh, May 1999, tim-taylor.com, accessed January 15, 2010.

8 Arthur W. Burks, OH 136. Oral history interview by William Aspray, June 23, 1987, Ann Arbor, Michigan. Charles Babbage Institute, University of Minnesota, Minneapolis.

and during the 'reading' process the information on the line is regenerated. Insertion of new information on a line, which may be done over old information is known as 'writing.'"[9] It was not simply the raw computational power of the ECP machine that fit Barricelli's scientific requirements so well, but also the way in which it organized information in parallel series of forty-letter words.

Barricelli applied for a position as a visiting research scholar sponsored under the Fulbright program and the Smith-Mundt Act of 1948. "I have made a preliminary investigation of the coding and time requirements of Mr. Barricelli's problem," von Neumann wrote in response to an initial query from Barricelli about the computational speed of the new device in Princeton.

> Our machine should be able to handle it on the scale that [Barricelli] suggests, i.e. with lines of 1000 cells each, and dealing with 200 lines in each block. The time to deal with one such block whould [sic] be approximately one and one-half hours to two hours, if all goes well, but in view of the peculiar contretemps that one has to expect in machine operation, the duration may well be doubled. It is, therefore, reasonable to assume that one should be able to dispose of approximately three 200-line blocks in one eight-hour day. Mr. Barricelli's program of 3000 lines, i.e. fifteen blocks of the above kind, would therefore seem to correspond to about five days, i.e. one week.[10]

Already intrigued by Barricelli's project, von Neumann wrote a recommendation letter in support of his Fulbright application, in

---

9 Frederic Williams and Tom Kilburn, "Information Storage Means" (US Patent 2777971 filed May 16, 1949), 1.

10 John von Neumann to Ragnar Frisch, letter, December 10, 1951. Barricelli member file, IAS Archives. Von Neumann's reference to "lines of 1000 cells" leads one to believe that Barricelli had originally specified a universe with a breadth of 1000 "genes" (represented as numbers) in parallel. Be that as it may, when Barricelli eventually mounted his experiments in Princeton in early 1953 his universe was set to a breadth of 512 genes.

which he stated that he was familiar with Barricelli's work on genetics, which struck him as highly original and interesting.[11]

Barricelli arrived in Princeton in either late 1952 or early 1953.[12] He was accepted as a visitor to the ECP for 1952–1953, and was later granted "member" status in the school of mathematics for his return in 1954. (Barricelli returned again in 1956 in an unspecified capacity not officially documented at the institute.)[13] His membership letter was signed by nuclear scientist Robert Oppenheimer, the institute's director since 1947. For membership Barricelli received a grant-in-aid of $1,800.

11 John von Neumann to Fulbright committee, letter, February 5, 1952. Barricelli member file, IAS Archives.

12 Von Neumann wrote to Barricelli again just before Thanksgiving in 1952 saying that he was looking forward to Barricelli's visit, and there is a record of Barricelli's signature dated February 10, 1953, in the "Director's signing book" at the institute, so it is likely that Barricelli didn't arrive in the US until early 1953.

13 See the operation log books for the ECP, which show entries from Barricelli on June 22 and other days during the summer of 1956. Records of the ECP, Box 15, IAS Archives.

16

Conjectural Biology

After arriving at the institute, Barricelli was granted access by von Neumann to some of the processing time offered by the Electronic Computer. During those years, the machine was busy chunking through ballistics numbers for use in national defense. But that happened primarily during daylight hours. Barricelli took over the night shift, spawning in the computer's memory scores of artificial organisms and then erasing them as dawn approached. His simulations first ran in the springtime nights of 1953, research that he summarized in a paper written that late spring and summer. During his return visits in 1954 and 1956, he modified and restaged his original experiments with the goal of achieving better results.

Barricelli spoke several languages and published in a few of them. Barricelli's signal research on bionumeric evolution spanned two decades from the 1950s to the early 1970s. First, during the period 1953–57, Barricelli drafted his initial substantial writings in the wake of his trip to Princeton. A twenty-six-page white paper (which likely did not circulate widely) titled "Experiments in Bionumeric Evolution Executed by the Electronic Computer at Princeton, N. J." was submitted to the institute in August 1953 and accompanied by a stunning series of large blueprint illustrations (figures 17 and 18), which were published the following year in an Italian cybernetics journal. Second, during the period 1962–63, a much longer paper was published in a Dutch theoretical biology journal. This paper synthesized and extended his work from the 1950s, adding additional sections summarizing the way in which he had trained his artificial organisms to play and win certain computer games. Third, in 1972, he published another essay that synthesized and extended all his research and thinking stemming from the 1953 Princeton experiments.[1]

These three series of papers—from 1953–57, 1962–63, and 1972—described how Barricelli created artificial organisms inside computers. In general, Barricelli owed a great deal to von Neumann and his work on cellular automata, as well as the biological theory of symbiogenesis.[2] But Barricelli's projects were uniquely his own. He started with a series of numbers, which he called "genes" after the term borrowed from the biological science of heredity. Into this primitive ecosystem of genes Barricelli introduced mutation and

---

1 See Nils Aall Barricelli, "Experiments in Bionumeric Evolution Executed by the Electronic Computer at Princeton, N. J."; Barricelli, "Esempi Numerici di processi di evoluzione," *Methodos* 6 (1954): 45–68; Barricelli, "Symbiogenetic Evolution Processes Realized by Artificial Methods," *Methodos* 9, nos. 35–36 (1957): 143–82; Barricelli, "Numerical Testing of Evolution Theories: Part I, Theoretical Introduction and Basic Tests," *Acta Biotheoretica* 16, nos. 1–2 (1962): 99–126; Barricelli, "Numerical Testing of Evolution Theories: Part II, Preliminary Tests of Performance Symbiogenesis and Terrestrial Life," *Acta Biotheoretica* 16, nos. 3–4 (1963): 69–98; and Barricelli, "Numerical Testing of Evolution Theories," *Journal of Statistical Computation and Simulation* 1, no. 2 (1972): 97–127.

2 Although they doubtless had numerous conversations about cellular automata during his stays in Princeton, in his 1957 paper Barricelli cited in particular the influence of von Neumann's Hixon Symposium lecture, given in Pasadena on September 20, 1948, which was edited and published as "The General and Logical Theory of Automata" in *Cerebral Mechanisms in Behavior: The Hixon Symposium*, ed. Lloyd Jeffress (New York: Wiley, 1951), as well as some of Claude Shannon's writing on automata. Barricelli also made note of pioneering work in symbiogenesis by the Russian botanist Boris Kozo-Polyansky and the American Ivan Wallin.

reproduction rules, dubbed "norms of action," "shift norms," or often just "norms" for short, to govern how each gene could propagate over successive reproductive cycles. Iterating the reproductive cycle over hundreds and thousands of generations, Barricelli was able to reproduce phenomena roughly resembling Darwinian evolution. Over many generations, the genes would coalesce into symbiotic groups, which Barricelli called "organisms." These organisms, existing in a more or less stable fashion, could nevertheless butt up against a neighboring organism or a rogue infectious gene, thereby mutating the original organisms into new equilibriums of genes. With his genes, norms, and organisms, Barricelli created something akin to living systems, all within the strictly numerical simulation universe of the Electronic Computer.

How did it work? "Instead of DNA or protein molecules reproducing by autocatalytic processes," Barricelli explained, "we use numbers reproducing according to conventional laws chosen in a suitable fashion."[3] Barricelli established a "universe" consisting of a horizontal row of 512 genes represented as an array of numbers. The universe could extend vertically as long as needed. The universe also wrapped around the left and right borders, meaning anything leaving the left border of the universe would reappear on the right, and vice versa. Overall the universe resembled a large rectangular raster grid, with each cell of the grid containing a single gene. Genes were represented using integers from negative 18 to positive 18. Barricelli seeded the first row of genes with initial values by means of a system for generating random numbers using a deck of playing cards.[4] Then he developed several norms (rules for mutation and

---

3 Barricelli, "Symbiogenetic Evolution Processes Realized by Artificial Methods," 147.

4 The playing cards system was defined in Barricelli, "Experiments in Bionumeric Evolution," 5, and later in Barricelli, "Symbiogenetic Evolution Processes Realized by Artificial Methods," 154. This conformed to Barricelli's essentially nonreligious view of the world. According to him the world consisted of random things assembled and transformed via the mundane, terrestrial rules of science. In this sense Barricelli was a strict materialist. Beauty, life, etc., appeared as a result of the complexity of material interactions, not because of a divine power.

reproduction) that when applied to each of the 512 genes would determine what new integer would appear in the successive generation; that is, in the column immediately below each original gene. In this way, the norms would translate rows of "parent" genes into subsequent rows of "child" genes, which in turn would be reproduced again and again by repeatedly applying the same norms to subsequent generations. If and when gene numbers reappeared in a sustained group, Barricelli would term each group an "organism." Thus, the cluster of numbers 5, -3, 1, -3, 0, -3, 1 might indicate an organism, provided the numbers persist as an uncorrupted cluster over subsequent generations of reproduction. To persist as an uncorrupted cluster, the numbers had to remain lined up in a segment, populating neighboring cells in Barricelli's grid table. If the 5 mutated into a -7, for example, the organism as a whole would have to be redefined.

Barricelli's universe was composed graphically from top to bottom line by line, filling in the top line first, then the second line, the third, and onward for hundreds or thousands of generations. Proceeding in lines from top to bottom, Barricelli's algorithm produced a rectangular image consisting of a grid of genes appearing as individual pixels. When finished, the image yielded a snapshot of evolutionary time, with the oldest generations of organisms at the top and the youngest at the bottom.

The output of Barricelli's experiments was highly visual. He did not simply print the integers in a grid. He used a simple graphical technique that made each integer appear differently to the naked eye—not unlike how alphanumeric characters can approximate a primitive gray scale in so-called ASCII images. Barricelli was drawing directly in binary numbers, converting zeros and ones into pixels in on or off positions.[5] He was able to benefit

---

5 Barricelli illustrated each gene as a vertical strip of dashes. Each dash acted like a pixel. Genes were one dash wide and eight dashes tall. To fill in the dashes he simply rendered each integer as a binary number: "binary numbers with less than 8 digits are used. The digits are disposed vertically in groups of 4 without marking the 0's. Negative numbers are designated by replacing 0's by 1's and 1's by

aesthetically from the interesting textures these binary markings afforded him. Because he represented each gene as a set of pixels, organisms were discerned visually based on how the pixel patterns self-organized into texture fields, which were identified as shapes or zones within the image. Variations in texture delineated one organism from another, and the width and height of any given texture field indicated the lifespan of the organism. Part of Barricelli's "evidence" thus lies in the unique visualizations he produced of his experimental trials.

Interestingly though, these visualizations were at the same time an image of the computer memory itself. Thanks to the Williams Tube, which merged pixel with bit on the screen of the oscilloscope, there was little to differentiate between what counted as a gene (which to Barricelli was just an integer) and what counted as a pixel. Number, pixel, and gene were all three quite literally the same thing.

Given what was available at the Institute for Advance Study in 1953, it is likely that Barricelli produced his images using a printer called the Teledeltos Outprinter, custom-made by institute engineer Willis Ware circa 1950. As Ware described it, the Teledeltos Outprinter "provides for the rapid printing-out of the contents of the internal memory of the main machine. Provision is made for printing each line of data from one to eight times. Two words are printed across each line so that a 1024 memory load occupies 512 'lines' of Teledeltos printing. (Each 'line' may consist of from one to eight passes of the stylus)."[6] Whether or not he used the Teledeltos

---

0's." To assist the reader Barricelli also provided a figure illustrating how each of the integers from positive 18 to negative 18 should look. See Barricelli, "Symbiogenetic Evolution Processes Realized by Artificial Methods," 155.

6 W[illis]. H. Ware, "Instruction Manual: Teledeltos Outprinter" (17 July 1951), 1. ECP West Storage Bldg. Box 1, folder 22, IAS Archives. The paper spool for the machine was about eight or nine inches wide. "I built a gadget that depended upon—what used to be called teledeltos paper, which is a thermally sensitive paper that you'd run a stylus across and spark it," Ware recalled years later in an oral history. "It worked great." See Willis H. Ware, OH 37. Oral history interview by Nancy B. Stern, January 19, 1981. Charles Babbage Institute, University of Minnesota, Minneapolis.

Outprinter, Barricelli initially printed a series of small images, each approximately eleven by eight inches. He then arranged the smaller prints side-by-side in groups of six or nine to form larger composites, which were reproduced using blueprint. As Barricelli's writings confirm, the blueprints should themselves be arranged side-by-side, resulting in a single mega-image measuring approximately three feet wide and eight feet tall. This large composite image consisted of three small images arranged side-by-side in the horizontal axis, and nine in the vertical axis. Taller than a person, Barricelli's universe of creatures would thus cascade downward eight feet through alternations of turbulence and consistency.

A computer-generated digital illustration of such magnitude would have been rare if not impossible in the early 1950s. Of art historical importance due to their early date, Barricelli's blueprints and other diagrams nevertheless suggest a generic continuity across all manner of pixel-based raster images stretching back to the eighteenth and nineteenth centuries and indeed to more ancient representational regimes using mosaics or textiles, which, as we saw already in section 2, are often mechanized and information-based in ways not entirely unrelated to modern computing.

Barricelli's 1953 paper documented nine reproduction norms. By 1957, he had regularized his system into a core set of five: the 0 or "zero" norm, A norm, B norm, C norm, and D norm. Each norm had its own personality. "The C norm favors disorganization and makes it difficult for any single species to invade the entire gene universe," he noted, while "the D norm produces mutations in the organisms and disqualifies organisms with few genes."[7]

---

7 Barricelli, "Symbiogenetic Evolution Processes Realized by Artificial Methods," 156. In the 1953 paper four years earlier, Barricelli had included two additional norms that were later discarded. He also had called the zero norm the "exclusion norm," and had given his norms slightly more vivid names: red norm, yellow norm, blue norm, blue modified norm, green norm, and purple modified norm. See Barricelli, "Experiments in Bionumeric Evolution," 3–4.

The norms have more technical definitions, but in essence they followed a technique of shift, collision, and mutation: genes shifted laterally left or right as they reproduced, based on their integer values (thus, a 4 gene will move four cells to the right, a -2 gene will move two cells to the left, and so on); if two genes happened to land on the same cell, a collision occurred, sparking a mutation based on the two genes in question; mutations were governed by whatever norm had been given jurisdiction for that cell; using a unique mathematical equation, each norm determined a new integer based on the values existing above and in neighboring cells to the cell currently under mutation.

Barricelli's norms had a limited scope. While they might be globally applied to an entire universe, each norm was inherently local, governing the behavior of each individual cell based on variables derived from the cell's relative position. Macro rules—such as transcendental identity or essential behavior—were eschewed in favor of local rules. Such a principle is consistent with how cellular automata systems operate more generally. Cellular automata systems tend to empower each small cell with relative autonomy while limiting the scope of what each cell can see or do.

Through close readings of these number spaces, Barricelli was able to identify not only symbiosis between genes but also smaller clusters acting as "germs" that might feed into an organism, as well as "parasites" that attach themselves to organisms. Biological phenomena such as heredity, gene transfer, adaptability, and mutation were also observed. In 1962, Barricelli summarized the different kinds of "life-like properties" he had observed in his symbioorganisms: "(A) Selfreproduction; (B) Crossing; (C) Great variability; (D) Mutation . . .; (E) Spontaneous formation; (F) Parasitism; (G) Repairing mechanisms; (H) Evolution."[8]

Barricelli's universe was strictly its own organizational domain, supervening the vital. "Just because the special conditions

8 Barricelli, "Numerical Testing of Evolution Theories: Part I" (1962), 80.

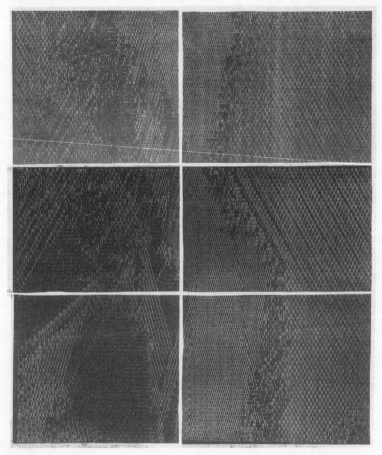

Figure 18. Composite image from Nils Aall Barricelli's 1953 demonstration of bionumeric evolution. Source: Nils Barricelli, "blueprints" Figures 1c and 1d (composite), Electronic Computer Project records, Series I – Oversize. From the Shelby White and Leon Levy Archives Center of the Institute for Advanced Study, Princeton, NJ, USA.

Figure 19. A 2010 restaging of Nils Aall Barricelli's original 1953 experiments, with the vertical axis scaled down by a factor of 8 to reveal a longer span of evolutionary time. Texture fields represent different organisms. Borders between textures indicate that an organism has perished, mutated, or otherwise evolved. Striped or interwoven textures contain multiple organisms in symbiosis.

prevailing on this earth seem to favor the forms of life which are based on organic compounds, this is no proof that it is not possible to build up other forms of life on an entirely different basis."[9] While admitting a connection to Darwinian theory, Barricelli ultimately had no interest in merely simulating the realm of biology. His experiments were not models. Rather, he wished to open up an autonomous field of life that was exclusively bionumeric. Barricelli's numerical organisms were, first and foremost, "alive" within a mathematical machine. If they also revealed something about the biological realm, so be it.

Many scientists would have doubted—and religious believers condemned—Barricelli's claim of creating artificial life. He must have felt the heat, because Barricelli went to great lengths to clarify to his readers whether or not his bionumeric organisms were "alive." By 1962, he felt obligated to preface his scientific paper with a special "note by the author," reinforced a few pages later by a reiterative footnote, aimed at ameliorating potential anxieties. "Some of [my] conclusions may be surprising to the reader," he admitted.[10] Yet Barricelli ultimately dodged the question of life. He pointed out that the term "living being" had not yet been fully defined, neither by him nor by anyone else. Instead, Barricelli proposed that living beings, such as those found in the terrestrial life of trees, animals, and humans, are simply one part of a higher classification tier that he labeled "symbioorganisms." The fact that bionumeric organisms also inhabit this higher tier of symbioorganisms, he argued, says nothing pro or con about the relative God givenness or scientific definability of life on Earth.

Even so, if his readers still harbored doubts, Barricelli advised them to cast aside their prejudicial emotions and act like

---

9 He argued that nothing about symbiogenesis required a chemical or biological substrate (for example, the substrate of DNA molecules). See Barricelli, "Symbiogenetic Evolution Processes Realized by Artificial Methods," 146.

10 Barricelli, "Numerical Testing of Evolution Theories: Part I" (1962), 69–70.

mountain climbers who "hold on solid ground" in moments of peril. "Proven facts and rigorous deduction are the solid ground on which scientific knowledge can be based. Feelings and opinions and any form of instinctive resistance to new ideas are not."[11]

11 Barricelli, "Numerical Testing of Evolution Theories: Part II" (1963), 7.

17

Intensity and Survival

The year 1953 was crucial for Barricelli. He had never achieved true evolution in his previous mathematical experiments. After that summer, he returned to Oslo, and in October wrote a letter (in French) to von Neumann underscoring the profound leap forward that the Electronic Computer had afforded him.

> No process of evolution had ever been observed prior to the Princeton experiments. The organisms that had appeared in previous experiments had never sustained any change. Only at Princeton did the organism prove capable of sustaining the process of evolution.[1]

Barricelli spent the late summer and fall of 1953 touring his results, presenting at an international congress on genetics in Bellaggio,

---

1 Nils Aall Barricelli to John von Neumann, letter, October 22, 1953. Member file on Barricelli, IAS School of Mathematics, Members, Ba-Bi, 1933-77, IAS Archives. One may assume that Barricelli meant such achievements were unprecedented both in terms of his own research and also in terms of the work of other scientists.

Italy, on August 30 and a few weeks later at the Institute for Telecommunications in Rome on October 10.

Yet the 1953 tests were still inconclusive. He returned to Princeton in 1954 to refine the algorithm in pursuit of better results. As he wrote, "It will be one of the most important aims of the next bionumerical experiments to find the way to start an unlimited evolution."[2] The 1953 experiments had been plagued by parasite genes. Even more ominous, Barricelli had noticed that the experiments tended to result in standard, homogeneous patterns after a relatively short number of generations. The stand-ard patterns came in two varieties, either pure uniformity or pure disorganization. Either a single organism killed off all others, creating a monoculture, or no organisms gained a foothold, result-ing in sustained randomness. Barricelli would later label the two patterns "organized homogeneity" and "disorganized homogeneity."[3] They were his Scylla and Charybdis. After return-ing in 1954, Barricelli's goal was to balance the experiments more carefully in the hopes of achieving an "unlimited evolution" between these two fatal extremes.

In 1953, Barricelli lamented the shortcomings of his early test results:

> All experiments have shown that the use of a single norm in the whole gene universe leads—in most cases in less than 500 generations—to *uniform conditions* in the whole universe, for instance by progressive disorganization or by a single species expanding to the whole gene universe. Where uniform condi-tions are established every further evolution stops.[4]

But a year later, he had already made some progress on this front.

---

2 Barricelli, "Experiments in Bionumeric Evolution," 12.

3 Barricelli, "Numerical Testing of Evolution Theories: Part I" (1962), 88.

4 Ibid., 6, emphasis added. Or later in the paper: "When a relative maximum of fitness is reached, the evolution process may stop for a long time," 18.

The chief purpose of the experiments of 1954 has been to find some methods to prevent the destruction of the species submitted to evolution and to realize some *durable evolution* process which could be carried on for any desired number of generations.[5]

In order to achieve "durable evolution" and avoid the twin dangers of monoculture and chaos—the two types of "uniform conditions"—Barricelli discovered a trick. He began to deploy three or more norms in parallel. For example, the first hundred cells might follow the A norm, the second hundred cells might follow the B norm, the third hundred cells might follow the C norm, and so on. Having different norms bump up against one another proved advantageous. (He also eventually devised a system in which multiple universes were run concurrently; he would copy entire sectors of genes from one universe to another in order to cross-fertilize them with new blood.) Mixing two mathematical norms across such thresholds generated points of genetic friction, increasing the complexity of the gene pool and thereby increasing overall biodiversity. By introducing multiple norms into his reproductive cycle, Barricelli was able to achieve a continuous form of evolution from generation to generation. The evolution was judged to be successful if an equilibrium persisted between pure stasis and pure change. If, after a few thousand evolutionary cycles, the gene pool had disintegrated into randomness with no symbiotic organisms emerging, the experiment was deemed a failure; it was likewise a failure if the gene pool was overrun by a single super-organism killing off all other living things. The goal was balance. Each kind of "positive feedback," whether assistive or disintegrating, was odious to life.

In this sense, Barricelli was a kind of biological Keynesian. He wished to mitigate the dangers lurking within his ecosystem by

---

5 Barricelli, "Symbiogenetic Evolution Processes Realized by Artificial Methods," 168, emphasis added.

deliberately bridling the more unhealthy tendencies that, when left unregulated, would lead to systemic disaster. To sustain creative evolution, he sought the equipoise of moderation through regulation.

Barricelli's "durable evolution" described a view of the world shared by the so-called process philosophers evoked previously. (Whether Barricelli was aware of Whitehead, Bergson, Spinoza, or others in this philosophical tradition is not known.) In reference to Hegel, Malabou wrote that historical evolution "is the correct proportion between maintaining and annihilating."[6] Certain things persist, while others fade away. Such a correct proportion was precisely what Barricelli sought in order to ensure the vitality of his bionumerical organisms.

Barricelli's tone was also similar to that of philosophers like Whitehead (before him) and Deleuze (after). Whitehead's so-called philosophy of organism—which he admitted was "closely allied to Spinoza's scheme of thought" and which he published in 1929 as *Process and Reality: An Essay in Cosmology*—fits with the kind of problem Barricelli was aiming to solve in his experiments twenty-five years later. "This doctrine of organism," wrote Whitehead in *Process and Reality*, "is the attempt to describe the world as a process of generation of individual actual entities, each with its own absolute self-attainment."[7] Or, later in the same text: "The problem for Nature is the production of societies which are

---

6 Catherine Malabou, "L'autre monde," *Fresh Théorie* 2 (Paris: Léo Scheer, 2006), 336. In the preface to the 1888 English edition of the *Communist Manifesto*, Friedrich Engels associated not Hegel but Marx with Darwin's evolutionary biology. As Engels wrote, Marx was "destined to do for history what Darwin's theory has done for biology." Friedrich Engels, "Preface to the English Edition of 1888" in Karl Marx and Friedrich Engels, *The Communist Manifesto*, trans. Samuel Moore (London: Penguin, 2002), 203. Indeed, following in the wake of Hegel, each scientist—Marx an economist, Darwin a biologist—had a view of history in which contingency ruled over necessity and essence gave way to evolution.

7 See Alfred North Whitehead, *Process and Reality: An Essay in Cosmology* (New York: Free Press, 1978), 7, 60.

'structured' with a high 'complexity,' and which are at the same time 'unspecialized.' In this way, intensity is mated with survival."[8]

Barricelli, too, sought an alliance between intensity and survival. In order to persist over time his symbioorganisms had to be suitably "intense." They had to cohere within themselves but also had to be "unspecialized," allowing themselves to undergo metamorphosis via genetic collisions with other organisms. "I may express my conclusions in the following manner," Barricelli wrote in a rich summarizing passage:

> Make life difficult but not impossible for a simbioorganism [sic], let the difficulties be various and serious but not too serious; let the conditions be changing frequently but not too radically and not in the whole universe at the same time; then you may see an evolution transforming the symbioorganism with a surprising rapidity and creating properties and organs which will make the symbioorganism able to face all the difficulties and all the new situations it meets. But do not expect to observe an evolution process if you let the symbioorganism vegetate in peace and safety in a perfectly homogenious [sic] universe. In that case you will probably observe nothing essentially more complicated than the simplest molecule.[9]

These are fascinating claims when taken as a whole. In one fell swoop, Barricelli offered a biology, an ethics, and a theory of history.

---

8 Ibid., 101.
9 Barricelli, "Symbiogenetic Evolution Processes Realized by Artificial Methods," 175.

18
Parallel Causality

Barricelli's computational creatures spotlight the problem of causality. While causality has appeared many times in the history of philosophy—in Aristotle's four causes, René Descartes's mind–body problem, or David Hume's critique of causality—only during the twentieth century did investigators begin to address directly the question of causality within complex and chaotic systems. Fueled by advances in fields such as thermodynamics, nonlinear mathematics, biology, complexity theory, and (eventually) cybernetics, systems theory, and chaos theory, scientists began to develop approaches for dealing with physical realities that had henceforth fallen outside classical scientific explanation.

Nonlinear causality refers to the way in which an effect is produced through indirect, compound, or multiple causes. Thermodynamics is illustrative in that it entails numerous independent variables operating in parallel, for example, the forces that make up complex eddy movements, laminar stresses, air viscosity, turbulence, heat flows, or conductivity.[1] Many such

---

1 On heat in media studies, see Nicole Starosielski's forthcoming book *Media Hot and Cold.*

nonlinear and "massively parallel" phenomena, which had previously been considered too complex to be modeled using existing methods, were now falling under the gaze of scientific knowledge (figure 20).

Figure 20. Étienne-Jules Marey, smoke trails encounter an obstacle creating turbulence, 1901. Source: Cinémathèque Française.

Philosophy and the social sciences had also pursued a more sophisticated theory of causality, beyond the simplistic notion that *a* causes *b*. In his *Wealth of Nations*, Adam Smith famously used the metaphor of the "invisible hand" to explain how individual self-interest at the micro level will end up having a beneficial outcome at the national or societal level.[2] That Smith had to

2 Adam Smith, *The Wealth of Nations*, Books IV–V (London: Penguin, 2000), 32. As Susan Buck-Morss reminded us: "There seems little doubt that Smith's use

resort to metaphor is a symptom of his inability to correlate small-scale behavior with large-scale results. By contrast, dialectics (whether from Hegel or Marx) proposed a novel form of causality rooted in negation and inversion. In dialectics, a cause produces an effect not directly but through an encounter with its opposite, eventually consuming and destroying this opposite through a "negation of the negation."

"I am not particularly taken by this term *overdetermination*," French Marxist Louis Althusser said of his signature concept, "but I shall use it in the absence of anything better, both as an *index* and as a *problem*."[3] Drawing on Freud, Lenin, Mao, Engels, Marx, and others in his essay "Contradiction and Overdetermination," Althusser set out to differentiate the Hegelian dialectic from the Marxian one. "Indeed, a Hegelian contradiction is never *really overdetermined*, even though it frequently has all the appearances of being so."[4]

For Althusser, overdetermination referred to the existence of multiple historical causes. Something is "overdetermined" when several influencing factors all act to affect it. These multiple causes mix and combine to bring about actual historical events. Yet the multiplicity of causes is never "resolved" or unified in the result. Rather, the result preserves the conflict between multiple root causes.

Althusser evoked what he called Marx's "two ends" of cause, the first the mode of production, the second the superstructure:

Here, then, are the two ends of the chain: the economy is determinant, but *in the last instance*, Engels is prepared to say, in the

---

of [the term 'invisible hand'] derived from the tradition of natural theology, which saw effects of the hand of God everywhere in the natural world." See Susan Buck-Morss, "Envisioning Capital: Political Economy on Display," *Critical Inquiry* 21 (Winter 1995): 434–67.

3 Louis Althusser, "Contradiction and Overdetermination," *For Marx*, trans. Ben Brewster (London: Verso, 1996), 101.

4 Ibid.

long run, the run of History. But History "asserts itself" through
the multiform world of the superstructures, from local tradition
to international circumstance . . . In short, the idea of a "pure
and simple" non-overdetermined contradiction is . . ."meaning-
less, abstract, senseless."[5]

In Althusser's analysis, no cause can simply effect a result in a
linear sense. Rather, the economy is filtered through the superstructure in complex ways. Only later does this historical base
"assert itself" and appear as a logical cause.

Deleuze also proposed an unusual theory of causality. He
labeled it the "quasi-cause," preferring to underdetermine rather
than overdetermine its potency. Deleuze's quasi-cause is an obscure
and slippery concept with an extensive backstory. To explain the
quasi-cause, Deleuze evoked the spirit of Joë Bousquet, the French
surrealist poet who was paralyzed in World War I. "My wound
existed before me," claimed Bousquet. "I was born to embody it."[6]

---

5 Ibid., 111–13. The Marxian concept of "determination in the last instance,"
was also discussed by Stuart Hall in "The Problem of Ideology: Marxism without
Guarantees," collected in *Stuart Hall: Critical Dialogues in Cultural Studies*, ed.
David Morley and Kuan-Hsing Chen (New York: Routledge, 1996). "We have to
acknowledge the real indeterminacy of the political" (45), he wrote. And, in a
clever reversal, Hall suggested that, in its indeterminacy, the political is not
economic in the last ·instance, but economic in the *first* instance (45).
"Determination in the last instance" has also found an unusual afterlife in the
work of François Laruelle, most notably in his book *Introduction au non-marxisme*
(Paris: PUF, 2000).

6 Gilles Deleuze, *The Logic of Sense*, trans. Mark Lester (New York: Columbia
University Press, 1990), 148. For more on the quasi-cause see pages 6, 124, 125,
and 146–7. Deleuze's language leads up to a magical climax, embedding normative
language directly into his discussion of causality and events, in this, one of
philosophy's most noble sentences: "Either ethics makes no sense at all, or this is
what it means and has nothing else to say: not to be unworthy of what happens to
us" (149). Such visions of the good life as the assumption of an affirmative practice
based on one's allotted fate have a long history in philosophical and theological
writings, including quite vividly in the work of Maurice Blondel and his claims
that man must align the "will-as-willing" (*volonté voulante*) with his "will-as-
willed" (*volonté voulue*). See Maurice Blondel, *Action (1893): Essay on a Critique*

In a reversal of temporal sequence, Bousquet's wound predated his wounded body. Bousquet's body (and his identity) must graduate into a fate already assigned to it.

Deleuze addressed the quasi-cause in Series 14, Series 20, and Series 21 of his book *The Logic of Sense* from 1969. "The quasi-cause does not create, it 'operates,' and wills only what comes to pass,"[7] Deleuze wrote, highlighting the elusive, retrospective glance of a cause that can appear only after its effects become evident. The quasi-cause is something like a primordial force that makes things communicate, but only after they have formed as such. A quasi-cause is inserted into a state of affairs; it cannot be said to precipitate a state of affairs. Or, in informal language, the quasi-cause "takes credit" after the outcome.

This weird form of causality has also captured the interest of Mark B. N. Hansen, the philosopher and media theorist who has, among other things, explored Whitehead's theory of the subject. How can subjectivity operate at multiple levels of experience simultaneously? How can a subject exist at the level of conscious thought, but also at the level of physical sensation, or the level of atomic particles? For example, do the interactions of molecules cause certain sensations in the human body, and do these sensations cause higher-order conscious thoughts? What about the reverse?

To answer these questions, Hansen proposed the concept of "indirection."[8] Indirection refers to the way in which one level of

---

of Life and a Science of Practice (Notre Dame, IN: University of Notre Dame Press, 1984).

7 Deleuze, *The Logic of Sense*, 147.

8 Mark B. N. Hansen, "Speculative Phenomenology (Whitehead, Nonrepresentational Experience, and 21st Century Media)," lecture given in the University Seminar on the Theory and History of Media, Columbia University, New York, NY, November 8, 2010. See also Mark B. N. Hansen, "System-Environment Hybrids" in *Emergence and Embodiment: New Essays on Second-Order Systems Theory*, ed. Bruce Clarke and Mark B. N. Hansen (Durham, NC: Duke University Press, 2009).

a heterogenous system "indirectly" sends out causal effects upward into another layer of the system. These are not causes in the traditional sense of *a* causing *b*. They are nonlinear causes that emanate from one magnitude of scale to another magnitude, for example from the macro to the micro.

In Hansen's view, life operates at different levels. At each level, phenomena remain autonomous and contained to their local milieu. Yet such phenomena can also produce epiphenomena that ripple upward or downward in the nested system of levels. These epiphenomena are not direct, causal results within the local milieu, but "indirect" results seeping orthogonally into other plateaus of the heterogeneous assemblage that constitutes subjective experience in the most general sense.

These various theories begin to describe the strange kind of causality at the heart of Barricelli's mathematical ecosystem. How could Barricelli simply draw a grid of integers and thereby generate a living creature? How can a simple sequence of numbers come to life? Further, how could such living creatures reproduce and propagate, thereby "causing" and mediating effects in future generations?

Barricelli's system was not so much a system of mediation as it was a system of "intermediation," to borrow a term from N. Katherine Hayles. Similar to Althusser's overdetermination, Deleuze's quasi-cause, and Hansen's indirection, Hayles's intermediation described a causal relationship in which multiple, parallel causal inputs cohere and conflict to effect a result.

An important aspect of intermediation is the recursivity implicit in the coproduction and coevolution of multiple causalities. Complex feedback loops connect humans and machines, old technologies and new, language and code, analog processes and digital fragmentations. Although these feedback loops evolve over time and thus have a historical trajectory that arcs from one place to another, it is important not to make the mistake of privileging any one point as the primary locus of attention, which can easily result in flattening complex interactions back into linear causal chains.[9]

Yet by the end of his 1963 paper "Numerical Testing of Evolution Theories," Barricelli had unfortunately committed the mistake Hayles warns against.[10] In his 1963 paper, Barricelli addressed games, those most emblematic of nonlinear systems. Moving beyond simply modeling evolutionary behavior, he posed the question "whether it would be possible to select symbioorganisms able to perform a specific task assigned to them."[11] In other words, could artificial organisms acquire a specific goal? Could they take on a task? Could they play and win games? Or, in Hayles's language, could the complex interactions be flattened back into linear causal chains?

Barricelli selected a simple game called Tac Tix, devised by Piet Hein, who had adapted it from the ancient Chinese game *nim*.

----

9 Hayles herself borrowed the term from Nicholas Gessler. See N. Katherine Hayles, *My Mother Was a Computer: Digital Subjects and Literary Texts* (Chicago: University of Chicago Press, 2005), 31.

10 The 1963 paper was essentially about games. But it carried greater historical significance because in it Barricelli proposed a "chemo-analogical computer" using DNA molecules as the computational substrate—a mere ten years after the discovery of DNA by Watson and Crick. Today it would simply be called a DNA computer, the origins of which are typically attributed to Leonard Adleman and his description of a DNA computer published in 1994. According to Barricelli's conjectures thirty years prior such a computer would consist of a normal "hardware" computer connected to a "wetware" environment made up of DNA molecules. Barricelli constructed a "DNA-norm" to govern the cellular phenomena of the base–pair interactions. Computations would first be transferred from hardware to wetware; the DNA molecules would perform the computations; and the results would be fed back into the computer. "Such a computer could essentially consist of an automatic, programmed chemical laboratory with read-in and read-out devices and other gadgets to perform the following operation: Interpret and transform information contained in IBM cards or magnetic tape into a specific arrangement of nucleotides and other molecules. Perform the chemical operations specified by the program (also contained in IBM cards or magnetic tape). Punch or read out the results into IBM cards or magnetic tape." See Barricelli, "Numerical Testing of Evolution Theories: Part II" (1963), 121.

11 Ibid., 100.

Barricelli read about Tac Tix in the February 1958 issue of *Scientific American* and devised a way to superimpose his cellular grids onto the grid of the game.[12] In essence Barricelli merged genetic pattern and game strategy. He ran his tests on the IBM 704 computer at the A.E.C. Computing Center at New York University in the fall of 1959, again in the summer of 1960 at Brookhaven National Laboratory, and a third time at Vanderbilt University. The result was a primitive form of machine learning—Barricelli is sometimes credited as the first to work in this domain—in which individual organisms would evolve in ways that were more suitable for game play, thereby becoming stronger opponents. "There is no doubt," he wrote, that "the symbioorganisms are 'learning' the game by a sort of 'evolutionary learning process' based on mutation, crossing and selection."[13]

In Barricelli's hands, parallel causality unfolded according to the virtues of organizational fitness and environmental competition, principles he had borrowed first from Darwinian evolution and later from game theory. What had originally opened up into a massively parallel system of inductive, emergent behavior was now

---

12 Nim is binary in nature. "Since digital computers operate on the binary system, it is not difficult to program such a computer to play a perfect game of nim, or to build a special machine for this purpose. Edward U. Condon, the former director of the National Bureau of Standards who is now at Washington University of St. Louis, was a co-inventor of the first such machine. Patented in 1940 as the Nimatron, it was built by the Westinghouse Electric Corporation and exhibited in the Westinghouse building at the New York World's Fair. It played 100,000 games and won 90,000. Most of its defeats were administered by attendants demonstrating to skeptical spectators that the machine could be beaten." See Martin Gardner, "Mathematical Games: Concerning the Game of Nim and Its Mathematical Analysis," *Scientific American* 198, no. 2 (February 1958): 108. The name "Tac Tix" is both a reference to tic-tac-toe and a homonym with the word "tactics."

13 Ibid., 116. On the topic of games, physics professor Øystein Aars noted in his 1993 obituary of Barricelli that concurrent with his research on game-playing automata Barricelli made a computerized chess game and actually sold some games to the Norwegian game publisher Damm; details are not forthcoming, but this would have most likely been during the 1970s or possibly the late 1960s. See Øystein Aars, "Nils Aall Barricelli" (obituary), *Aftenposten* (February 8, 1993).

focused, enchained, canalized, and disciplined by a new pedagogical goal. Barricelli did not just want his creatures to live and evolve. He wanted his creatures to learn optimal behavior within a game space. He wanted his creatures to win.

"The contemporary indoctrination into linear causality is so strong," wrote Hayles, "that it continues to exercise a fatal attraction for much of contemporary thought."[14] Barricelli would have been wise to heed such a warning. Why cripple an emergent system by reintroducing the soft fascisms of mastery and teleological discipline? Why reduce the multiple to the unitary? According to Hayles, the temptation to lapse back to linear causality "must be continually resisted if we are fully to realize the implications of multicausal and multilayered hierarchical systems, which entail distributed agency, emergent processes, unpredictable coevolutions, and seemingly paradoxical interactions between convergent and divergent processes."[15]

In ignoring Hayles's advice, any system of organization, any life whether organic or inorganic, will find itself misconstrued and poorly drawn. Worse, it risks reintroducing the same kinds of "uniform conditions" that Barricelli spent the months and years of the 1950s trying to escape.

14 Hayles, *My Mother Was a Computer*, 31.
15 Ibid.

PART V.
Crystalline War

19

Times of Crisis

"I await the end of Cinema with optimism," Jean-Luc Godard announced in 1965. And, indeed, the end was near. "The cinema seems to me to be over," was Guy Debord's blunt assessment by the spring of 1978. Much happened in those intervening years, with the progressive explosion of the middle to late sixties engendering a crisis and retrenchment in the early to middle seventies. The transformation was evident in a number of events and pseudo-events: student revolts in Paris and elsewhere, the French left's flirtation with Maoism and other militancies, the oil crisis of 1973 and 1974, a painful renovation in the economic base of developed societies coinciding with the rise of information networks and the concomitant changes in the role of the individual in society. The rise of the information age was also a time of crisis. In fact, scholars like Mary Ann Doane and Wendy Hui Kyong Chun have reflected on how crisis itself is not incidental to the information age, but rather part of its very essence.[1]

1 See Mary Ann Doane, "Information, Crisis, Catastrophe," in *New Media, Old Media: A History and Theory Reader*, ed. Wendy Hui Kyong Chun and Thomas Keenan (New York: Routledge, 2006), 251–64, and Wendy Hui Kyong Chun, "Crisis, Crisis, Crisis, or Sovereignty and Networks," *Theory, Culture & Society* 28, no. 6 (2011): 91–112.

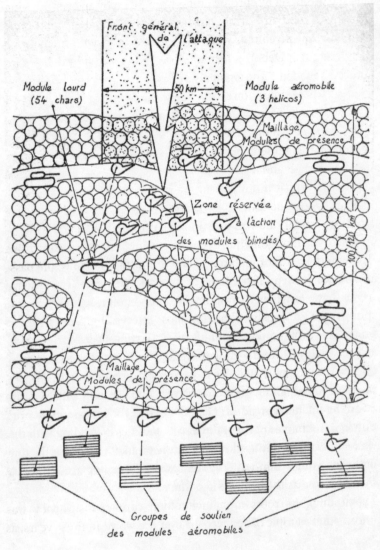

Figure 21. Guy Brossollet, "Non-Battle." Source: Guy Brossollet, *Essai sur la non-bataille* (Paris: Belin, 1975), 82.

Guy Debord never recovered from the crisis of the 1970s. His later life was beset by chronic illness brought on by an ever-growing gluttony in food and drink. He deserted the capital city and grew more introspective in his work, mixing manifesto with memoir. By March 8, 1978, Debord's former glory as a radical filmmaker and author had faded. "The cinema seems to me to be over," he wrote in a letter. "These times don't deserve a filmmaker like me."[2]

The 1970s was a long decade. It "began in 1967–68 and ended in 1983," recalled Antonio Negri. "In 1967–68, as in all the developed countries, the student movement took to the barricades."[3] Much has been said about Debord being at those May barricades, certainly in spirit if not also in the flesh, with Situationist graffiti festooning the pediments of respectable French society. But a frontline militant he was not, and Debord soon left Paris to settle in one of the hexagon's more remote outposts, the rural Auvergne. There he stayed for much of the rest of his life, watching the passing parade from a safe distance. The new social movements of the 1960s, having swollen in importance, were soon met by an iron fist and eventually crushed by the freshly transformed post-Fordist economies of the middle to late 1970s. If the 1960s represented a certain triumph, the 1970s were a decade of defeat. "The first to be defeated were the social movements," remembered Negri, reflecting on the kidnapping and killing of Italian Prime Minister Aldo Moro by the Red Brigades. "Having cut themselves off totally from the representatives of the traditional left . . ., the social movements were thus dragged into the abyss of an extremism that was becoming increasingly blind and violent. The kidnapping and killing of Aldo Moro was the beginning of the end."[4]

Although its roots are much older, counter-insurgency was increasingly a topic of concern around the world in those years, as

2 Guy Debord, *Correspondance*, vol. 5, *janvier 1973–décembre 1978* (Paris: Librairie Arthème Fayard, 2005), 451.

3 Antonio Negri, "Reviewing the Experience of Italy in the 1970s," *Le Monde diplomatique* (September 1998).

4 Ibid.

state and nonstate actors alike were perfecting the art of subduing popular upheaval. Viewing individuals and populations as liabilities, even threats, the army and the police adopted a series of tactics, from urban warfare and occupation, to ideological campaigns and the winning of "hearts and minds," to torture and other forms of nonlethal force.

All this comes under the heading of asymmetric warfare, a topic explored in books like Robert Taber's classic *War of the Flea* (1965) or in American military field manuals produced during and after the war in Vietnam. *Essai sur la non-bataille* [*Essay On Non-Battle*], written in 1975 by the French military officer Guy Brossollet, added an interesting dimension to the literature on asymmetric warfare. Brossollet's perspective was more explicitly networked and topological. Military theory has long identified the existence of asymmetric threats—within which popular movements play an important part—but Brossollet gave a rather unusual piece of advice to his colleagues in the French military. Brossollet advised them to adopt the very structure and tactics of the opposition, to fight asymmetry with asymmetry. (The American Pentagon started to adopt a similar strategy twenty years later in the 1990s under the banner of so-called Fourth-Generation Warfare.) Brossollet thus stands as a kind of historical precursor, a harbinger of the coming net war.

Brossollet's essay on "non-battle" was a military text. The book was written from the perspective of a military insider and for an informed audience. Nationalistic and promilitary, the book was not critical of French power, but nevertheless it advocated reform of the military in the face of a changing world. The book was firmly situated in the Cold War, as would be expected for a military text written in Europe during the 1970s. Brossollet's primary example throughout the book concerned a ground invasion coming from the northeast, through Belgium. The French military must "Connaître l'Autre," he insisted, with the Soviets playing the role of this particular "Other."[5]

---

5 Guy Brossollet, *Essai sur la non-bataille* (Paris: Belin, 1975), 13.

Yet Brossollet was not primarily thinking in terms of bilateral antagonism along the lines of Self/Other or West/East. Like Lewis Richardson before him, Brossollet's language was also one of heterogeneity and complexity. "The Other and the others, these are the heterogeneous elements of the environment of conflict, elements that may be friendly or unfriendly, meek or powerful, contestational or allied—but even then each party is part of the multipolar dialectic of the antagonisms of our times."[6] Algeria had recently obtained independence from France in 1962, and the Algerian conflict must have been a key reference for Brossollet. But he was also likely thinking of the popular uprisings of May 1968 and the various revolutionary movements across Europe such as the German Red Army Faction or the Italian Red Brigades active during the 1970s.

The coming warfare will be network-centric, Brossollet argued. The coming battle will be a non-battle. No longer gaining power from its "fists," France must think in terms of "pinpricks."[7] "The principle that is at the heart of this research," wrote Brossollet, is that "for the events that we wish were determined but which remain unpredictable (i.e. battle), we must substitute a series of minor but statistically consistent actions that we call, by contrast, non-battle."[8] From fists to pinpricks, from major to minor, from deterministic strategy to stochastic tactics—he speculated that the coming warfare will be "multiform, maneuverable, omnipresent."[9]

Brossollet imagined a battlefield of bubbles and meshes, connected by corridors (figure 21). The corridors allow military assets that are not network-appropriate, such as tanks, the ability to move quickly in and among the mesh. Yet tanks or missiles are less important in non-battle. Complimenting the strategic nuclear deterrent, Brossollet argued that the military should shift toward

6 Ibid.
7 Ibid., 67
8 Ibid., 78, emphasis removed.
9 Ibid., 15.

maneuver forces, which he described in terms of probing and test-ing. Four types of teams make up the "testing" forces: presence, destruction, shock, and transmission units.[10] The *module terrestre de présence* or "mesh" forces act as a kind of "tiger team," each equipped with armaments and a jeep and mobilizable in a cellular formation.[11]

A few years later, in their book *A Thousand Plateaus*, Gilles Deleuze and Félix Guattari made a distinction between what they called the "smooth" and the "striated," the former being nomadic, fractal, and rhizomatic, the latter more sedentary, organized, and arborescent.[12] As the Brossollet example indicates, networks are not smooth by default, but can be both smooth or striated. While the term "striated" means a kind of layered organization, and has a connection in Deleuze and Guattari to geology, striated networks can be understood in terms of *cellular* spaces. These are the kinds of network spaces developed in the 1950s by people like John von Neumann and Nils Aall Barricelli. Cellular spaces, be they grids or more elastic topologies, rely on a hard and fast distinction between links and nodes, and thus between one node and another. Contrast this with smooth or *non-cellular* spaces, for instance architect Konrad Wachsmann's "grapevine structure" (figure 22) or the kinds of structures imagined by Lebbeus Woods. In the buildings and landscapes of Woods, there was often no clear distinction between node and edge, likewise between node and node. Instead, the "smooth" form took over, governed by altogether different logics: hydraulics, metallurgy, a pure difference "in movement, in flux, in variation."[13]

---

10 Ibid., 67–77.

11 For an exploration of networks and the architecture of antagonism, see Branden Hookway, *Pandemonium: The Rise of Predatory Locales in the Postwar World* (New York: Princeton Architectural Press, 1999).

12 Gilles Deleuze and Félix Guattari, "14. 1440: The Smooth and the Striated," in *A Thousand Plateaus*, trans. Brian Massumi (Minneapolis: University of Minnesota Press, 1987), 474–500.

13 Deleuze and Guattari, *A Thousand Plateaus*, 409.

Brossollet derived a language of multilateral, rhizomatic network warfare, strictly out of the Cold War context of bilateral, nuclear-armed states. The concept of deterrence provided the key; nuclear deterrence created a kind of absolute state of exception within which only non-battle could be thought and deployed. In other words, nuclear weapons, in making battle obsolete, allowed battle to become virtual or superpositional. Deterrence led to the virtualization of war. And, in the best tradition of Sun Tzu, the most effective battle became the one that did not arrive.

At the same time, Brossollet claimed that non-battle emerged from a position of weakness not strength. "During the period 1939–1975," France experienced a decline in offensive capacity, he lamented. "Our country changed from being a great military power to being a medium-level power."[14] Yet I suspect Brossollet was wrong on this point, unduly swayed by nostalgia for the French imperial past. Non-battle was not so much the waning of power, but rather an intensification of power to an ever higher degree. The reigning opinion inherited from Clausewitz, that everything comes to a head in battle, was rendered obsolete by the threat of nuclear war. But power, when extended to hyperbolic levels, inverted and produced its opposite.

This realization slightly modifies the origin myth of the network age, the old chestnut that scientists like Paul Baran developed distributed networks in 1964 as a way to resolve the nuclear threat. The myth is not wrong per se. Nevertheless network-centric warfare was not so much a deviation from or resolution of the threat of nuclear annihilation, but rather a *result* of the nuclear threat. Network-centric warfare was, in other words, an extension or refinement of the previous form of antagonism. As with the birth of terrorism, absolute power creates the absolute deviant. Or, one might say, the absolute produces the virtual.

---

14 Brossollet, *Essai sur la non-bataille*, 30.

Figure 22. Konrad Wachsmann, "Grapevine Structure," 1953. Source: Akademie der Künste, Berlin, Konrad-Wachsmann-Archiv, Nr. 164 F.1. © Konrad Wachsmann, courtesy Ray Wachsmann.

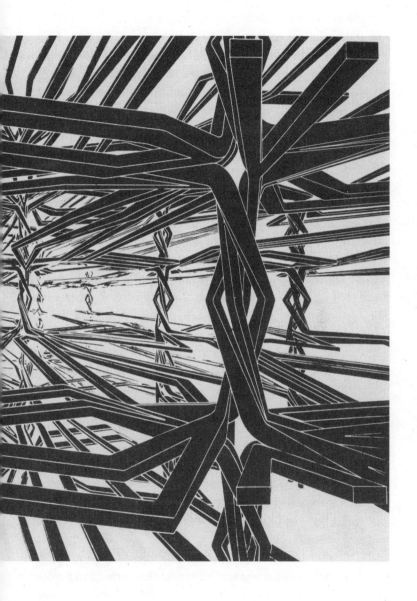

Addressing Moro and the Red Brigades in his 1979 preface to
the fourth Italian edition of *The Society of the Spectacle*, Debord
spat on the guerrilla movement, claiming that the Red Brigades
were in fact unknowing pawns of the state Stalinist forces. Writing
to Gianfranco Sanguinetti before the killing, Debord predicted
that Moro would be "suicided" by his own government, thus allowing the state forces to consolidate power—known in Italy as the
"historic compromise"—around the common fear of terror and
anarchy.

"Italy epitomizes the social contradictions of the whole world,"
warned Debord.[15] For him, Moro was an emblem of the newfound
asymmetrical conflicts plaguing developed nations, from France's
Algerian uprising in the 1950s to scores of militant splinter groups,
bombings, and airplane hijackings—the very form of conflict
Brossollet had in those years labeled "non-battle." Such encounters
were termed "unconventional" because they no longer resembled
the customs of so-called civilized, oppositional conflict, in which
professional armies meet in known theaters of conflict to thrash
out victory in blood and arms. With his life obscured today by the
romantic mist of apotheosis, it is easy to forget that Debord was
something of a fading violet when it came to actual conflict. He
preferred the mischievous potshot to the Molotov cocktail. Yet the
raw heroic drama of militancy forever excited him. Like many
political thinkers, it was the thrill of revolution that was so seductive, of the possibility that this depraved life might one day be cast
off and refashioned anew. And, while Brossollet's "non-battle"
synchronized with some of the Situationist experiments—drifting
and hijacking—an older Debord drifted back toward an older style
of antagonism.

"I am very interested in war," Debord confessed unapologeti-
cally in his late autobiographical work, *Panegyric*, amid glowing

---

15 Guy Debord, "The State of Spectacle" (preface to the 4th Italian edition of
The Society of the Spectacle), in *Autonomia: Post-Political Politics*, ed. Sylvère
Lotringer and Christian Marazzi (New York: Semiotext(e), 2007), 96.

citations from Clausewitz on the emotional intensity of going to battle. "I've thus been studying the logic of war. And I even had some success, already some time ago, in realizing the essence of these processes in the context of a simple chessboard."[16]

16 Guy Debord, *Panégyrique, tome premier* (Paris: Gallimard, 1993), 69–70. While his fascination with war was not ironic and indeed perhaps uncritical, it is plausible that Debord knew of Engels's famous assessment of Clausewitz, contained in a 1858 letter from Engels to Marx. Clausewitz's approach to philosophy was "odd," cautioned Engels, but "*per se* very good." More than anything else, war resembles commerce, he told Marx. "Combat is to war what cash payment is to commerce; however seldom it need happen in reality, everything is directed towards it and ultimately it is bound to occur and proves decisive." Karl Marx and Friedrich Engels, *Marx/Engels Collected Works*, vol. 40 (London: Progress Publishers, 1929), 241. I thank Richard Barbrook for bringing this letter to my attention.

20

The Game of War

As Brossollet was theorizing about "non-battle," Guy Debord was at his rural home playing war games and toying with the idea of fashioning one of his own. The backdrop of asymmetrical conflict in the 1970s makes Debord's penchant for playtime all the more intriguing. One such game was called Djambi, a four-person game played on an extruded chess board of nine by nine squares. Instead of chess's medieval court of kings, queens, knights, and bishops, Djambi's game characters are modeled after the various political actors that make up advanced liberal democracies: the news reporter, the provocateur, the activist militant, and the assassin. A distinctly late-modern game, Djambi allows players to stage forms of media spectacle and asymmetrical warfare. If the then incipient postmodernity were distilled and sanitized into the form of an intellectual diversion, as chess did for feudal skirmishes, Djambi would be that game.

"Thanks for Djambi," Debord wrote on May 7, 1978, to his friend and benefactor Gérard Lebovici in a letter otherwise disdainful of the game. "As long as the only goal of the game is to eliminate all the others, there can exist but one absolute mode of winning, which can't be shared in any way, to the point that in this game of trickery, you can't trick anyone. The rules suffer from a contradiction between the game's totalitarian goal and its representation of the struggles of an 'advanced liberal democracy.'"[1] The ridiculous subtext of Djambi was clear to Debord: How could a board game ever correctly model the types of complex political dynamics encircling France, or Italy, or what Jean-François Lyotard in his book on postmodernity would soon call "today's most advanced societies"? What is to be done, after the power elite goes global in order to hide itself from the base of society? What is to be done, when control and organization are no longer hierarchical or repressive, but instead rhizomatic and flexible?

In fact, at that moment, Debord had been intensely focused on trying to work through the challenges of advanced liberal

Figure 23. Playing Guy Debord's Game of War. Photograph by Diana Martinez.

1 Debord, *Correspondance*, vol. 5, 462.

democracy, and particularly how armed struggle could be simulated in the form of simple parlor games. The cinema was over. A new format was required. So, in the winter of 1977, after having been a filmmaker and author, Debord did something rather unconventional for an avant-garde leftist intellectual: he formed his own company for making games.[2] Not chess exactly; it was a variation of his own design, dubbed first in his notes the Kriegspiel

2 Play was always central to Debord's work. "The situationist project was ludic above all else," wrote one of his biographers. "Debord's life revolved around games, seduction and warfare, provocation and dissimulation, labyrinths of various kinds, and even catacombs where the knights of the lettrist round table played a game of 'whoever loses (himself) wins.'" Vincent Kaufmann, *Guy Debord: Revolution in the Service of Poetry* (Minneapolis: University of Minnesota Press, 2006), 265. Debord's interest in games coincided with his self-imposed exile to a small town in the center of France after the events of 1968. "I have long tried to lead a life of obscurity and evasion so that I may better develop my experiments in strategy," he confessed in 1978. "My research results will not be delivered in cinematic form." One may assume that "not in cinematic form" is a reference to the new ludic form of the Kriegspiel; a footnote reminds us that this was Debord's last film. See Guy Debord, *In girum imus nocte et consumimur igni* (Paris: Gallimard, 1999), 50.

There is also an interesting overlap between the Situationist International and the work of Johan Huizinga, author of *Homo Ludens: A Study of the Play Element in Culture*. The Situationist architect Constant, in particular, was inspired by Huizinga, as evidenced in a late interview with Benjamin Buchloh in which Constant aimed to reconcile Huizinga and Marx: "It is not so difficult, I should think, to make a link between Huizinga and Marx . . . Huizinga, in his *Homo Ludens*, was speaking about a state of mind, not about a new kind of humanity; of human being, but in a certain sense a state of mind, of certain temporary conditions of human beings. For instance, when you are at a carnival, a feast, a wedding party. Temporarily you become the *homo ludens*, but then the next day you can be the *homo faber* again." See "A Conversation with Constant," in *The Activist Drawing: Retracing Situationist Architectures from Constant's New Babylon to Beyond*, ed. Catherine de Zegher and Mark Wigley (Cambridge, MA: MIT Press, 2001), 24–5. The final phrase refers to the forward of Huizinga's book in which he evokes, first, the classical notion of *homo sapiens*, followed by the modern, industrial (and one may assume, although Huizinga resists using the name, Marxian) notion of *homo faber* or "man the maker." Yet Huizinga's politics were more *ancien régime* than progressive revolutionary, a detail often overlooked in the frequent connections made between Huizinga and Situationism.

(from the German for "war game") and later more formally The Game of War.[3]

"I insist on the opportunity to throw the Kriegspiel into this stunned world as soon as we can," Debord wrote to Lebovici. "It's quite obvious that its time has come."[4] In January 1977, the two founded a company called Strategic and Historical Games and set out to produce an edition of the game. (Debord also worked on a naval warfare game called Jeu de la bataille navale, though the rules were never transcribed.) Debord's Game of War is a Napoleonic chess-variant played by two opposing players on a game board of 500 squares arranged in rows of 20 by 25 squares. (By comparison, a chess board is eight by eight, while a go board is nineteen by nineteen.) Like chess, the Game of War contains game tokens of varying strengths and speeds that one must maneuver across a grid landscape in an attempt to wipe out one's enemy. Unlike chess, one must also maintain "lines of communication" that crisscross the terrain, keeping all friendly units within transmission range of one's home bases. These lines of communication are a special part of the game; they propel player strategy and are key to winning.

---

3 In his letters and notes Debord referred to the game as the "Kriegspiel"— although my German friends will insist on *Kriegsspiel* as the correct spelling. Nevertheless when the game was fabricated and released in France, Debord officially titled it "Le Jeu de la guerre." A short discussion on the most appropriate translation of the game exists in Debord's letter of May 9, 1980, to Lebovici. After reviewing the English proofs, the last question remaining was the English title: "The Game of the war" or "The Game of war"? "We must choose the more generalizing and glorious title," he insisted. "Even if *kriegspiel = wargame* is the most 'linguistically' exact, it doesn't fit at all historically. *Kriegspiel* connotes 'a serious exercise by commanders,' but *wargame* connotes 'an infantile little game played by officers.'" See Guy Debord, *Correspondance*, vol. 6: *janvier 1979–décembre 1987* (Paris: Librairie Arthème Fayard, 2006), 55–6.

4 Debord, *Correspondance*, vol. 5, 451. In fact, Debord had tinkered with Kriegspiel in some form or another since the 1950s. The first recorded mention of the game dates to 1956, where, in the text "Project for an Educational Labyrinth," Debord mentioned the game by name and described it as a mixture of chess and poker. See Guy Debord, *Œuvres* (Paris: Gallimard, 2006), 285. A prototype of the game, inscribed with the title "Kriegspiel Clausewitz-Debord," was fabricated in 1965 by René Viénet.

Debord was delighted with his creation. "The surprises of this Kriegspiel seem to be inexhaustible," he confessed later in his memoir *Panegyric*. "It might be the only thing in all my work—I'm afraid to admit—that one might dare say has some value."[5]

With the assistance of Lebovici, Debord produced the game in a limited edition of four to five during the summer of 1977. The edition included an 18- by 14 ¼-inch game board and player tokens fashioned in copper and silver metal (figure 23). The game was fabricated by a certain M. Raoult, a Parisian artisan whom Debord trusted implicitly, referring to him as the "intrepid Raoult," and admiring him for his "politeness, rationality, and capacity to recognize what is essential in the matter at hand."[6]

By the end of June 1978, after a setback due to poor health, Debord finished drafting a written copy of the game rules. "I am sending you soon the rules for the Kriegspiel," he wrote to Lebovici. "Its main section, given over to a juridico-geometric writing style, has cost me innumerable headaches."[7] As illustrated also in his jab at Djambi, Debord was thus intimately aware of the true reality of games, that they are a conjunction of two elements: the "juridical" element, meaning the spheres of law and rule, and the "geometrical" element, meaning the realm of mathematical arrangements and spatial logics. This was no longer an intervention in spectacle or in narrative, as were his films, but now an intervention at the level of a "juridico-geometric" algorithm, that is, at the level of a finite set of rules that, when executed, result in a machine for the simulation of political antagonism.

The game board is divided into a northern territory and a southern territory, each with a single mountain range of nine squares, a mountain pass, three forts, and two arsenals. In addition each faction has nine infantry, four cavalry, two artillery (one on

5 Guy Debord, *Panégyrique*, vol. 1 (Paris: Gallimard, 1993), 70.

6 Debord, *Correspondance*, vol. 5, 426, and Debord *Correspondance*, vol. 6, 26–7.

7 Debord, *Correspondance*, vol. 5, 466.

foot and one mounted), and two transmission units (one on foot and one mounted). Each combat unit has an attack and defense coefficient, and may move either one or two squares per turn depending on the unit type. The forts, arsenals, and mountains are welded to the game board, and thus immobile. Combat and noncombat units are mobile and may be positioned in any desired formation prior to the beginning of a match.

Arsenals radiate lines of communication vertically, horizontally, and diagonally. In addition, transmission units propagate any line of communication aimed at them. All units must remain in direct connection with their own lines of communication, or be adjacent to a friendly unit in communication. If stranded, a unit goes out of communication and becomes inert. The lines of communication are immaterial constructs, and thus have no game token to represent them. Instead, they must be mentally projected onto the game board by each player. The lines of communication are in essence a network of patterns superimposed onto the basic grid of squares—similar to the "knight's tour" in chess—helping to determine where and how each piece may move. As the game unfolds, these patterns can and will shift, adding to the complexity of possible games and possible strategies.

The metal game of 1978 is stunningly modernist in its formal simplicity and reduction of ludic function into plain, abstract shapes.[8] The cavalry units, far from aping a horse, are represented by a tall wire spike, mounted on a hexagonal base, while the infantry are represented by an upright, snubbed peg, affixed to a square base. To indicate their communicative duties, the transmission units sport a crisp flag, protruding at ninety degrees. The artillery emblem is equally spare: a horizontal hollow tube to indicate a cannon barrel. The most representational design is reserved for

---

8 "Before deciding on abstract designs for the different types of combat troops in the game," wrote archivist Laurence Le Bras, "Debord had considered figurative designs. With this in mind, he acquired a number of toy soldiers, now conserved along with his archives in the Manuscript Division" at the National Library of France. Guy Debord, *Stratégie* (Paris: L'échappée, 2018), 20.

the mountains and the forts, the only two elements not aligned to a faction: the mountains are hulking chunks of metal, appealingly chiseled to bring out miniature crevices and peaks; the forts resemble gallant storybook parapets, hexagonally cut for the North faction, and solidly square for the South. The mountain passes have no representational form at all, but are merely the absent spaces residing at gaps in the mountains. None of the pieces displays any sort of ornament, or additional engraving or color. All of them conform to an extremely muted, almost ascetic, formal design.

The game proceeds in turns. A player may move up to five units each turn, followed by a single attack against an enemy unit. An attack is determined by summing all the offensive power in range of an enemy target square, then subtracting this number from a summation of all the defensive power supporting the same target square. Offensive and defensive power emanates from a unit in a straight line, either vertically, horizontally, or diagonally. If the offensive power is less than or equal to the defensive power, the unit resists. If the offensive power is two or more, the unit is destroyed.

Like the lines of communication, which require a certain amount of mental energy to be maintained in the imagination of each player, the combat mechanic for the game requires a nontrivial amount of player arithmetic, particularly as multiple units are involved in attack and defense at any given moment.

A player wins the game by either (A) destroying all enemy combat units, or (B) destroying the enemy's two arsenals.[9] If both sides agree to quit, the game is a draw.

While stressing the symmetrical quality of Clausewitzian warfare, Debord at the same time designed the terrain of the game board to be asymmetrical. Here is revealed Debord's talent for

---

9 Although not mentioned in Debord's rulebook, it is possible to deduce one additional win state: a player wins if the enemy's two transmission units are destroyed and all enemy combat units are offline.

game design. His aim was to achieve balance through asymmetry, such that the game would not lapse into predictable strategies and styles of play. Thus, while certain approaches are better than others, there is no "optimal" overall formation in the game. Instead, one plays through a series of compromises, always having to adjudicate between "contradictory necessities."[10] For each offensive movement of aggression, one's rear flank becomes that much more vulnerable. This dialectical tension was part of what Debord aimed to achieve with the game. Thus, the two mountain ranges in the game are arranged asymmetrically: North's mountain cleaves the terrain sharply between east and west, inhibiting lateral movement but leaving a cramped passage across the top; South's mountain is a wall expelling downward advances and making any penetration into its territory difficult. Even more significant is the placement of the arsenals. South's two arsenals are split wide apart and held flush to the baseline, while North's two arsenals are staggered closer to the middle. This makes for two very different styles of play. South must run a split defense, or else sacrifice one arsenal and hunker down with the remaining one. North, on the other hand, can use the terrain to its advantage, gaining protection from the mountains (which block fire) plus a defense boost from the mountain pass in range of its westerly arsenal.

In 1986 as his publishing imprint was suffering hard times in the wake of the death of Gérard Lebovici, Debord suggested a scheme to Floriana Lebovici, Gérard's widow, to relieve the publisher's debts by commercializing the Game of War. It was merely a business matter, Debord wrote, like selling a game of Monopoly. "Or is my judgment of the strategic, and thus economic, value of this Kriegspiel distorted by a certain indulgence? We shall see."[11] But while Debord and Lebovici had originally formed a company around the game—Strategic and Historical Games—it is unclear how serious they had ever been about making the game

---

10 Debord, *Correspondance*, vol. 5, 352.
11 Debord, *Correspondance*, vol. 6, 448–9.

commercially viable. Debord never trusted Kessler, the intellectual property lawyer hired to assist with the game. "You worry me greatly by bringing up 'strange things about Kessler,'" he wrote in 1985 to Floriana Lebovici. "Of anyone in the world, Kessler is in the best position to swindle us."[12] In the end, the game was not a particularly large commercial success.

While distilled to a simple essence, Debord believed that the Game of War represented in gamic form all the necessary principles of war. He did admit, however, that three things were missing from his near-perfect simulation: climate conditions and the cycles of day and night; the influence of troop morale; and uncertainty about the exact positions and movements of the enemy. "That said," he continued, "one may assert that the [Game of War] exactly reproduces the totality of factors that deal with war, and more generally the dialectic of all conflicts."[13] Indeed, Debord's ambitions for the game were grandiose. By evoking the "dialectic of all conflicts," he was appealing backward to the power of 1968 and the days of the Situationist International, but also forward to the game's future potential in training and cultivating a new generation of militants.

12 Ibid., 306.

13 Alice Becker-Ho and Guy Debord, *Le Jeu de la Guerre: Relevé des positions successives de toutes les forces au cours d'une partie* (Paris: Gallimard, 2006), 151.

21

A Nostalgic Algorithm?

Debord's game was missing more than just climate conditions. In fact, viewed against the silhouette of his other work, it is surprisingly square. The spirit of "wandering" or "hijacking," from the Situationist days, is absent in the game. There is no mechanism for overturning society, no temporary autonomous zones, no workers' councils, no utopian cities, no imaginary landscapes of desire, no cobblestones and no beach, only grids of toy soldiers fighting a made-up war in a made-up world.

It invites the question: Why was this game relatively unadventurous, while Debord's other work was so experimental? Can it be explained through an analysis of media formats, that Debord had a certain panache for radical filmmaking and critical philosophy, but lapsed back into the predictable habits of the bourgeois parlor game when he tried his hand at game design?[1] Or did Debord

---

1 McKenzie Wark called the game "Debord's 'retirement project.'" See McKenzie Wark, *50 Years of Recuperation: The Situationist International 1957–2007* (Princeton, NJ: Princeton Architectural Press, 2008). Tom McDonough said something similar about Debord's mature work: "We might say that Debord was born into this class [the petty bourgeoisie] and, at the end of his life, returned to it." In McDonough's assessment the late Debord was "marked by the deployment

simply lose his radical zeal late in life, with his Hegelianism finally winning out over his Marxism? Why, when the guerrillas were staging assassinations in Italy, was Debord playing with toy soldiers in France?

Was there a link between Moro's killing and Debord's late work? Of course, there was none, nothing more than a coincidence of dates. Yet this very incompatibility frames in stark relief a crisis within the work. Why an *objet d'art* instead of a cobblestone?

A number of explanations are possible. The abrasively anachronistic Debord was already well-known for masquerading inside the very thing he found most repulsive. For instance, the "reactionary" format of cinema was taken up by Debord precisely in order to critique that same medium as spectacle. Perhaps now he was merely making a "reactionary" game in order to explode the logic of play from within. In this way, Debord might have simply been restaging the same Trojan Horse logic he had deployed many times before.

Alternately, it is plausible the game was never intended by Debord to be a theoretical proposal, and therefore should not be evaluated as one; the game existed simply to train militants in basic strategic thinking. Thus if, in Debord's view, *any* tactical training helped unlock radical consciousness, then it mattered little that the Game of War stresses Clausewitz (instead of Sun Tzu) or the legacy of the Napoleonic wars (instead of Parisian street revolts).

Debord admitted that the game was bound to a historical period. "This doesn't represent wars of antiquity," he explained, "nor those of the feudal period, nor modern warfare refashioned by technology after the middle of the nineteenth century (railways, machine guns, motorization, aviation, missiles)."[2] Instead, the

---

and consolidation of a normative—if not archaic—conception of selfhood." See Tom McDonough, "Guy Debord, or The Revolutionary Without a Halo," *October* 115 (Winter 2006): 42, 40.

2 Becker-Ho and Debord, *Le Jeu de la Guerre*, 149.

game referred to warfare as it was practiced in the early and middle modern periods up to about 1850. The "classic equilibrium" of the eighteenth century was his model, a mode of warfare best represented by the Seven Years' War, and characterized by symmetry, regularity, professional armies, the preciousness of personnel, and the importance of supply stockpiles.[3] So the Game of War *is* indeed historically specific. But it is historically specific for a century long past, not the time in which Debord was living. Or, as Philippe Sollers would later quip, Debord was not much interested in the twentieth century.

In comparisons made between his game and chess, Debord accentuated the question of historical specificity. He positioned chess firmly in what the French term the "classical" period, consisting of kings and corporal fiat, while the Game of War belonged to a time of systems, logistical routes, and lines of communication. In chess "the king can never remain in check," but in the Game of War "liaisons must always be maintained."[4] Debord's rules stipulate that all pieces on the board must stay in contact with a communication liaison, or else risk destruction.

Spatial relationships between pieces are indeed paramount in chess, the "knight's tour" serving as a classic mental projection of pattern and recombination. Debord preserved these spatial relationships, accentuating them further by sewing them directly into the game mechanic. The "liaisons" in the Game of War are not simply the projections of possible troop maneuvers, but a supplementary layer linking game tokens back to their home base. The king in chess must be fortified through the protection of its allied footmen. But Debord's arsenals are extensive nodes; they too must be protected, but even more, they serve as the origin point for a radiating fabric of transmission. Chess presents a set of challenges in proximity to the opponent's king—a consecrated corpus, a prize—but the Game of War is a game of decentralized space itself,

---

3 See Debord, *Correspondance*, vol. 5, 351.
4 Becker-Ho and Debord, *Le Jeu de la Guerre*, 165–6.

the assets of war strung out in long lines and held together by a tissue of interconnection. "This 'war' can be fought as much on the plane of communication as that of extensible space," wrote McKenzie Wark on the Game of War.[5] In short, Debord's game is something like "chess with networks."

The transmission lines thus are a kind of allegory for the new information society emerging in the 1970s, even as they harken back to the logistical lines of Napoleon. Debord's game is both nostalgic for a bygone era and anticipatory of a newly dawning age.

Chess required intense strategy, but it was ultimately too boring for Debord. The Game of War "is completely contrary to the spirit of chess," he insisted. "Actually it was poker I was trying to imitate. Less the randomness of poker and more the powerful sense of battle."[6]

Ultimately, what attracted Debord to the Game of War was not a philosophical or theoretical argument about history or even technology. He considered theory to be an inferior form, one beholden to passing fancy. Debord was enamored with war for precisely this reason. For him, "war" meant "not theory," just as, for Napoleon, war meant "not ideology."[7] War was proven in the execution of things, thought Debord. War sprang from the heart and from a sensible and practical empiricism. War was the opposite of the absolute. War was *contingency*— that special term so dear to late-twentieth-century progressive movements.

---

5 Wark, *50 Years of Recuperation.*

6 Becker-Ho and Debord, *Le Jeu de la Guerre,* 166. Indeed, chance has no place in the Game of War; after an opening coin toss to determine who moves first, the game plays out dice-free.

7 Napoleon was responding at the time to the recent coinage of the term "ideology" by Destutt de Tracy in 1796. Napoleon scorned the concept, calling ideology a "diffuse metaphysics" responsible for "all misfortunes which have befallen our beautiful France." These quotations are cited without reference in Raymond Williams, *Keywords: A Vocabulary of Culture and Society* (New York: Oxford University Press, 1976), 154.

"I'm not a philosopher," Debord confessed to Giorgio Agamben, "I'm a strategist."[8] Or as he put it in *In girum imus nocte et consumimur igni,* his final film, which was produced concurrent with the game: "no vital periods ever began from a theory. What's first is a game, a struggle, a journey."[9]

In that film, Debord incorporated footage stolen from Hollywood scenes of epic pitched battles. One such film sampled by Debord was Michael Curtiz's *The Charge of the Light Brigade* of 1936, a movie adapted from the Tennyson poem of the same name, which itself mythologized the notorious and bloody defeat of the British cavalry in 1854 during the Crimean War. What did it mean to hijack such horse-mounted heroics and crosscut them with footage of the Game of War? As Debord wrote later with only a hint of irony, "In a very heavy-handed and congratulatory way, *The Charge of the Light Brigade* could possibly 'represent' a dozen years of interventions by the Situationist International!"[10] This "representation" takes center stage in the Game of War, in the form of the cavalry game tokens, the most powerful units in the game due to their elevated speed and special "charge" ability, resulting in compounded, focused damage of up to twenty-eight attack points. Debord was thus able to revisit, albeit in a mediated game environment, the types of heroic monumentality attained in his previous interventions, even as they faded into silence. "The SI is like radioactivity," he joked in a letter to one of his Italian translators. "One speaks little of it, but detects some traces almost everywhere. And it lasts a long time."[11]

---

8 Quoted in Giorgio Agamben, "Repetition and Stoppage—Debord in the Field of Cinema," in *In Girum Imus Nocte et Consumimur Igni—The Situationist International (1957–1972),* ed. Stefan Zweifel et al. (Zurich: JRP Ringier, 2006), 36.

9 Debord, *In girum imus nocte et consumimur igni,* 26.

10 Debord, "Note sur l'emploi des films volés," *In girum imus nocte et consumimur igni,* 66.

11 Debord, *Correspondance,* vol. 6, 45–6.

But the arc of time is nothing if not warped. What had started with popular revolts in the 1960s would culminate in combat coefficients and win-loss percentages. What had started on the streets of Paris would end as a game algorithm.

22

Some Problems with the Data

First published in 1987, Alice Becker-Ho and Guy Debord's book *Le Jeu de la Guerre: Relevé des positions successives de toutes les forces au cours d'une partie* [*The Game of War: Record of the Successive Positions of All Forces During a Match*], was an unusual volume, not least in its format.[1] As its subtitle indicated, the book documented a full match played by the married couple, complete with snapshot diagrams for each configuration of game pieces after each move. From the opening gambit to the final capitulation, the two players annotated each turn with play-by-play commentary on the progress of the game, along with notes about strategy.

Most unusual, though, is that the 1987 book was a meditation on losing. After fifty-five rounds, the South player conceded to North, and the match was over. But who played South? Who lost the match, was it Alice or Guy? Unfortunately, no explicit answers exist in the text as to who played the North faction and who played

---

1 First published as Alice Becker-Ho and Guy Debord, *Le Jeu de la Guerre: Relevé des positions successives de toutes les forces au cours d'une partie* (Paris: Éditions Gérard Lebovici, 1987), the book was reissued by Gallimard in 2006, and translated into English as Alice Becker-Ho and Guy Debord, *A Game of War*, trans. Donald Nicholson-Smith (London: Atlas, 2007).

the South. Nevertheless, we may say it with precision. Debord played the South. He is the one who perished in the end.

To explain, I must broach a topic of some delicacy. It concerns a number of mistakes that exist in the original book from 1987, mistakes that largely persist in both the 2006 French reprint, and also in the 2007 English translation.[2] In addition to a few minor graphical errors, the book contains one patently illegal move, plus five additional moves that, while more subtle in nature, are also illegal given a proper interpretation of the game rules.[3]

Alternating between North and South, the turns of the match are numbered 1, 1′, 2, 2′, 3, 3′, etc. The first illegal move occurs in turn 9′. A South infantry unit moves two squares to position I17, whereas infantry can only move one square at a time. The five additional illegal moves are as follows: the K15 infantry in move 14′; the L12 cavalry in move 17′; the I9 infantry in move 35′; the

---

2 In addition to the problems in the match documentation, the two existing English translations of the game rules—Donald Nicholson-Smith's translation for Atlas Press and an inferior translation bundled at the end of Len Bracken's biography of Debord—both misstate details. Whereas Debord indicated that a charge consists of any number of cavalry in a contiguous, straight line and immediately adjacent to the enemy, Nicholson-Smith has no fewer than "all four" cavalry in series, while Bracken allows for noncontinuous series. Bracken also mischaracterizes the combat mechanic when he states that, after successful destruction of the enemy, "the destroyer must occupy the empty square." Debord stipulated the opposite, that it is not obligatory to occupy the empty square, nor could it be, given how movement and attack function more generally in the game. Bracken inverts another rule when he states that communication units can destroy arsenals by occupying them (they cannot). See Len Bracken, *Guy Debord: Revolutionary* (Venice, CA: Feral House, 1997), 240–49; and Becker-Ho and Debord, *A Game of War*, 11–26. I thank Allison Parrish for first discovering some of these discrepancies. In fact, the publication of 1987 contained, by Debord's own admission, five mistakes in placement of pieces during various points in the game. Many of the mistakes were only pointed out by readers, one of which he acknowledged in a letter of March 9, 1987. See Debord, *Correspondance*, vol. 6, 458–9.

3 I gratefully acknowledge the contributions of Stephen Kelly and Jeff Geib, who first pointed out some of these mistakes to me and also helped refine and clarify in my mind the manner in which these mistakes appear in the book. A more detailed summary of errata is at r-s-g.org/kriegspiel/errata.php.

J10 infantry in move 36′; and the J14 infantry in move 46′. In each of these instances, the unit in question would be thrust out of communication during the course of the player's turn. However, according to a strict interpretation of the game rules, noncommunicating pieces are inert and cannot move.

Two additional details help unspool the mystery. First, all of the mistakes are committed by the same player, the South player; North commits no fouls. Second, (almost) all of these mistakes remain unremedied through multiple authorial and editorial stages: the couple's original playing of the match in question; their documentation of the match and writing of the annotations contained in the book; then subsequent rounds of editorial oversight, in 1987 and 2006 (not to mention the English translation of 2007). Yet, after all that, roughly one out of every eight full turns documented in the book contains an error. How could so many mistakes pass through so many rounds of scrutiny? What can explain this blindness?

A topic of some delicacy, indeed. What do these mistakes mean? And why so many of them? Of course, the issue is not that Debord and Becker-Ho failed to publish an error-free book. All publications contain mistakes. The point is that these mistakes furnish a different sort of "evidence" than revealed in the identification of a typo, a misspelled word, or even a minor grammatical blunder in a work of literature. These mistakes are not orthographical or even simply syntactical in nature, they are *algorithmic*. Which is to say, the mistakes deal not with a relatively localized condition of correct writing—in, for example, the case of a misspelled word—but with the correct execution of rule-bound action. So, these errors are not typos. They are more like glitches, or even cheats, no doubt executed innocently if not also unconsciously.

Let me summarize: first and foremost, a number of nontrivial mistakes in gameplay; but also, a hypothesis that Debord played the South. How are these two things connected? Did Debord cheat and lose? Or did he play clean and win?

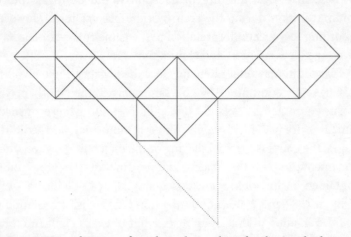

Figure 24. Visualization of combat relationships for the South player in Guy Debord's The Game of War, "Turn 22'." Derived from Alice Becker-Ho and Guy Debord, *A Game of War* (London: Atlas Press, 2007), 83.

After learning of the mistakes in the documentation of the Game of War, some might conclude that Debord played North, that he committed no fouls and won the match. The argument goes that, since Debord was the game designer and had been playing the game, or some form of it, since the middle 1950s, he would have had such intimate knowledge of the game's rules that he would not break any of them. This line of reasoning locates Debord as the North player, and the more casual player Becker-Ho as the South.

While such an argument is somewhat appealing, a different argument strikes me as ultimately more persuasive. Instead of relying on a psychological rationale—what Debord did or did not know, what he did or did not intend—we might turn our attention to a structural rationale, indeed an algorithmic rationale. Instead of relying on how they played the game, we might investigate how the game played them.

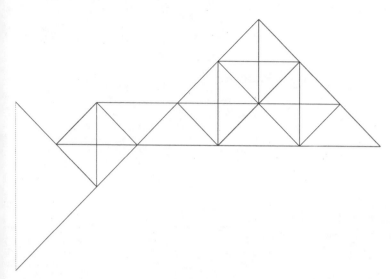

Figure 25. Visualization of combat relationships for the South player in Guy Debord's The Game of War, "Turn 44'." Derived from Alice Becker-Ho and Guy Debord, *A Game of War* (London: Atlas Press, 2007), 127.

The correct execution of rules is rarely ever localizable; it induces repercussions only legible later as the game unfolds. The status of a fault in an algorithmic text is of a very different order than the status of a fault in a traditional text. In this way, the mistakes in the famous match are not so much a red herring as they are decoys for what is actually happening. Instead of a style of mind, let us instead explore a style of code. Let us explore the game at the level of its algorithmic and structural aesthetics.

23

Crystal Aesthetics

The concept of optimization is important to algorithmic aesthetics. In any rule-based system, there will be an optimal state of affairs in which the structure at play is exploited to the fullest. To optimize a system means to increase its efficiency, to eliminate redundancy, and to exploit advantages.

In Debord's Game of War, optimal troop formations are identified by crystalline shapes such as latices, ladders, X formations, crosses, and wings (figures 24 and 25). The reason for this is straightforward. The game rules are a kind of algorithm; they define specific states of affairs and specific kinds of action. In particular, the rules define things like attack coefficients and defensive coefficients, plus the commutativity of these combat coefficients to both friendly and hostile players across the grid of the game board. Since attack and defense propagate in straight lines, the game tends to privilege truss structures built from struts and crossbars. This generates latices, ladders, crosses, and other frameworks. These structures can be described as "crystalline" because they grow like salt crystals: simple boxes and regular shapes that iterate outward to form a mass. Crystalline media begin with a local, microstructure—for example, a square or an

X-formation—and then repeat the structure multiple times in order to create a durable, material grid.

Algorithms do not have to be optimized, of course. For art historian Rosalind Krauss, grid formations are "schizophrenic" because they move centrifugally and centripetally at the same time, propagating outward while also collecting and repeating themselves.[1] The grid is "what art looks like when it turns its back on nature," Krauss has claimed, suggesting a kind of structural excess.[2] Such structural forms frequently remain unoptimized, whether by choice or by design. Yet if a system of rules is followed, and followed closely, the rules themselves will shine through and become legible. If an algorithm is sufficiently simple, the point of maximal exploitation may be known. And if gamers are sufficiently experienced with the rules of a game, they will learn the point of maximal exploitation. If players are keen on winning, they will enact these techniques of optimal exploitation as often as possible. In the Game of War, those players will tend to be crystalline players, those who play with a crystal aesthetics of boxes, crosses, ladders, and wings.

With this knowledge in hand, one can build a profile for each player based on their degree of crystallization, on how well they optimize gameplay. The results are emphatic: South relied heavily on latices, X formations, crosses, and all the other crystal building blocks, while North displayed none of the same ticks anywhere in the book. (The same is true for the book's "Explanatory Diagrams," which were authored by Debord, not Becker-Ho; here the South player was the protagonist, albeit for purposes of explanation.) In other words, each player left a signature of their own unique play style. One may read those signatures and build a profile from them.

---

1 Rosalind Krauss, *The Originality of the Avant-Garde and Other Modernist Myths* (Cambridge, MA: MIT Press, 1985), 18.

2 Ibid., 9. See also Svetlana Alpers, *The Art of Describing: Dutch Art in the Seventeenth Century* (Chicago: University of Chicago Press: 1983), 138, for a discussion of grids in the context of mapping.

The South player loses, yet South is more crystalline. Assuming Becker-Ho played North, she was indeed the better player, at least during the match documented in the book. Still, as the game designer, as the one who had tested and crafted the rules over many years, Debord's relationship to the game was undoubtedly more structural and intimate, like an architect to a building. She won, but he was the crystalline player. Debord played South.

The highly structured, crystalline forms displayed here are all the more interesting when compared to the unstructured, wandering, topographical forms featured in much Situationist work. See, for example, Debord's famous map from the late 1950s titled "The Naked City." Now, several years later, he appears to have shed that style, preferring rigidity over flow, structure over drift.[3]

But how could this crystalline player with his affection for optimal troop formation repeatedly make small mistakes (in turns 14', 17', 35', 36', and 46')? The answer requires a sense of how algorithmic knowledge works. The answer lies in the fact that it is possible for a single individual to be skilled at low-level knowledge of pattern formation and rule-bound behavior while still failing at more superficial operations. Even the most skilled philosophers will inadvertently write typos, just as the most skilled computer programmers will inadvertently generate bugs. Most programmers have a cultivated sense of algorithmic knowledge, and yet even the most skilled programmers are unable to identify certain bugs that for the machine are trivial to identify. Debord was a crystalline machine, adept at the programmer's level, that is, at the level of gameplay. But, like most of us, Debord was perfectly fallible at the level of the real.

In the end, the mistakes in turns 14', 17', 35', 36', and 46' are something of a decoy. When identifying a play profile, it is more

---

3 Soyoung Yoon has written on Debord's geometry and "the temporal-spatial continuum of the *dérive*" in her essay "Cinema Against the Permanent Curfew of Geometry: Guy Debord's *Sur le passage de quelques personnes à travers une assez courte unité de temps* (1959)," *Grey Room* 52 (Summer 2013): 38–61.

important to focus on low-level algorithmic skill such as knowledge of how rules can be exploited for optimal game states than it is to worry over small, largely technical mistakes.

So Debord played the South. He is the one who lost in the end. But he did not just lose, worse, he threw in the towel, punishing himself with a stern lecture on the necessity of better strategic knowledge and planning. Here is the final annotation of the match, at the moment of South's concession:

> The South ceases its hostilities. It's time now for him to reflect on the operations of the campaign, recalling the unchanging theories of war, in order to understand the string of circumstances, the assumptions, and maybe also any relevant mental traits recognizable in his command, that this time led the North to victory.[4]

What are these relevant mental traits? Has he gone mad? One wonders if Debord ever really won anything, or if the entire history—the Situationist International and all the rest—was always leading up to this end and this end alone. First cinema and philosophy, and now finally the bourgeois parlor game.

———

Ever since Marx indicted exchange value and alienation, progressive movements have looked with skepticism at the domain of abstraction and optimization. A similar anxiety lurks beneath the surface of Debord's game. Is there a benefit in optimization? Or should simulation and modeling be indicted as well? The immaterial, or Spirit, or the *logos* are not, by necessity, contrary to progressive political movements. Nevertheless, the lofty realm of rational idealism has always been something of a hindrance to those suffering from the harsh vicissitudes of material fact. And while the left

---

4 Becker-Ho and Debord, *Le Jeu de la Guerre*, 127.

has suffered at the hands of abstraction, it also has long pursued an agenda of utopian creativity and invention, Debord included. Such a dynamic has fueled many of the debates in world history, those between traditionalism and transformation, between positivism and dialectics, or between social science and "theory."

Progressive art movements are very good at beginnings, but terrible at endings. As Debord said in 1978 amidst his losses, from the death of the Situationist International and the "end" of the cinema: "avant-gardes have but one time."[5]

One might say something similar about leftist cultural production in general: (1) the left is forever true in the here and now, always in the grip of its own immediate suffering; but (2) it will forever be defeated in the end, even if it finds vindication there. This is why Debord can occupy himself with both struggle and utopia. It is also a window into why Debord became obsessed late in life, not with street revolt, but with the sublimation of antagonistic desire into an abstract algorithm. It is not that the past is always glorious and the future antiseptic. Quite the opposite, both past and future are internally variegated into alternately repressive and liberating moments. For the left, the "historical present" is one of immediate justice won through the raw facts of struggle and sacrifice. The historical present is always *true*, and at the same time *bloody*. But the future, the utopian imagination, is a time of complete liberation forged from the mold of the most profound injustice, meaning that utopia is always *false*, but forever at the same time *free*.

---

5 Debord, *In girum imus nocte et consumimur igni*, 47.

PART VI.
Black Box

24

Black Box Cypher

Of all the revivals in recent years, the revival of Hegel is the most startling, although certainly not for those involved. Hegelianisms of all shapes and sizes prevail today, from Catherine Malabou's dutiful reconstruction of dialectical plasticity to Slavoj Žižek and the inescapable bind between the "determinate negation" and the "wholly Other," from which explodes the terror of proletarian power. Or consider the Hegelianism of Alain Badiou, who stakes everything on being as a pure formalism that only ever realizes itself through the event, an absolute departure from the state of the situation.

Only the Hegelian dialectic, and not the Marxist one, can snap back so cleanly to its origins like this, suggesting that *Aufhebung* was always forever a spectralization and not a mediation in general, that the ultimate truth of the Hegelian dialectic was spirit, not negation or becoming or anything so usefully mechanical. The negation is thus *revoked* during synthesis, much more than it is resolved. This would be one way to read the current intellectual landscape, as so many revoked materialisms, so many concepts too terrified by matter to matter.

And so, the question comes again, always again: is the dialectic a medium, or does the dialectic demonstrate the absolute impossibility of any kind of mediation whatsoever? What is the status of negation, of the obscure, of the dark corners of being that are rarely ever subsumed by dialectical becoming, or even strategically excluded from it?

Tiqqun's essay on the cybernetic hypothesis is interesting not so much for its description of the late twentieth century, a description of cybernetic society that has become increasingly common today. Rather the essay is notable for how the authors described the appropriate political response to such a hypothesis. They spoke of things like panic, noise, and interference. They proposed counter-strategies of hypertrophy and repetition. They implored their comrades "to execute *other* protocols."[1]

Yet there is often a strategic obscurantism in their prescriptions, what Tiqqun called "invisible" revolt. "It is invisible because it is unpredictable to the eyes of the imperial system," they wrote, lauding the virtues of mist and haze: *"Fog is the privileged vector of revolt . . . Fog makes revolt possible."*[2]

In order to increase opacity and ramify interference, Tiqqun presented two techniques:

All forms of interference start out from these two gestures: exterior and interior lines of flight, sabotage and pull-out, searching out forms of struggle and assuming forms-of-life. From now on the revolutionary problem will be to bring these two moments together.[3]

First create a short circuit, second unplug. After that, during the ensuing states of interference, Tiqqun sought what they called "branch points," that is, "critical thresholds from which a new state of the system becomes possible."[4]

1 Tiqqun, "L'Hypothèse cybernétique," *Tiqqun* 2 (2001): 69, emphasis added.
2 Ibid., 73, 80. See also Tiqqun's concept of the "human strike," particularly in the text "Comment faire?," *Tiqqun* 2 (2001): 278–85.
3 Tiqqun, "L'Hypothèse cybernétique," 74.
4 Ibid., 72.

Together, this created what Tiqqun called "the encounter": "The encounter is found below language, beyond words, in the virgin lands of the non-said, at the level of a suspension, of this power of the world that is at the same its negation, its 'power-to-not-be.'"[5]

Invisibility is not a new concept within political theory. Yet Tiqqun's essay indicated a specific kind of invisibility that has begun to permeate cybernetic societies. Further, they indicated that this invisibility, this blackness, is not simply an effect of cybernetic societies but is, in fact, its necessary precondition.

The black box, an opaque technological device for which only the inputs and outputs are known; the black bloc, a tactic of anonymization and aggregation often associated with the direct action wing of the left—somehow these two things come together near the end of the twentieth century. Is there a reason for it?

—

Close your laptop tight and what do you see? A smooth outer opaque shell, hiding and housing a complex electronic machine within. With the lid down, there is little with which to interact. Pick it up, put it down, not much more.

Open it again to find the situation reversed. Now concave, the external surface of the machine is no longer opaque and smooth, rather it is plastered over with buttons and sockets, speakers and screens, boxes and windows, sliders and menus. Splayed open, the box begs to be touched, it exists to be manipulated, to be interfaced.[6]

---

5 Ibid., 78.

6 On the design of technical interfaces, see in particular Branden Hookway, *Interface* (Cambridge, MA: MIT Press, 2014). On the use of sensing interfaces, see Jennifer Gabrys, *Program Earth: Environmental Sensing Technology and the Making of a Computational Planet* (Minneapolis: University of Minnesota Press, 2016).

There are many kinds of black boxes.[7] One is the black box as *cypher*. Another is the black box as *function*. With the lid closed, the laptop is a black box cypher. With the lid up, a black box function.

The black box cypher was common during modernity. Marx articulated the logic cleanly in *Capital*, volume 1 with his description of the commodity as having both a "rational kernel" and a "mystical shell." The commodity was thus a kind of cypher, impervious from without. Never announcing its own history of production, the commodity needed to be decoded, unveiled, or otherwise illuminated. As Sarah Kofman has shown, this follows a logic of visuality—what can be seen, what cannot be seen—and indeed the metaphor of the *camera obscura* has long been important in Marxist critique, the metaphor of perceiving in and through shadow.[8]

Such logic appeared quite frequently in Marx. It was a useful device for him, portable and deployable at will. Thus, the commodity was a black box cypher, but so was value, and so was the relationship between exchange and production, and also the class relation, and on and on. Scrutinize the cypher and begin to decode. Such is the "rational kernel, mystical shell" logic at its purest. Untouched, the phenomena of the world are so many cyphers, so many mystical black boxes waiting to be

---

7 Of the many investigations into the black box, see in particular the work of Bruno Latour in *Pandora's Hope: Essays on the Reality of Science Studies* (Cambridge, MA: Harvard University Press, 1999) and *Science in Action: How to Follow Scientists and Engineers Through Society* (Cambridge, MA: Harvard University Press, 1988); Langdon Winner, "Upon Opening the Black Box and Finding It Empty: Social Constructivism and the Philosophy of Technology," *Science, Technology, & Human Values* 18, no. 3 (Summer 1993): 362–78; and Christopher Kelty, "Opening the Brown Box: Networks, Science and Infrastructure," in *Feelings Are Always Local*, ed. Joke Brower et al. (Rotterdam: V2_Publishing/NAi Publishers, 2004), 82–103.

8 Kofman calls this "perspectivist knowledge." See Sarah Kofman, *Camera Obscura: Of Ideology*, trans. Will Straw (Cornell, NY: Cornell University Press, 1998), 49.

deciphered to reveal the rationality (of history, of totality) harbored within.

Like Leibniz's monad, the black box cypher "has no windows." The cypher is a cloaked node with no external connectivity. Think again of the laptop with its lid closed. The operating system is sleeping, but, more than that, the network sockets and interface buttons are inactive as well, even if the machine itself has not vanished. The case is a turtle shell designed to keep out what is out, and keep in what is in.

This is what the commodity is, to be sure, but it is also what the sign is, what spectacle is, and what all the other cultural phenomena are that model themselves after the commodity logic. Interiority is all; interface is but a palliative decoy, a flourish added for humans who require such comforts.

These days the cypher logic has become synonymous with critique itself, for any number of things mimic the logic of the commodity. As such, they elicit all manner of demystifications, denaturalizations, or unveilings. When a book like Guy Debord's *Society of the Spectacle* indicted the image, it did so on the grounds that images were cyphers. Images may be bought and sold, of course, but that is not what makes them similar to commodities, at least not only. The image was a commodity for Debord due to the specific organization of its constructed innards, a complex arrangement requiring representation and "forms of appearance" along with hiding and obfuscation, the latter terms being special synonyms for the former.

Marx began *Capital* with an analysis of the commodity form. But even Marx's grand demystification of the commodity was itself a kind of obfuscation, mere prologue for a subsequent step. Focusing on the commodity form, no matter how much it could be demystified or critiqued, was ultimately a kind of distraction. The heart of the matter, Marx reminded his readers, resided not in the object cypher but on the factory floor. Discard the object, and journey instead inside an even more important black box, the "hidden abode of production":

> Let us therefore, in company with the owner of money and the owner of labour-power, leave this noisy sphere, where everything takes place on the surface and in full view of everyone, and follow them into the hidden abode of production, on whose threshold there hangs the notice "No admittance except on business."[9]

The opening sections of *Capital* were thus Marx's concession to all those political economists who still thought that commodities and markets were the key to capitalism. Marx knew the truth lay elsewhere, in production.

Marx was envisioning thresholds, the steel doors that open up onto the factory floor. But he also envisioned thresholds of another kind, the cognitive thresholds breached by the dialectic. In this sense, the opening sections on the commodity were a sort of dialectical foil deployed to actuate its own subsequent negation.

In other words, history changes, and one's critical apparatus ought to change with it. The computers of the new millennium are not like the mechanical tools and machines of Marx's time. Likewise, labor has changed a great deal, and, with it, the structure and status of objects. As a capitalist machine, the computer traffics in symbols and information rather than durable goods. The computer is constantly demystifying things, so too obfuscating them. It is as if the computer absorbed the logic of the black box cypher, then rearranged it into a new form.

Hence the story of Marx's "hidden abode" is only half the story. Having served quite nicely for decades, Marx's story nevertheless needs a new chapter. The productive abode is today a new place with new demands, new systems, new commodities, and new workers. And thus, if one were to restage Marx's theater of production, it might go something like this:

> Let us reconnect to this noisy sphere where everything takes place on the surface and in full view of everyone, for this is the

---

9 Karl Marx, *Capital*, vol. 1 (New York: Penguin, 1976), 279–80.

plane of production, on whose threshold is already encoded a million mantras for the new economy: "Do what feels right." "Reach out and touch someone." "Play hard." "Don't be evil."

Fortified with a bright array of windows and buttons, the monad ceases to be a monad. It is still the old cypher, but now it has an interface. Consider a network socket, or an application programming interface (API), or how a function works in a computer language. What is consistent across all these technologies is the notion that access should be granted, but only selectively and according to specific grammars of action and expression. Today the black box is connected to the things around it, but its external connectivity is heavily managed. It is still a cloaked node, only now it is covered in symbolic skin.

Marx's original injunction was to illuminate the black box by decoding it. Today the suggestion is slightly different: functionalize the black box by programming it. What was once a black box cypher has evolved into a black box function.

25

Black Box Function

While its conceptual origins go back to Marx and the nineteenth century, the term "black box" entered discourse proper in the 1940s via military tech slang. Media historian Philipp von Hilgers has written about the Battle of Britain during World War II and particularly the Tizard Mission, an emergency diplomatic expedition that shepherded sensitive British technologies out of the United Kingdom to the relative safety of the United States. The Tizard Mission arrived in Washington, DC, on September 12, 1940, carrying vital items packaged inside of a black metal box in the hope that American scientists could assist their British allies in developing new technologies for the war effort.[1] Inside the black box was another black box, the magnetron, a small microwave-emitting tube suitable for use in radar equipment. The magnetron had been modified in recent years from a transparent glass housing to an opaque, and therefore "black," copper housing.

1 Philipp von Hilgers, "Ursprünge der Black Box," in *Rekursionen: Von Faltungen des Wissens*, ed. Philipp von Hilgers and Ana Ofak (Berlin: Fink, 2009): 127–45.

The black box emerged directly from a tactical challenge faced by scientists during the war effort. Warren McCulloch described one particular moment at a meeting in Princeton during the winter of 1943/44 attended by Norbert Wiener, Lorente de Nó, Walter Pitts, and others:

> Lorente de Nó and I, as physiologists, were asked to consider the *second* of two hypothetical black boxes that the allies had liberated from the Germans. No one knew what they were supposed to do or how they were to do it. The first box had been opened and exploded. Both had inputs and outputs, so labelled. The question was phrased unforgettably: "This is the enemy's machine. You always have to find out what it does and how it does it. What shall we do?"[2]

The *second* of two boxes? The first one had exploded. The second had better be kept intact, else risk a second explosion like the first one. But how to analyze the box without opening it?

By the time the question had become that well defined, Norbert [Wiener] was snoring at the top of his lungs and his cigar ashes were falling on his stomach. But when Lorente and I had tried to answer, Norbert rose abruptly and said: "You could of course give it all possible sinusoidal frequencies one after the other and record the output, but it would be better to feed it noise—say white noise—you might call this a Rorschach." Before I could challenge his notion of a Rorschach, many engineers' voices broke in. Then, for the first time, I caught the sparkle in Johnny von Neumann's eye. I had never seen him before and I did not know who he was. He read my face like an open book. He knew

---

2 Warren McCulloch, "Recollections of the Many Sources of Cybernetics," *ASC Forum* 6, no. 2 (Summer 1974 [1969]): 12, emphasis added. For a critical assessment of McCulloch, see Leif Weatherby, "Digital Metaphysics: The Cybernetic Idealism of Warren McCulloch," *Hedgehog Review* 20, no. 1 (Spring 2018), hedgehogreview.com.

that a stimulus for man or machine must be shaped to match nearly some of his feature-filters, and that white noise would not do. There followed a wonderful duel: Norbert with an enormous club chasing Johnny, and Johnny with a rapier waltzing around Norbert—at the end of which they went to lunch arm in arm.[3]

The refrain of the "enemy's machine," opaque and locked tight, was echoed by McCulloch a few years later in a comment made during the discussion that followed John von Neumann's lecture on "General and Logical Theory of Automata":

I confess that there is nothing I envy Dr. von Neumann more than the fact that the machines with which he has to cope are those for which he has, from the beginning, a blueprint of what the machine is supposed to do and how it is supposed to do it. Unfortunately for us in the biological sciences—or, at least, in psychiatry—we are presented with an alien, or enemy's, machine.[4]

What did McCulloch mean by the "enemy's machine"? The "hypothetical" black boxes "liberated from the Germans" were in fact based on real tactical scenarios. The British protected their magnetron because they knew how valuable it would be to the enemy if it fell into the wrong hands. Warplanes often contained technologies such as radar that, if the plane were shot down, could be acquired by the enemy. To avoid this, such technological devices were often equipped with self-destruct mechanisms. Thus, when McCulloch said that the first black box exploded, he meant just that: its self-destruct mechanism had been triggered. Box number two remained intact, though, and no telling if there would ever be

---

3 McCulloch, "Recollections of the Many Sources of Cybernetics."

4 John von Neumann, "General and Logical Theory of Automata," in *Papers of John von Neumann on Computing and Computer Theory*, ed. William Aspray and Arthur Burks (Cambridge, MA: MIT Press, 1987), 422.

a chance to capture additional boxes with which to experiment. Thus, the second box was inviolable. No attempt should be made to explore the innards of the second box, to avoid the least risk of a second explosion. Any knowledge to be gained from the second box would have to be gained purely through noninvasive observation. The threat of an auto-destruct mechanism made it inadvisable—if not also impossible—to open up any device captured from the enemy. The box must stay closed. The box must stay black. The investigator should rather concentrate on the outside surface of the box, its inputs and outputs.

This was not just a problem for engineers, however, but indicative of a larger paradigm. For instance, the same logic was evident in the definition of behaviorism given by Arturo Rosenblueth, Norbert Wiener, and Julian Bigelow in their influential essay "Behavior, Purpose, and Teleology":

> Given any object, relatively abstracted from its surroundings for study, the behaviorist approach consists in the examination of the output of the object and of the relations of this output to the input. By output is meant any change produced in the surroundings by the object. By input, conversely, is meant any event external to the object that modifies this object in any manner.[5]

Wiener gave a more specific definition of the black box in a footnote to the 1961 preface added to his influential 1948 book *Cybernetics*:

---

5 Arturo Rosenblueth, Norbert Wiener, and Julian Bigelow, "Behavior, Purpose, and Teleology," *Philosophy of Science* 10, no. 1 (January 1943): 18. While functionalism and cognitive science would appear later as responses to behaviorism, I classify them more as friendly amendments to the black-box logic, not disruptions of that general trend. Thus, while functionalism might be *more* willing to engage directly with the mind than behaviorism, one should not read this as a new translucency of the box. In fact, for a black box function, it is *necessary* to describe (in functional terms) the inner operations of the black box. Such a description in no way diminishes the obfuscation of the box's innards. On the contrary it provides the conditions of possibility for obfuscation in the first place.

I shall understand by a black box a piece of apparatus, such as four-terminal networks with two input and two output terminals, which performs a definite operation on the present and past of the input potential, but for which we do not necessarily have any information of the structure by which this operation is performed.[6]

Whether in human or object form, a black box performs a definite function, yet it is not known *how* the function is performed; the observer only knows *that* it is performed, via access to the inputs and outputs of the box.

On a small scale, devices like the magnetron were black boxes that allowed the Allies greater flexibility with their radar. But, on a larger scale, the confrontation of the war itself was a veritable black box theater in which enemy objects and messages were frequently intercepted and had to be decoded. The new sciences of behaviorism, game theory, operations research, and what would soon be called cybernetics put in place a new black-box epistemology in which the decades if not centuries old traditions of critical inquiry, in which objects were unveiled or denaturalized to reveal their inner workings—from Descartes's treatise on method to both the Kantian and Marxian concepts of critique to the Freudian plumbing of the ego—was replaced by a new approach to knowledge, one that abdicated any requirement for penetration into the object in question, preferring instead to keep the object opaque and to make all judgments based on the object's observable comportment. In short, the behaviorist subject was a black-boxed subject. The node in a cybernetic system was a black-boxed node. The rational actor in a game theory scenario was a black-boxed actor.

"[T]he cybernetic philosophy was premised on the opacity of the Other," wrote historian Peter Galison. "We are truly, in this view of the world, like black boxes with inputs and outputs and no

---

6 Norbert Wiener, *Cybernetics: or Control and Communication in the Animal and the Machine* (Cambridge, MA: MIT Press, 1961), xi n1.

access to our or anyone else's inner life."[7] In other words, the black box was not simply an isolated device. The black box grew to become a constituent element of how entities and systems of entities were conceived more generally.

Was this the death of Freud and Marx and hermeneutics in general? At the very least Marx's principle for the commodity had finally come full circle. Instead of Marx's rational kernel in the mystical shell, the late twentieth century had birthed a new reality, *the rational shell and the mystical kernel*. Today the shell is a keyboard, the kernel a microprocessor. Our skins come already tattooed. Our surfaces invite symbolic interaction, selectively allowing passage from a visible exterior to an opaque interior. The shell is rational, even as the kernel remains absolutely illegible.

These new black boxes are therefore labeled *functions* because they are nothing but a means of relating input to output, they articulate only their exterior grammar, with their innards remaining black boxed. Computer scientists quite proudly, and correctly, call this technique "obfuscation." Black box functions include the computer, the protocol interface, data objects, and code libraries. RFC 950 on subnetting procedures put this principle quite clearly: "each host sees its network as a single entity; that is, the network may be treated as a 'black box' to which a set of hosts is connected."[8] This new industrial scenario is one in which a great premium is placed on interface, while interiority matters very little, assuming of course that everything is online and in its proper place. These black boxes have a purely functional being; they do not have essences or transcendental cores.

The enemy's machine is thus not simply a device in a German airplane, it is ourselves: a call center employee, a card reader at a security check point, a piece of software, a genetic sequence, a

---

7 Peter Galison, "The Ontology of the Enemy: Norbert Wiener and the Cybernetic Vision," *Critical Inquiry* 21, no. 1 (Autumn 1994): 256.

8 J. Mogul et al., "Internet Standard Subnetting Procedure," RFC 950, www.faqs.org/rfcs/rfc950.html.

hospital patient. The black box is no longer a cypher waiting to be unveiled and decoded, it is a function defined exclusively through its inputs and outputs.

- This is why one must invert the logic of Marx's "hidden abode of production." To repeat: It is no longer a question of illuminating the black box by decoding it, but rather that of functionalizing the black box by programming it. The point is not to ignore the existence of the new hidden sites of production, from *maquiladoras* to co-working facilities. On the contrary, these sites are part and parcel of the new industrial infrastructure. The point instead is to describe the qualitative shift in both the nature of production, and, perhaps more importantly, the nature of consciousness.

In the nineteenth century Marx allegorized critical thought as a "descent" into a "hidden abode." But if the illumination of hiddenness no longer reveals a way out, how else are we to make our way through?

26
The Tyranny of Structurelessness

Black boxes imply a form of interaction, a particular network architecture. This network is not new, of course. It is as old as Agamemnon's chain of triumph and Clytemnestra's web of ruin. But in the 1960s, computer engineer Paul Baran gave it a name, the distributed network.[1]

The distributed network spreads out horizontally with a thicket of links connecting the nodes together. No single node acts as master of the mesh. Instead, organization and control propagate broadly across the entire web. Each node makes local decisions about network topology and message sending.

Baran contrasted the distributed network with the centralized or "star" network, characterized by a singular hub from which a number of peripheral nodes extend. A third network form, the decentralized network, was a mixture of the first two. Decentralized networks contain a number of hierarchical "star" subnetworks, the hubs of which are interconnected via backbone links into a larger amalgam. Thus, distinct from its centralized or decentralized

---

1 See Paul Baran, *On Distributed Communications* (Santa Monica, CA: RAND, 1964).

cousins, the distributed network is a specific network architecture characterized by equity between nodes, bidirectional links, a high degree of redundancy, and a general lack of internal hierarchy.

Each node in the network is treated as a black box. Each node reveals an array of functionality. Two nodes may interact by interfacing between functions, sending messages back and forth, and realizing specific services. The distributed network is thus a black box network.

For message sending, Baran's distributed network relied on a technology called packet-switching, which allowed messages to break themselves apart into small fragments. Each fragment, or packet, was able to find its own way to its destination. Once there, the packets reassembled themselves to create the original message. The ARPAnet, started in 1969 by the Advanced Research Projects Agency (ARPA) at the US Department of Defense, was the first network to use Baran's packet-switching technology. In fact, the term "packet-switching" was not invented by Baran, but instead by British scientist Donald Davies, who also invented a system for sending small packets of information over a distributed network, all the while unaware of Baran's work. (It was Baran's institutional affiliation with RAND and his proximity to the newly emerging ARPA network in America that solidified his historical legacy.) At the same time, Leonard Kleinrock published his research on network flow and queuing theory. Kleinrock's focus was to analyze stochastic flow through networks, that is to say, flow that is not steady or predictable but in which "both the time between successive arrivals to the system and the demand placed on the channel by each of these arrivals are random quantities."[2] Kleinrock's research on queuing would become important for the design of network nodes such as routers.

During the 1970s and 1980s, the ARPAnet, later dubbed the Internet, benefited from the drafting of a number of technological standards called protocols. A computer protocol is a set of

2 Leonard Kleinrock, *Communication Nets* (New York: Dover, 1964).

recommendations and rules for implementing a technical standard. The protocols that govern much of the Internet are contained in what are called RFC (Request for Comments) documents.[3] The expression derives from a memorandum titled "Host Software" sent by Steve Crocker on April 7, 1969, which is known today as RFC 1. The Internet protocols are published by the Internet Engineering Task Force (IETF). They are freely available and used predominantly by engineers who wish to build hardware or software that meets common specifications. Since 1969, a few thousand RFC documents have been released, and they, along with a larger constellation of global technological standards, constitute the system of organization and control known as protocol. Protocols are systems of material organization; they organize the flow of bits and atoms through the networks in which they are embedded.

Working during the Cold War, under the threat of a nuclear exchange with the Soviet Union, Baran saw a strategic advantage in the flat and flimsy quality of distributed networks. During World War II, target lists had been assembled according to strategic locations and facilities: factories, airports, bridges, cities. But in Baran's distributed network, no single node was inordinately important. Hence no node was any more of a military target than another node. In essence, the target list became binary, either swelling to the total number of nodes, or falling to zero.

Baran's plans demonstrated how Clytemnestra's web of ruin could be highly effective. Compared to pyramidal hierarchies, distributed networks are indeed flimsy, ineffective, and disorganized. But this relationship of asymmetry was precisely what, in the long run, made them so formidable. Baran understood that distributed networks did not remove organization and control. Rather, distribution provided a new structure of organization, at once malleable and robust, fragile but also agile.

---

3 The RFCs are archived online in a number of locations and can be retrieved via a normal web search.

This sort of distributed perspective existed in the same lineage as Dietz's algebraic textiles and Barricelli's cellular creatures, the same lineage as chronophotography and photosculpture. Multiple agents and parallel perspectives transgressed the threshold of the computable.

In other words, the web of ruin has finally outclassed the chain of triumph. Today the Furies are the operative divinity, not Iris or Hermes. This is true across the board, both for hegemonic forces but also for more progressive political movements. "We're tired of trees," wrote Deleuze and Guattari. But it did not take long for those same words to be spoken in the highest echelons of the transnationals, or behind the closed doors of the Pentagon, or deep within other former bastions of pyramidal hierarchy. On the one hand, distributed organization was evident in the new social movements of the 1960s, in what Jo Freeman so interestingly assessed in her 1970 essay "The Tyranny of Structurelessness."[4] But at the same time, power itself has also become distributed. As Michael Hardt and Antonio Negri wrote, today's global empire is "a dynamic and flexible systemic structure that is articulated horizontally."[5] Empire is *formally* similar to the very movements intent on abolishing it.

The normative status of networks has thus changed. In the old scenario, the web of ruin (here refashioned as the distributed network) was perceived as a solvent or threat vis-à-vis more centralized control. In the new scenario, the web of ruin has become entirely vital, even necessary. Or, as Peter Galison so succinctly put it, Cold War tech waged a "war against the center," ultimately replacing centralization with decentralization and distribution.[6] Today we live amid the ruins of centerlessness.

---

4 Jo Freeman, "The Tyranny of Structurelessness," jofreeman.com/joreen/tyranny.htm.

5 Michael Hardt and Antonio Negri, *Empire* (Cambridge, MA: Harvard University Press, 2000), 13.

6 Peter Galison, "War Against the Center," *Grey Room* 4 (Summer 2001), 7–33.

Yet distributed networks have become hegemonic only recently. Because of this, it is tempting to reminisce about when networks were disruptive of power centers, when the guerrilla threatened the army, when the nomadic horde threatened the citadel. But this is no longer the case. The distributed network is the new citadel, the new army, the new power. As Foucault said of the Furies, "What makes them precarious also makes them sovereign."[7]

---

7 Michel Foucault, *Madness and Civilization* (New York: Random House, 1965), 113.

27

The Tragedy of Interactivity

Software is often described as having various levels, like the layers of an onion. Software exists as "source code," a human-readable text file containing commands written in a computer language such as C++. When this source code compiles, the commands translate into machine-readable code called an executable application, consisting of basic operations that can be understood by the hardware of the machine. This application creates a third instance of software, the "runtime," when the code is run by an actual user interacting with it.

These three aspects—source, executable, and runtime—are crucial in any computer technology. But which one is the most important? The runtime interface is often considered to be primary, because it is the actually existing experience of the software, as it relates to a user. Yet from a different perspective, the executable is the determining moment, since it contains the actual commands necessary for the software to function. But, third, the executable is merely the result of a compilation of the source code, which is thus considered essential—as the recipe is to the created work, or the musical score is to the performance. So for "source" code to run it must appear in a form it is not (the executable), only to be experienced in a third form different entirely from the other two (the runtime). One aspect hides itself while another takes control. This is what might be called the occult logic of software: software hides itself at exactly the moment when it expresses itself most fully. Or as Wendy Hui Kyong Chun has noted in her work, code is never merely a source, it is always a "resource."[1]

The dynamic between surface and source has led to social movements around open source software, that is, a type of software in which both source code and executable are made available to users. Yet the surfacing effect of software is much more insidious than it might seem. The black box logic runs deep. For instance, the computer science design style known as *encapsulation* pervades almost every computer language and programming environment, regardless of whether that code is open source or not. Encapsulation is a technique whereby an engineer segregates code into specific modular units, sometimes called objects or libraries, then provides a legible interface for others to use.

In this sense, software itself acts like a network, a network of message-sending, simulated entirely within an abstract informatic space. Software objects are the nodes in the network and messages are sent via an "edge" consisting of any two objects' interfaces. The interface acts as the sole conduit for communication into and out of the object or library. The source of the object or library itself is hidden. In general, encapsulation is valued by computer scientists because it makes code easier to maintain and simpler to implement.

Black box architecture thus signals a crisis in legibility. Or, if not a crisis, then a reconfiguration of what it means to read and write. Following Claude Shannon's work on information science, information is relatively indifferent to semantic content and interpretation. Data is parsed; it is not "read" in any conventional sense. In

1 Wendy Hui Kyong Chun, *Programmed Visions: Software and Memory* (Cambridge, MA: MIT Press, 2011).

this way, information is anti-hermeneutic; it does not inherently contain meaning, only pattern.

In fact, digital objects themselves are defined as the intersection between two protocols (two technologies), not as a result of some human being's semantic projection of meaning into form. Once material is digitized, any recognizable "content" is merely the artificial parsing of the digital substrate into a predictable, template-driven chunk—what computer scientists call a "struct." Any sense of the "content" of data emerges as an epiphenomenon of human behavior previously collected, as seen in the page-rank algorithms used by search engines, or the output of machine learning.

In short, a new model of reading will have to be explored, one that is not simply hermeneutic in nature, but also about cybernetic parsing, scanning, rearranging, filtering, and interpolating. This new model of reading will need to be based on an immanent or machinic notion of software. The question now is not simply *logos* (discourse) but *ergon* (work). Networks are not simply textual entities, they are entities in a constant labor with themselves.

This form of activity, this form of labor—two-way interactivity via networks—was famously described as utopian by Bertolt Brecht in his short fragments on radio, and later reprised by Hans Magnus Enzensberger as the heart and soul of an "emancipated" media.[2] However, today interactivity is one of the core instruments of control and organization. Like the web of ruin, networks ensnare in the very act of connection. Yet like the chain of triumph, networks are exceedingly efficient at articulating and conveying messages bidirectionally (in what graph theorists call an "undirected" graph).

Call it the political tragedy of interactivity. Organisms must communicate whether they want to or not. Indeed, in Wiener's

---

2 See Bertolt Brecht, *Brecht on Film and Radio*, trans. Marc Silberman (London: Methuen, 2000), and Hans Magnus Enzensberger, "Constituents of a Theory of the Media," in *Electronic Culture: Technology and Visual Representation*, ed. Timothy Druckrey (New York: Aperture, 1996).

original definition of cybernetics, "communication" and "control" were inextricably linked. Organisms are "captured," to use Phil Agre's terminology, using any number of informatic codes and rubrics.[3] Clicks are accumulated. Behaviors are mined for meaningful data, or tracked for illegal data. Even the genome is prospected for rare or otherwise useful sequences. Interactivity is a political tragedy. What was once so liberating for Enzensberger is today the very site of informatic exploitation, regulation, and control. Enzensberger's desire to change the media from the unidirectional model of fascism to the bidirectional model of radical democracy was laudable and germane to the political movements of his time. Yet today bidirectionality is not the savior it was once thought to be. Today, interactivity means total participation, and thus universal capture.[4]

Still, networks define nodes and edges, but they do not define the holes in the net, the gaps that let things pass while others are ensnared. Indeed, the science of networks, dubbed graph theory, has no theory of the gap. Graphs are nets without holes. Or at least they are nets for which the holes are marginally evident. Graphs assert the hole, but only as an exclusion from the whole, as something that is present but unable to act. Graphs are nets for which the "unconnected" has been prohibited from discourse.

Such a shortcoming is also a liability. More and more, politics issues from the holes in the graph, from those who are formally excluded. With the general augmentation of network technologies throughout social space, this formal exclusion encompasses all manner of extra-network concerns: precarious labor and post-Fordism; conceptions of the human as "flesh" (Hortense Spillers)

---

3 See Phil Agre, "Surveillance and Capture," *New Media Reader*, ed. Noah Wardrip-Fruin and Nick Montfort (Cambridge, MA: MIT Press, 2003), 737–60.

4 The rise of digital capture has swelled the importance of prophylactic techniques such as blocking, obfuscating, hiding, suspending, and withholding. For more on resistance to digital capture, see Finn Brunton and Helen Nissenbaum, *Obfuscation: A User's Guide for Privacy and Protest* (Cambridge, MA: MIT Press, 2016).

or "bare life" (Giorgio Agamben); the politics around imprisonment, extradition, and *habeas corpus*, with today's "dark sites" a restaging of the old penal colony or Devil's Island.[5] Who or what is excluded from networked presence? And how do structural dynamics—for instance, mechanisms of social reproduction and racialization—persist across the transition from chain to web?[6]

But while politics unfolds beyond the perimeter, it also reemerges from the inside. Consider all the network-centric diagrams for political resistance evident during modernity and the passage into postmodernity: guerrilla warfare, anarcho-syndicalism, "grassroots" organizations, and other rhizomatic movements. These are all "formally within" the network mode because they are themselves formally constituted as distributed or decentralized networks of some kind or another.[7]

Yet after the powers-that-be have migrated into the distributed network, thereby co-opting the very toolbox of leftist militancy, new models for political action are required. A new exploit is necessary, one that is as asymmetrical in relationship to

5 See Hortense J. Spillers, "Mama's Baby, Papa's Maybe: An American Grammar Book," *Diacritics* 17, no. 2 (Summer 1987): 64–81, and Giorgio Agamben, *Homo Sacer: Sovereign Power and Bare Life*, trans. Daniel Heller-Roazen (Stanford, CA: Stanford University Press, 1998). For a critique of Agamben using the work of Spillers, see Alexander Weheliye, *Habeas Viscus: Racializing Assemblages, Biopolitics, and Black Feminist Theories of the Human* (Durham, NC: Duke University Press, 2014).

6 For a particularly compelling account of chains and webs in the context of racialization and mass incarceration, see Jackie Wang, *Carceral Capitalism* (Los Angeles: Semiotext(e), 2018). On the labor of social reproduction (as it relates to the problem of the family), see Sophie Lewis, *Full Surrogacy Now: Feminism Against the Family* (London and New York: Verso, 2019).

7 Consider how the question of "noise" is defined in information theory. One might romantically think that "noise" is inherently corrosive of the predictable patterns of digital code. However, in information science, noise is not the opposite of information, defined by Shannon and Weaver as the amount of entropy in message construction. Simply put, more noise (generally) means more information. Hence noise is an intra-informatic problem, not an extra-informatic problem. See Claude Shannon and Warren Weaver, *The Mathematical Theory of Communication* (Urbana: University of Illinois Press, 1963).

distributed networks as the distributed network was to the power centers of modernity, as asymmetrical as Clytemnestra's "vast voluminous net" was to Agamemnon's militaristic efficiency.

This new exploit may be found outside the network. It may be found within it. Examples might include Hakim Bey's concept of the temporary autonomous zone, or the Electronic Disturbance Theatre's system of online electronic swarming. Or, in the realm of the nonhuman, computer viruses and worms have developed, perhaps totally haphazardly, a new model of contra-network infection and disruption that takes advantage of the homogeneity of distributed networks to propagate far and wide with ease. At the same time, hackers seek out logical exploits in networked machines that allow for inversions and modulations in the normal functionality of code.

Many of these techniques are not yet fully formed. In some cases, they might even appear politically naïve, if not retrograde, as with the case of the virus. Yet they do begin to sketch out a new model of networked organization and, via silhouette, an image of a counter-network practice that is entirely native to the network form.

28
Toward a Practical Nonexistence

From student occupations in California and New York, to Black Lives Matter, to the *indignados* in Spain and the anti-austerity movement in Greece, to Tiqqun and the Invisible Committee, and back further to Zuccotti Park and the Occupy Wall Street movement, a new political posture emerged after the turn of the millennium, a new political bloc with an acute black-box profile.

Some of these movements have made demands on power. Some of them have even won concessions. At other times, a strange sort of insistence was heard from the lips of the defiant: *no, we have no demands*. Our movement does not want political representation. We do not want collective bargaining. We are not angling for a seat at the table. We want to leave be, to leave being. We have no demands—at least no demands articulable in your language. My life is the demand. Remaining present is the demand.

Some criticize this new posture as defeatist, impractical, or utopian. Some even criticize it as a form of privilege. For who but the privileged could afford to protest for nothing at all? Yet the power behind the "no demands" posture is precisely that it makes no claim about power. Instead, it seeks to upend the power circuit entirely through a kind of political nonparticipation or *degrowth*. It would be wrong to discard these movements using the typical epithets of cynicism or nihilism, or even to explain them away using the language of state power versus terrorism—which was the language of Lenin just as much as it was the language of Obama, Bush, and all the rest. The key to this new political stance is in *subtraction*, in its subtractive quality vis-à-vis the dimensions of being.

Consider the grand declension narrative beginning over a century ago from time to space and now to appearance itself. The nineteenth and early twentieth century was the moment when time entered Western thought, only to be supplanted after World War II by space as a new organizing principle. One may speak therefore of an aesthetics and politics of time, back to Hegel and Darwin and Marx to be sure, but also in the work of Bergson and Heidegger, in Benjamin with his interest in nostalgia and reproduction, in Einstein's scientific treatment of time, or in the great 1900 media (as Kittler called them) like the gramophone, the cinema, and other technologies for the recording of time in series.

Nevertheless, if the earlier phase introduced a politics of time, the post–World War II period ushered in a new politics of space. By the 1970s and 1980s, fueled in part by Henri Lefebvre's landmark *The Production of Space* (1974), discussions turned toward "situations" and "geographies," toward "territorializations" and "lines of flight," toward "heterotopias" and "other spaces," toward "nomadic" wanderings and "temporary autonomous zones." Indeed, Fredric Jameson argued that postmodernism was not simply a historical period but quite literally the spatialization of culture. More recently, Jameson has called for a reinvention of the dialectic itself, not as a so-called engine of history, but as an engine of spatiality, a "spatial dialectic."[1]

---

1 Fredric Jameson, *Valences of the Dialectic* (London and New York: Verso, 2009), 66–70.

From the fourth dimension, time, to the three dimensions of space, the subtraction of dimension points forward like an arrow. Next come the two dimensions of surface—Deleuze with his topologies—followed by a politics of the singular dimension. Binary in nature, the singular dimension reduces all politics to the on/off logic of appearance and disappearance.

Perversely, today's binary is ultimately a false binary, for unlike the zeros and ones of the computer, which share a basic numeric symmetry at the level of simple arithmetic, the binaries of offline and online are so radically incompatible that they scarcely interface at all. In fact, the "interface" between inclusion and exclusion is defined exclusively through the impossibility of interfacing: the positive term carries an inordinate amount of power, while the negative term carries an extreme burden of invisibility and alterity. Today's politics, then, is a kind of rampant "dark Deleuzianism" in which the affirmation of pure positivity and the concomitant acceptance of the multiple in all its variegated forms resulted nevertheless in the thing it meant to eradicate: a strict binarism between the wired world and the dark continents, between state power and the terrorists, between us and them.[2] The "no demands" posture flies in the face of all of this. Our lives are the demand. Remaining present is the demand.

The politics of the new millennium will thus be a politics not so much of time or space but of appearance. Beyond Debord or Jameson or Lefebvre, a new radical syllabus is shaping up today: Virilio's *The Aesthetics of Disappearance,* Lyotard's *The Inhuman,* or Levinas's *On Escape.* Instead of a politicization of time or space, consider the politicization of absence and presence around issues like invisibility, opacity, and anonymity, or the relationship between identification and legibility, or the tactics of nonexistence and disappearance, new struggles around prevention, the therapeutics of the body, piracy and contagion, informatic capture and

---

2 See Andrew Culp, *Dark Deleuze* (Minneapolis: University of Minnesota Press, 2016).

the making-present of data (via data mining).[3] Consider Hito Steyerl's 2013 video on "how not to be seen," or Simone Browne's work on black luminosity.[4] Or recall Claire Fontaine's concept of *human strike*.[5]

"For us it's not about *possessing territory*," wrote the Invisible Committee, deemphasizing space in favor of illegibility. "Rather, it's a matter of increasing the density of the communes, of circulation, and of solidarities to the point that the territory becomes unreadable, opaque to all authority. We don't want to occupy the territory, we want to *be* the territory."[6] The question for them was not one of territorial "autonomy" (Hakim Bey) or a reimagining of space (Debord and the Situationists), but rather a question of opacity and unreadability. "There is a politics of the unrepresentable," McKenzie Wark wrote in *A Hacker Manifesto*, "a politics of the presentation of the nonnegotiable demand."[7]

Tracking this current from the higher attributes downward, from time, to extension (space), and ultimately to existence

---

3 While disappearance and withdrawal may evoke white male privilege— Henry David Thoreau retreating to his cabin, or John Rawls withdrawing behind a "veil of ignorance"—I am inspired here more by theories of opacity and disappearance drawn from feminist and black theory. See in particular Rosi Braidotti, "The Ethics of Becoming-Imperceptible," in *Deleuze and Philosophy*, ed. Constantin V. Boundas (Edinburgh: Edinburgh University Press, 2006), 133–59; Édouard Glissant, *Poetics of Relation*, trans. Betsy Wing (Ann Arbor: University of Michigan Press, 1997); Elizabeth Grosz, "A Politics of Imperceptibility," *Philosophy & Social Criticism* 28, no. 4 (2002): 463–72; Kevin Quashie, *The Sovereignty of Quiet: Beyond Resistance in Black Culture* (New Brunswick, NJ: Rutgers University Press, 2012).

4 See Hito Steyerl, "How Not to Be Seen: A Fucking Didactic Educational .MOV File" (2013), and Simone Browne, "Everybody's Got a Little Light Under The Sun: Black Luminosity and the Visual Culture of Surveillance," *Cultural Studies* 26, no. 4 (July 2012): 542–64.

5 Claire Fontaine, *The Human Strike Has Already Begun & Other Writings* (London: Mute, 2013).

6 Invisible Committee, *The Coming Insurrection* (Los Angeles: Semiotext(e), 2009), 108.

7 McKenzie Wark, *A Hacker Manifesto* (Cambridge, MA: Harvard University Press, 2004), 231.

(presence/absence), the raw condition of the political reveals itself. The new politics of being is not simply a politics of durational or historical authenticity, not simply a politics of territorial dominance or even identification and appearance, but quite literally a newfound struggle over what is and what can be. Substitute prevention with *preemption*. Substitute the activist mantra "no one is illegal" with "no *being* is illegal." These are not just skirmishes over the politics of the body—from body modifications to designer pharmaceuticals—but struggles over the politics of being. Who is allowed to be? And who is allowed to flourish at the expense of others who do not?

The new illegibility of being will not resemble the twentieth-century debates around essentialism and anti-essentialism, since post-Fordism put an end to that discussion once and for all. It will be a material confrontation, to be sure, but also at the same time an immaterial or idealist struggle in which that old specter of the "thought crime" will rear its ugly head again. People will be put in jail for ideas and forms and scripts and scriptures. And others will triumph by capturing and valorizing pure form. Indeed, the future is already here, as the "source fetishists" are already running rampant, bioprospecting for new genetic sources deep within the Amazon jungle and mining for consumer essences deep within the Amazon website.

What this means for thinking is another question altogether. The determining aspect of the dialectic today is not so much contradiction as such, or synthesis or negation or even the group of terms related to becoming, process, or historicity, but rather that of the asymmetrical binary, a binary so lopsided that it turns into a kind of policed monism, so lopsided that the subjugated term is *practically nonexistent*, so lopsided that synthesis itself becomes a mirage, a mere pseudo-technique floated with the understanding it will be recouped, like a day trader floating a short-term investment. As Godard famously said: this is not a just image, this is just an image. So, if anything can be learned from the present predicament it might be that a practical nonexistence can emerge from a being that is practically nonexistent, that subtractive being ($n - 1$) might be the best way to degrow the abuses of power.

We shall not say that there is a new blackness. We shall not ratify the rise of the obscure and the fall of the transparent. But do not proclaim the reverse either. Simply withdraw from the decision to ask the question. Instead ask: what is this eternity? What is this black box—this black bloc—that fills the world with husks and hulls and camouflage and crime? Is it our enemy, or are we on the side of it? Is this just a new kind of nihilism? Not at all. It is the purest form of love.

Afterword: A Note on Method

Introspection is often necessary in scholarly work, not simply concerning the objects of the mind but also the actual manner in which intellectual work is done. This typically comes under the heading of methodology. Yet the meaning of methodology is not always clear, particularly within the so-called theory disciplines that span Marxism, feminism, poststructuralism, psychoanalysis, and related fields. Some prefer the self-serving and somewhat vain conviction that theory and methodology are one and the same pursuit. Hence "doing theory" would seem to preempt the thorny exercise of methodological introspection, rendering it moot. Why speak of method when theory is nothing but method? Why worry about other tasks when theory is king? Yet the reality of scholarship contradicts such pat conclusions. In fact, academic halls are teeming with a vast array of different research methods, from the positivistic expediency of quantitative investigation, to the staging of ethnographic interviews, to the narrative reductions of historiography, to the various instrumentalized strains of hermeneutics such as the Marxist reading, the feminist reading, or the psychoanalytic reading.

In other words, methodology today has a distinctly liberal profile. For every taste, there is a method to match. For every

predilection, there is a satisfaction to be had. In order to be successful today, a student or scholar must internalize the many options
and enact them appropriately given the task at hand; this method
for that problem, followed by a new method for the next. In this
sense, methodology today is often more a question of appropriateness than existential fit, more a question of personal style than
universal context, more a question of pragmatism than unwaver-
ing conviction.

But appropriateness is a thorny business, and not everyone
agrees on matters of taste. Many methodological discussions
devolve into a sort of popularity contest. Who advocates what
method and for what purpose? Which general equivalent trumps
all others? Is it sexuality, or is it class, or is it the *logos*, the archive,
the gaze, desire, play, excess, singularity, resistance, or perhaps life
itself, elevating one methodological formation above all others in
a triumphant critique (to end all future critique)?

A contradiction thus emerges: the historical forces that generate
liberal ecumenicalism are the same forces that strive to canalize
and entrain such heterogeneity under a single symbolic order. The
liberal profile of contemporary scholarly methodology is thus a
kind of method-effect in which diversity of method is simultaneously asserted and withheld.

The situation is even more puzzling, however, as many humanities disciplines have in recent years marked a shift away from
qualitative methods, as diverse and multitudinous as they are, in
favor of more quantitative and empirical research techniques. In
an apparent rebuff to methodological ecumenicalism, the
positivistic expediency of quantitative research has tended to
outflank other methods within modern thought, as recent
debates around digital humanities again make clear. Appeals to
empirical verification, to the reduction of complexity into
simplicity, to the principles of repeatability and objectivity, to the
sequential logic of the syllogism or the deductive argument—
appeals, in short, to the paradigm of Enlightenment reason
handed down since the Baroque turn of Descartes, Kepler,

Galileo, and Leibniz—have gradually edged out all the others. A liberal array of possibilities galvanized to a single methodological tendency—but why, and how?

Perhaps the very question of method refers to that moment in history when knowledge becomes production, when knowledge loses its absolute claims to immanent efficacy, when knowledge ceases being intuitive and must be legitimized via recourse to some kind of metadiscourse. The ability to speak authoritatively is not a newfound right bestowed on humanity in the modern period, as recounted in the various narratives around triumphant secularism, the death of God, and the rise of reason. Today, such authority is precisely the thing corrupted and debased into all manner of intellectual haggling. Method is already fragmented when it arrives; the apotheosis comes later.

So to observe that quantitative, rationalistic methods became dominant is not simply to claim that scientific positivism won the battle of wits, having transformed the nature of knowledge production and truth since the early modern period. It is also something else, for the liberal iteration of methodologies (in the plural) is itself a method-effect. The liberal iteration is precisely the only flavor available to anyone subscribing to the cult of scientific positivism in the first place.

What other mode could possibly be as efficient as pure suitability itself, pure individual appropriateness, the raw granularity of every body satiated by its own unique specificity? As with post-Fordism, what results is a field of infinite customization, where each thinker has a method tailored to his or her preferences. Such capacious liberalism takes great pride in the fact that no single methodological authority can ever truly be triumphant, whether that authority be God, *jouissance*, pragmatic reasonableness, or positivistic verifiability. In other words, even in the face of the seeming liberal fragmentation of the many methodologies, such liberalism nevertheless simultaneously enshrines the law of positivistic efficiency, for what could be more efficient than infinite customization? What better way to wrangle this rainbow coalition than to grant everyone in it the freedom to do what they will? Standardize the world and kill the spirit, but empower difference and the individual is unchained. In short, under post-Fordism, liberal ecumenicalism and positivistic efficiency share a special relationship.

For cultural workers, this presents something of a problem. The triumph of quantitative methods seems to devalue and exclude much of what cultural workers do. And the reverse is true as well, since many cultural workers often see little point in positivistic pursuits, regularly writing them off as wrongheaded, soulless, or myopic. Faced with such crises of method, some cultural workers prefer to withdraw into a more rigorous critical practice, not, as their detractors might claim, to cling to some sense of cloistered security granted to the armchair philosopher, but because of the newfound perspective gained from thinking in a way that is asymmetric to the current state of affairs.

Yet humanists pursuing quantitative research methods face an additional challenge, for today's corporate titans consist of little more than highly evolved modes of quantitative research. An Internet search company's page rank algorithm taps into a mass of intellectual labor performed in the field. It supplements this laboring mass with its own intellectual labor, the labor of data extraction, storage, and processing. So, in many cases, what used to be intellectual work is now industrial work. When using quantitative methodologies in the academy (spidering, sampling, surveying, parsing, and processing), one must compete broadly with the sorts of media enterprises at work in the contemporary technology sector. A cultural worker who deploys such methods is little more than a lesser Amazon or a lesser Equifax.

A century ago, capital had a monopoly on the physical materiality of production. Now it has a monopoly on the immaterial sphere of information. Industry has finally moved into the realm of intellectual labor, and by most reports it is excelling beyond all expectations. Many writers and scholars must therefore face a startling fact: the corporate sector simply has far superior data reserves at its disposal. Thus, in the information society the scholar of information will forever be trapped in a deficit of resources, playing catch-up behind the scads of mathematics PhDs on staff at Google. Never before in history have immaterial and informatic assets been so closely intertwined with capital.

But beyond the challenge of unequal talent and resources is the question of critical efficacy. Is it appropriate to deploy positivistic techniques against those selfsame positivistic techniques? In a former time, such criticism would not have been valid or even necessary. Marx was writing against a system that laid no specific claims to the apparatus of knowledge production itself—even if it was fueled by a persistent and pernicious form of ideological misrecognition. Today the state of affairs is entirely reversed. The new spirit of capitalism is found in brainwork, self-measurement and self-fashioning, perpetual critique and innovation, data creation and extraction. In short, doing capitalist work and doing intellectual work—of any variety, bourgeois or progressive—are more aligned today than they have ever been.[1] Hence there appears something of a moral crisis concerning the very validity of scholarly methodologies. Such methods are at best underfunded and impotent cousins to the new algorithmic industries and at worst unknowing shills for that same system of canalization and debasement. Audre Lorde once asked whether the master's tools can be used to take down the master's house. Her question remains, along with a second one: *can we still use our own tools now that the master has taken them up?*

—

1 For three spectacular yet rather different testimonials to this effect, see Nancy Fraser, *Fortunes of Feminism: From State-Managed Capitalism to Neoliberal Crisis* (London and New York: Verso, 2013); Alan Liu, *The Laws of Cool: Knowledge Work and the Culture of Information* (Chicago: University of Chicago Press, 2004); and Luc Boltanski and Ève Chiapello, *The New Spirit of Capitalism*, trans. Gregory Elliott (London and New York: Verso, 2005).

Indeed, in the last few decades we have witnessed the fulfillment of the cybernetic hypothesis with the rise of computers and media in both academia and society at large. This has produced a number of contentious debates around the nature and culture of knowledge work. Perhaps the most active conversation concerns the status of hermeneutics and critique, or "what it means to read today." Some assert that the turn toward computers and media destabilizes the typical way in which texts are read and interpreted.[2] The discussion often hinges on the rise of digital media and the way in which they seem to disrupt the stalwart critical and interpretive techniques of reading. Some argue that digitality shifts the focus away from things like style, symbol, and allegory and toward things like technique, materiality, and the archive. As Stephen Best and Sharon Marcus recently argued, computers are "weak interpreters" that produce "more accurate knowledge about texts" and hence jibe well with a new kind of reader characterized by "minimal critical agency."[3] Franco Moretti's argument in *Distant Reading* was similar: computers are useful readers because they improve empirical accuracy by performing kinds of research that are difficult for humans, such as sampling from a vastly larger corpus of texts, identifying emergent phenomena via clustering algorithms, and mapping numerous data points spatially.[4] Many of these scholarly exchanges are still quite active today, and among a number of important references I will

---

2 For some of the basic contours of this debate, itself complex and divergent, see Bruno Latour, "Why Has Critique Run Out of Steam? From Matters of Fact to Matters of Concern," *Critical Inquiry* 30, no. 2 (Winter 2004): 225–48; Stephen Best and Sharon Marcus, "Surface Reading: An Introduction," *Representations* 108 (2009): 1–21; and Heather Love, "Close but Not Deep: Literary Ethics and the Descriptive Turn," *New Literary History* 41 (2010): 371–91. The various discussions around "close reading," "distant reading," "surface reading," and "descriptive reading" also clash and intermingle with the existing art historical discourse on close viewing and distant viewing, or what Aloïs Riegl called the tactile and optical qualities of art. See Aloïs Riegl, *Late Roman Art Industry*, trans. Rolf Winkes (Rome: Bretschneider, 1985).

3 Best and Marcus, "Surface Reading," 17.

4 See Franco Moretti, *Distant Reading* (London and New York: Verso, 2013).

merely cite Alan Liu's thorough description of the current state of digital humanities and Elizabeth Weed's response to Best and Marcus in defense of a certain kind of criticality.[5]

Beyond simply asserting or describing the existence of a social, cultural, and economic paradigm, beyond simply moralizing about it or fomenting some kind of reinvigorated "hermeneutics of suspicion" fashioned to debunk it, I have tried here to shift tone and provide a more detailed picture of the contemporary landscape. How and when were the seeds of the digital universe planted? What are the historical conditions that had to be developed in order for the concept of the digital to make sense? When and how did the creation and recombination of knowledge gain its distinctly liberal profile, in which each thinker may pursue their own autonomous goals? Why would such an arrangement be beneficial for the extraction of surplus value? The aim here was thus to explore the history of digital society in classic Foucauldian fashion, to explore some of the "conditions of possibility" for the computer age. Norbert Wiener invented the science of cybernetics, of course, but what conditions of possibility had to have been invented in years prior for him to be able to innovate? Claude Shannon put forth a new model of information science, but what conditions of possibility had to exist already for the world to be conceived as information in the first place? There are many ways to answer these questions; I have chosen a series of episodes, from Ada Dietz, Nils Barricelli, and others, not as a replacement for existing histories of computation, but as a way to widen the historical and conceptual window of what counts as computable.

The debate over digital computation is thus properly framed as a debate not simply over this or that research methodology but over a general regime of knowledge going back several decades at least. Given what we have established thus far—that digital

---

5 See Alan Liu, "The Meaning of the Digital Humanities," *PMLA* 128, no. 2 (2013): 409–23, and Elizabeth Weed, "The Way We Read Now," *History of the Present: A Journal of Critical History* 2, no. 1 (2012): 95–106.

methods are at best a benign part of the zeitgeist and at worst a promulgation of late-twentieth-century computationalism—let me end by itemizing a series of problems and challenges that anyone partaking in digital methods must consider.[6]

A) *Hegemony, Recapitulation, and Symmetry.* Given the hegemonic status of computers in contemporary life—a position endorsed by everyone from Kevin Kelly and Thomas Friedman to Manuel Castells and Michael Hardt and Antonio Negri—to propose computer-centric research methodologies is to propose that the humanities follow a trend toward normalization with the dominant rather than of differentiation from it. This will present a problem to certain intellectual endeavors that value deviation and heterodoxy over normalization and orthodoxy.

Moreover, the problem of hegemony is not simply limited to a hierarchy of domination and subordination. It also implicates the types of utterances that are made within such a hierarchy, particularly whether or not certain claims about knowledge or reality are recapitulative or critical of the hegemonic position. The nature and role of criticism is at the heart of contemporary debates over the digital humanities, with many wondering whether criticism is still necessary and interpretation still valid. It is thus obligatory to identify the changing fortunes of critique as a specific shift in the relative value of recapitulative versus contestational claims.

Given the problems of hegemony and recapitulation, one must also ask whether the role of humanities research is to be a symmetrical mirror of trends in larger society or an asymmetrical rethinking of those larger trends. When the social and economic infrastructure is structured in such and such a way, is it the role of humanities researchers to redesign their discipline so that it is symmetrical with that infrastructure? Silicon Valley views society as a network of value-producing agents (whose unpaid labor generates immense profits); is it, then, the role of university English

---

6 For more on computationalism, see David Golumbia, *The Cultural Logic of Computation* (Cambridge, MA: Harvard University Press, 2009).

departments also to propose that society is a network of value-producing agents? Object-oriented computer languages propose that entities can be abstracted into "objects" with codified interfaces that perform certain measurable functions; is it, then, necessary for literary researchers to view novels or poems as objects with codified interfaces that perform certain measurable functions? The issue here is not simply recapitulation (speaking the same or speaking different), but a structure of symmetry versus asymmetry (the propagation and extension of regular structure).

Whether or not critique remains viable, one must still ponder the original Kantian question: is thought as such dictated by the regularity of an inherited structure, or is thought only possible by virtue of an asymmetrical and autopositional posture vis-à-vis the object of contemplation? Having inherited the computer, are we obligated to think with it?

B) *Ideology, Deskilling, and Proletarianization.* A second cluster of terms reveals a different challenge faced by scholars of digital computation. Call it the *Zuhandenheit* problem: we live within the cybernetic universe without necessarily being conscious of it, and we use these digital tools without necessarily reflecting on them. Of course, the naturalization of tools can be good and useful in certain contexts, and literature and art are admittedly inseparable from *techne* at a more fundamental level. But the naturalization of technology has reached unprecedented levels with the advent of digital machines. Nature likes to hide itself, wrote Heraclitus, and it is no different with computers. One must be dispassionate about this infrastructure of obfuscation, identifying when and how it is beneficial, and when and how it is not.

Ever since Kant and Marx inaugurated the modern regime of critical thought, a single notion has united the various discussions around criticality: critique is foe to ideology (or in Kant's case, not so much ideology as dogma). Hence a new challenge to digital theory: if there is indeed an increase in naturalization and a corresponding decrease in criticality, does this entail a concomitant rise in the power of ideology? Digital methods tend to naturalize the process of data discovery. Do they also at the same time embolden an ideological infrastructure?

Yet beyond these heady inquiries into the relative validity of knowledge, a more prosaic challenge also appears: the deskilling problem, or what Best and Marcus call the "minimization of agency."[7] The digital humanities assume certain things about human subjects. While seeming to embed scholars and students more firmly in data, digital tools tend to do the opposite. Highly codified black-box interfaces reduce the spectrum of possible input to a few keywords or algorithmic parameters. Those who were formerly scholars or experts in a certain area are now recast as mere tool users beholden to the affordances of the tool—while students spend ever more time mastering menus and buttons, becoming literate in a digital device rather than an archive or corpus.

Thus, while Best and Marcus praise the minimization of agency—a spectacular reversal from the 1980s and 1990s, when agency was all the rage in theoretical circles—one might be wise to acknowledge the "dark side" of a dissipated human agency. Low-agency scholars are deskilled scholars, proletarianized thinkers denuded of their authority to make claims (at least claims that haven't been culled directly from a measurement device). Low-agency scholars are adjunct workers with precarious economic roles to play in the university, their standing diminished relative to the increased power of academic administrators, presidents, chancellors, and trustees. Critique is foe to ideology, but, particularly in Marx's case, critique is also a necessary technique for revealing the conditions of proletarianization. As the Marxist tradition has persuasively demonstrated, capital itself thrives most when the proletariat identifies positively with the very structure of its own debasement.[8] Thus the tools and trinkets

7 Best and Marcus, "Surface Reading," 17.

8 An important touchstone in such a tradition is Fredric Jameson's essay "Reification and Utopia in Mass Culture," *Signatures of the Visible* (New York: Routledge, 1992), 9-34.

we find so seductive, digital or otherwise, are the same devices that fragment and reorganize social life around specific economic mandates.

—

What I hope to suggest with these challenges and provocations is not so much a doom-and-gloom view of digital studies, but rather a sober assessment of the problems faced by the academy and a view, provisional at best, of the kinds of solutions that might be possible. Scholars must make their own assessments of the challenges posed by digital computation. How does the advent of the computer change humanistic research? How will it be possible to use computers while avoiding the difficulties just itemized, the epistemological challenges around hegemony, recapitulation, and symmetry and the more political challenges of ideology, deskilling, and proletarianization? Speaking as a programmer who has been writing and studying software for several years both within and without the research context, I hope to ally myself with those innovating with technical research methods, as they exist now and how they might exist in the future. Personally, my own efforts have followed a multimodal strategy of producing academic writing concurrent with software production, the goal of which being not to quarantine criticality, but rather to *unify* critical theory and digital media (around the technique of allegory, for instance). Others will find an approach that is most appropriate to them.

Still, this is not to advocate for some kind of rote digitization of the humanities; it is not to say that every child must be given a laptop. Few things will cripple the humanities more than the uncritical "adoption of tools" or the continued encroachment of positivistic research methods borrowed from cognitive science, neuroscience, computer science, or elsewhere. One should be very skeptical of the Googlization of the

academy.[9] Rather, one might hope to pursue the kind of creativity and care necessary for understanding and responding to
the growing industrialization of mind and body.

As scholars and students in the humanities and liberal arts, are
we outgunned and outclassed by capital? Indeed we are—now
more than ever. Yet as humanists we have access to something
more important. We have access to what François Laruelle has
called the "weak force" of persons in their generic humanity. The
goal, then, is not to challenge the data miners at their own game,
for we will always be underfunded and understaffed. The point is
to withdraw from the game altogether and continue to pursue the
very questions that technoscience has always bungled, beholden as
it is to specific ideological and industrial mandates. The weak force
grants us access to the generic commonality of history and society
and the various aesthetic and cultural phenomena that not only
populate this history but, as its flesh and blood, are history itself.

---

9 My home institution, New York University, announced an agreement with
Google in the fall of 2010 that migrated much of the university's data flow to
Google Apps for Education, including email, calendaring, document sharing,
and collaboration tools. The subsequent revelation that Google had been sharing
its data stream for several years with the National Security Agency only adds to
the moral shortcomings of this type of industrial outsourcing.

Acknowledgments

I am grateful to my colleagues and students at New York University, the University of Pennsylvania, and Harvard University, where much of this material was first presented and discussed. The writing and editing of the book were facilitated by fellowships at the American Academy in Berlin, Germany, and at the Institute for Advanced Study on Media Cultures of Computer Simulation (MECS) at Leuphana University in Lüneburg, Germany. The archivists at the Institute for Advanced Study (IAS) in Princeton, New Jersey, were particularly helpful when I first contacted them several years ago regarding Nils Aall Barricelli. The final book manuscript was finished during a subsequent fellowship at the IAS in the School of Social Science, for which I give special appreciation to Didier Fassin, Marion Fourcade, Alondra Nelson, and Joan Scott. Several colleagues and friends were good enough to read the penultimate draft and provide comments, including Andrew Culp, Seb Franklin, Eben Kirksey, Jason LaRiviere, Nicole Starosielski, and Leif Weatherby. Research assistants Shane Brennan, Sonaar Luthra, Alice Marwick, and Caleb Salgado improved the manuscript in innumerable ways, and I acknowledge their labor.

I thank and acknowledge Taeyoon Choi, who cooked up the title "Uncomputable," and who has proven to be an invaluable collaborator over the years. I also thank T'ai Smith, who first informed me of the work of Ada K. Dietz several years ago. Sina Najafi published two short texts of mine in *Cabinet* magazine— one on Guy Debord and one on Nils Barricelli—and thus helped propel this project at an early stage. I thank McKenzie Wark for sneaking into an art exhibit with me before it opened so we could play Debord's Game of War firsthand. And I gained much insight into Debord's game from countless conversations with Mushon Zer-Aviv. Jason E. Smith taught me a great deal about Tiqqun (and Debord), and has thus inflected the manuscript in many ways. Juliet Jacobson is an inexhaustible source of intellectual and editorial exchange.

This book includes adaptations of the following journal articles and book chapters: "Black Box, Black Bloc," in Benjamin Noys, ed., *Communization and Its Discontents: Contestation, Critique, and Contemporary Struggles* (Brooklyn: Minor Compositions/ Autonomedia, 2011), 237–49; "The Computational Image of Organization: Nils Aall Barricelli," *Grey Room* 46 (Winter 2012): 26–45; "Creative Evolution," *Cabinet* 42 (Summer 2011): 45–50; "The Cybernetic Hypothesis," *differences: A Journal of Feminist Cultural Studies* 25, no. 1 (2014): 107–31, republished by permission of Duke University Press; "Debord's Nostalgic Algorithm," *Culture Machine* 10 (2009): 131–56; "The Game of War: An Overview," *Cabinet* 29 (Spring 2008): 67–72; "Networks," in W. J. T. Mitchell and Mark Hansen, eds., *Critical Terms for Media Studies* (Chicago: University of Chicago Press, 2010): 280–96; "Our Best Machines Are Made of Sunshine," in *Sarah Oppenheimer: S-337473* (Columbus, OH: Wexner Center for the Arts, 2017), 36–49; "Polygraphic Photography and the Origins of 3-D Animation," in Karen Beckman, ed., *Animating Film Theory* (Durham, NC: Duke University Press, 2014), 54–67. I thank the publishers and editors of these texts for helping to make this book possible.

Index

Aars, Øystein, 172
Adam, Adolf, 73
Agre, Phil, 23, 237
Althusser, Louis, 167

Babbage, Charles, 146, 153
Badiou, Alain, 215
Bar, Alphonsine, 39
Barnett, Louise K., 55
Barricelli, Nils Aall, 8, 9, 10,
    141–143, 145, 147, 150, 154,
    156, 157, 160, 172, 182, 259, 260
Baudelaire, Charles, 40
Benjamin, Walter, 4, 31
Best, Stephen, 252
Blas, Zach, 6, 7
Blondel, Maurice, 168
Boundas, Constantin V., 243
Bowden, B. V., 70
Bracken, Len, 204
Braune, Christian Wilhelm, 44

Brossollet, Guy, 178, 180
Browne, Simone, 6, 7, 243
Buck-Morss, Susan, 166
Burks, Arthur W., 146

Charcot, Jean-Martin, 38
Chow-White, Peter A., 100
Chrétien, Gilles-Louis, 18
Chun, Wendy Hui Kyong, 6, 80,
    99, 177, 235
Clausewitz-Debord, Kriegspiel,
    191
Condon, Edward U., 172
Cornu, M., 26

Da, Nan Z., 11
de Lasalle, Philippe, 74
de Loménie, Louis, 41
de Nó, Lorente, 223
de Parville, Henri, 17
de Saint-Victor, Paul, 15, 16, 23

Dean, Aria, 8
Debord, Guy, 10, 126, 177, 179,
186–193, 195–197, 199, 201,
203, 204, 206, 207, 210, 219,
260, 266–268
Demenÿ, Georges, 26, 28
Didi-Huberman, Georges, 18
Dietz, Ada K., 8–10, 82, 84, 86, 87,
90, 92, 96, 260
Disdéri, André-Adolphe-Eugène,
41, 42
Doane, Mary Ann, 39, 177

Eder, Josef Maria, 26
Ensor, James, 30, 33
Escher, M. C., 55

Falcon, Jean Philippe, 73
Fazi, Beatrice, 2
Fontaine, Abbé D., 72
Fortis, François-Marie, 74
Foster, Ruth E., 82, 83, 87, 92

Geoghegan, Bernard Dionysius,
54, 120
Gödel, Kurt, 2, 145
Goldstine, Herman H., 70
Griswold, Ralph E., 86
Guattari, Félix, 5, 52, 126, 182

Hansen, Mark B. N., 169
Hardt, Michael, 5, 232, 254
Harich-Schwarzbauer, Henriette,
66
Harlizius-Klu, Ellen, 70
Hass, Robert, 42
Hayles, N. Katherine, 8, 170, 171

Hegel, G. W. F., 18
Heller-Roazen, Daniel, 238
Henderson, Ethel, 85
Hirshberg, Leonard Keene, 83
Hodge, James, 48
Hottinger, Sara N., 98
Hu, Tung-Hui, 6
Hui, Yuk, 6

Jacquard, Joseph Marie, 67, 78, 80
Janssen, Pierre-Jules-César, 26
Johnson, Nellie Sargent, 82, 87

Kane, Carolyn L., 102
Katchadourian, Nina, 102, 103
Kelty, Christopher, 218
King, Homay, 8
Kleinrock, Leonard, 230
Kofman, Sarah, 218
Kovalevskaya, Sofia, 98
Kozo-Polyansky, Boris, 150
Krauss, Rosalind, 40, 209

Laruelle, François, 8
Le Prince, Augustin, 39
Liddell, Henry George, 65
Light, Jennifer S., 99
Liu, Alan, 253
Londe, Albert, 32, 36–38, 40
Lovelace, Ada, 8, 69, 70, 76, 81, 98
Loyd, Mary, 18
Lyotard, Jean-François, 189

Marey, Étienne-Jules, 20, 25, 26,
28, 35, 166
McDonough, Tom, 197
Menabrea, Luigi Federico, 79

Merleau-Ponty, Maurice, 32, 33
Mill, John Stuart, 75
Mitchell, W. J. T., 260
Montucla, Jean Etienne, 61
Moore, Doris Langley, 70
Moro, Aldo, 179, 186
Muybridge, Eadweard, 26, 35

Nicholson-Smith, Donald, 203, 204
Nosch, Marie-Louise, 66

Oh, Yeon Ju, 100
Osen, Lynn M., 98

Pasolini, Pier Paolo, 55
Peters, John Durham, 101
Price, Seth, 7

Richardson, Lewis, 181
Rosner, Daniela K., 82

Sanguinetti, Gianfranco, 186
Sauvage, Pierre-Louis-Frederic, 18
Shannon, Claude, 3, 117, 118, 126, 150, 235, 238, 253
Silverman, Kaja, 21, 111

Smith Dexter, John, 83
Smith, Anthony Paul, 8
Smith, Jason E., 260
Spillers, Hortense J., 238
Starosielski, Nicole, 6, 101, 165, 259
Steyerl, Hito, 243
Stiegler, Bernard, 6
Syms, Martine, 7

Toole, Betty, 75

Wallin, Ivan, 150
Ware, Willis H., 153
Wark, McKenzie, 197
Weed, Elizabeth, 253
Whitehead, Alfred North, 142, 163
Wiener, Norbert, 116, 121, 223, 225–227, 253
Willème, François, 8, 15–17, 20, 22, 23
Winthrop-Young, Geoffrey, 36
Wright, Frank Lloyd, 88

Zemanek, Heinz, 73